ONLY

ONE

LIFE

A STORY OF MISSIONARY RESILIENCE

BIOGRAPHY
of
LEON ROSENBERG

The late founder and director
of the American European Bethel Mission

A compilation from archives and memory
by
Vera Kuschnir

American European Bethel Mission
Second Printing
2000

Kuschnir, Vera *"Only One Life"*

ISBN: 1-885024-04-5

Printed in the U.S.A.

*Dedicated to the glory of God
and to the numerous descendants
of Leon and Fanny Rosenberg.*

Many Thanks:

— To Dr. and Mrs. Theodore Fischbacher for the many hours of tedious proofreading of the English text and their fervent prayer support.

— To Maria Slort, the youngest Rosenberg daughter, for wracking her memory for tidbits of information and for reading and correcting the final draft.

— To Alexis Mihailitchenko, the late Home Office Administrator of the A.E.B.M., for many boring hours spent at the copying facility and for corresponding with several potential publishers.

— To all who offered prayer support and encouragement to me during the many months of my journeying through often unchartered waters of hundreds of pages of old material in search of chronology and continuity in this remarkable story.

Vera Kuschnir
(One of the five Rosenberg granddaughters)

"Only one life

T'will soon be passed —

Only what's done for Christ

Will last."

TABLE OF CONTENTS

ॐ

Part IV

ॐ

Part V

♔
Part VI

♔
Part VII

ψ

Part VIII

ψ

Part IX

ψ

THE LIFE STORY OF LEON ROSENBERG

Introduction

In the pages following this introduction, we gladly accede to the requests repeatedly made by our friends and co-workers in the Lord's vineyard, namely, that we should write and publish the life story of the Founder of the American European Bethel Mission.

The life story of this man is most unusual, if not actually unique. It represents personal experiences of a rabbinical student, who eventually became a veteran missionary of the Cross of Christ. It documents experiences which took place in two different "worlds" — the rabbinical "world" into which Leon Rosenberg was born and in which he spent his early years, being very strictly reared until he reached a mature age of twenty, and the Christian "world" in which he lived after his spiritual regeneration.

The latter part of the early years, until Leon reached his twentieth birthday and graduated from a rabbinical seminary, were spent mostly in the gloom of uncertainty, deep longings and inner conflicts due to his burning thirst for knowledge and his quest for *THE TRUTH*.

The depth of such a spiritual conflict is known only to those who have experienced it. The gap between Rabbinical Judaism on the one hand, and Biblical Christianity (which we might call *"Messianism"*) on the other, seemed to be insurmountable. The power of *THE LAW,* the rigid demands of the sages and their precepts, had already deeply influenced his life, while the Light of the "sure word of prophecy," as given in the prophetic books, was hidden and the study thereof forbidden.

It is indeed a miracle when one manages to find his way out of the confusing labyrinth of rabbinical "interpretations" and "explanations" of the Holy Writ as contained in the books of the Talmud.

On the other hand, the sometimes shallow and dogmatic way of presenting the claims of Jesus Christ, as the promised and expected Messiah of Israel on the part of those who represented Christianity, served only to deepen the inner conflict of the one whose life story we are venturing to publish.

It behooves the biographer to acquaint the reader with some of the early struggles of the subject of this biographical sketch in his search for proofs, substantiating the Messiahship of Jesus of Nazareth, and especially His deity as the Son of the Living God. The frequently heated arguments with those who presented those claims, will serve as an eye-opener to many, and introduce them to a type or kind of Jews who are Jews not only because they were born such, but are Jews by deliberate choice. (Rom. 2:28,29 & 9:6)

Rabbinical Talmudic Judaism is an entirely different world from that of Christendom. So are some of the customs and rites, as well as the significance, which this cast of Jews attaches even to their observance of the Sabbath and other festivals in their mystical aspects. All these facts will be displayed before the eyes of the reader in this unusual life story, and he or she will find it very enlightening and profitable. The arguments, used by young Rosenberg to defend his faith, and how he eventually overcame the obstacles and stumbling-blocks in his path to becoming a Christian, will be of assistance to many who are interested in the salvation of Israel as a nation, and of individual Jews.

The acceptance of Christ as his personal Savior was really a triumph of the grace of God in Leon Rosenberg's life, and a real proof that "the Gospel is the power of God unto salvation to every one that believeth, to the Jew first and also to the Greek." (Rom. 1:16)

Although Leon Rosenberg's struggle between "darkness" and "light" lasted for quite some time, praise God the final victory was the Lord's, because Leon's rabbinical zeal was reborn with him and was sanctified and yielded fully to "show forth the praises of Him Who had called him out of darkness into His marvelous light." (1 Peter 2:9)

The two different "worlds," mentioned earlier, had been packed with thrilling experiences which must be related in this biography as they are radically different from one another. The first "world" was the world of Leon's early childhood and youth, which were spent in rabbinical training, in preparation to follow in the footsteps of his father.

The experiences of the second "world," after Leon's conversion, fall into several time spans, the first of which began in czarist Russia, with its rigid laws prohibiting the spreading of the Gospel under Pobedonoszev, the Procurator of the Holy Synod of the official Russian Church, known as the Russian Orthodox Church.

The marvelous leading of the Lord of this missionary took him not only to glorious heights and outstanding blessings, but also into the depths of a Jewish *"pogrom,"* including banishment to Siberia.

The second time segment of Leon's Christian "world" was spent under the bloody communist regime of Lenin with all of its horrors: starvation, imprisonment and a death sentence.

The third time span was the time of Nazi cruelties, which cost the lives of Leon's own daughter and her husband, along with many other relatives, six assistants in his Mission, and a great number of dear children of the "Bethel" Orphanage in Poland, who had to drink the bitter cup of affliction and death, together with millions of men, women and children of their kindred.

The fourth time span, and the most wonderful of all, was the one spent in the USA after the rebirth of the Bethel Mission there, and the establishment of the Jewish State in the land of Palestine. It was the best part of Leon's Christian "world" with all the glorious experiences in the ministry of soul winning among many Jews in the USA and Israel. He repeatedly stated that the greatest lesson which God allowed him to learn through it all was that nothing in the world can separate us from the love of Christ. (Rom. 8:35)

Leon Rosenberg's life was lived largely under the shadow of the Cross, and in many ways it can be likened unto that of the Apostle Paul, concerning whom the Lord said, "I will show him how much he must endure for My name's sake." Like Paul, Leon, too, learned to say, "We rejoice inasmuch as we are partakers of Christ's suffering," and that all sufferings for the sake of Christ "are not worthy to be compared with the glory which shall be revealed in us" (Rom. 8:18). He "banked" upon the promises "Who shall separate us from the love of Christ? Shall tribulation, or distress, or persecution, or famine, or nakedness, or peril, or sword? Nay, in all these things we are more than conquerors through Him that loved us. For I am persuaded that neither death, nor life, nor angels, nor principalities, nor powers, nor things present, nor things to come, nor height, nor depth, nor any other creature, shall be able to separate us from the love of God, which is in Christ Jesus our Lord." (Rom. 8:35-39)

We are writing these pages with deep gratitude to God for His matchless Grace which has so gloriously enriched the life of this outstanding servant of His, and our prayer is that this story may be a blessing and a source of encouragement to all who read it.

Ψ

PART
I

Chapter 1

EARLY TRAINING STEEPED IN ANCIENT TRADITIONS

☰

Ancestry

☰

A word or two should be said about Leon's ancestors, or the closest of them at least. His grandfather, Akiva, was highly respected by his kindred for his integrity and generosity. In token of a special merit (Jews were generally not allowed to own land in Czarist Russia) he was granted by Nicholas I, Emperor of Russia, the unusual privilege of owning a tract of land of considerable size for farming purposes. He lived a very secluded life, spending his time in studying the Scriptures and the teachings of the Sages. The farming business was in the hands of an able administrator.

Leon's maternal grandparents enjoyed, in a special way, the respect of their entire community. The grandfather, Rabbi Jossele, was a noted *"Landon"* (a highly learned man). Because of his erudition and piety, he belonged to the "elite" of the famous *"Tzaddikim"* who had a following of many thousands of the, so-called, *"Chasidim."*

Leon Rosenberg was born on the 15th day of February, 1875, as the first child of Eleazar Rosenberg and his wife Gali.

His father was known as *"Rebb Eleazar ha-Cohan,"* meaning "the Priest." It is important at this time to explain the Jewish priesthood as it is observed in Israel today. We must state here that it is strictly observed even to this day, and cannot be usurped by others — either a rabbi or any other religious functionary. It is an office borne only by those recognized by the Synagogue as being descendants of the tribe of Levi and of the lineage of the high priest Aaron. (Num. 3:9,10) The question is frequently asked, "Can the priesthood be really established? Are there any genealogical documents to prove the priestly succession?" To that we must answer "no." There are perhaps no genealogical documents, but this heritage is one of the most carefully observed traditions which go down from father to son, from generation to generation. The Apostle Paul speaks of some traditions which he himself observed and recommended to the Church. (Gal. 1:14; II Thess. 2:15 and 3:6)

While according to Hosea 3:4, the Jewish priest could not officiate by bringing sacrifices or performing other ceremonies linked strictly to the Sanctuary of the Temple which was in Jerusalem, he had quite a number of obligations to fulfill, besides the redemption of the firstborn. To him was given preference in the Synagogue on the Sabbath day and at Festival Services. He had to open and read the Scroll. He alone was allowed to pronounce the Aaronic benediction at high Festivals, and in conformity with Num. 6:23-26, no one was allowed to do this except the priest, not even the rabbi or the official prayer-leader. This was in conformity with the 23rd verse of that chapter, where it is explicitly stated that only Aaron and his descendants might pronounce that blessing. A special ceremony accompanies the benediction.

The priest takes off his shoes, and after ritual washing of hands, takes his place before the Ark which is substituted for the Ark of the Covenant in the Sanctuary of old. In the Ark today there are only one or two (or more) scrolls of the Holy Torah. He covers his head with the *"Tallit"* (prayer-shawl) and lifts his arms to symbolize the Wings of the Cherubim which were upon the Mercy Seat in the Holy of Holies. By joining the two thumbs pointing down, and with his index and second fingers of each hand joined closely and pointing upward, and with the third and fourth fingers of each hand held together and pointing outward, the priest gives a picture of the Wings of the Cherubim.

As the benediction is pronounced, according to Num. 6:24-26, the priest pauses after each verse to give the congregation time to respond by chanting the appropriate prayers. The main object in so zealously preserving the office of the priesthood today, is to be ready for the service in the Sanctuary, which the Jew hopes some day to rebuild in Jerusalem as soon as the expected Messiah shall have come.

One of the rabbis under whom Leon Rosenberg studied in the Seminary, had exclusively sons of priests in his care whom he carefully prepared for that service in the future Temple. This rabbi, Chofez Chaim, (a kind of "nickname" given to him because of his extreme piety and his belief that the Messiah would come in his time) was especially interested in preparing the sons of priests for that purpose.

Leon had three "birthdays." His actual birthday was, as we mentioned earlier, the 15th of February 1875. However, because he was a child of a priest his real birthday could not be registered. His father, being strictly rabbinical, had some scruples in regard to registering his firstborn son with the Gentile authorities. His conscientious objection to this was based on the Holy Scriptures, Numbers 23:9, where the record reads: "Israel shall not be numbered among the nations." Another particular objection to registering his firstborn son was based especially on the words in the Book of Numbers 1:49 regarding the tribe of Levi, "Thou shall not number the tribe of Levi, neither take the sum of them among the children of Israel." However, in compliance with the civil law regarding registration of new-born children, the father was obliged to register his child. This he did, and it was done on the 22nd day of April of the same year. Only in doing so the father changed the name of his son somewhat, registering him not as Isaac Levi, the name which had been given to him on the eighth day after his birth, when the ritual of circumcision was observed on him, but under the name of "Leon, the son of Lazar Rosenberg." This date became Leon's official "birthday" and appeared in all of his personal documents ever after.

The third "birthday" came later at Leon's twentieth birthday and after his graduation from the Rabbinical Seminary. It came at the time of his conversion as the most essential factor for every one who accepts Jesus as his Savior and Lord, and was *THE NEW BIRTH* of which the Lord Jesus spoke to rabbi Nicodemus, saying, "Ye must be born again" (John 3:7).

The new registration did not make any difference in the Jewish Synagogue, nor was his name changed there. The name "Isaac Levi" which was given to him at the time of sacred ritual by which he was admitted into the Covenant of Abraham, remained the same. There he was known as "Isaac Levi, the son of Eleazar the Priest." No surname (last name) was ever mentioned in the Orthodox Synagogue of those days. The surnames, imposed upon Jews by a hostile government, involved much embarrassment and humiliation, but were completely ignored by the Jewish Synagogue.

The reason why Jews in those days objected to surnames was not only because they were a novelty in Jewish history, but also because in their opinion these names constituted a violation of their religious rights, as unequal to non-Jews.

It is well known that family ties in Israel were rigidly regulated by the Law of Moses — that Israel might be a "separated" nation — and the names given to children born into the family were usually of Biblical significance and were inseparably linked with the name of the father. This was carried on through many generations, until a cunning Emperor of Austria — who desired to replenish his empty treasury — decreed that every Jew under his dominion should purchase a surname and pay a price for the same, according to the name which he chose from a list of surnames presented to him by the tax collectors.

These names were classified according to their derivations from various plants, minerals, animals, etc. Hence we find a great variety of surnames among Jews, such as cat, dog, calf, cow, ox, bear, wolf, lion, silver, gold, diamond, stone, smith, taylor (tailor), carpenter — all, of course, in the Jewish version and not as they appear in English. The same was the case with names taken from various plants — a leaf, a blade of grass, a tree, a branch *("blatt"* — leaf; *"zweig"* — a branch; *"baum"* — a tree, or combination as in *"Birnbaum"* — pear tree; *"Greenzweig"* — a green branch; *"Rosenblatt"* rose leaf; *"Rosenblum"* — rose blossom; *"Rosenberg"* — a rose mountain or a hill of roses; *"Rosenthal"* — rose valley; *"Rosenfeld"* rose field, or a field of roses, etc. These were German words).

In the synagogue, however, Jewish identification remained in the old manner, "Moses, the son of Amram," "David, the son of Jesse," etc.

Following this rule, young Leon never appeared under the name *"Rosenberg"* in the synagogue. When he was invited to read the Holy Torah, the Scroll, in the synagogue on the Sabbath day or during the Festivals, he was called by the name given him at the time of his circumcision, namely, *"Yitzchak Ben Eleazar ha-Cohan"* ("Isaac, the son of Eleazar the Priest").

ψ

Circumcision

ψ

The rite of circumcision is still very strictly observed among Orthodox Jews. On the eighth day after a male child is born, he has to undergo the rite or ritual of circumcision, according to Genesis 17:9-13. This was the Covenant God made with Abraham, and no Jew can ever become a child of Abraham and a member of this Covenant without being circumcised. At that procedure the officiating rabbi or his assistant, the *"Mohel,"* the man who performs the actual circumcision — pronounces the name of the child, saying, "The name of this child shall be called in Israel (the name given by the parents)." And so it was in the case of little Isaac Levi. The entire ceremony was strictly observed in the presence of a praying congregation, in accordance with the rabbinical traditions.

Believing in the prophet Elijah as the guardian of the Holy Law, it is generally assumed in strict rabbinical circles that he is present at this sacred ceremony, and a special seat is reserved for him which is called "The bench of Elijah" *("Kysseh Shel Elijahu")*.

This seat is usually temporarily occupied by the rabbi, whose honor it is to hold the child during the procedure. In the absence of such a rabbi another person may be honored to take his place.

During the performance of the sacred ritual, a prayer is chanted as follows, "Blessed art Thou, O Lord our God, Who has sanctified us by giving us the command regarding circumcision." After the ceremony, the father of the child praises God for affording him the privilege of bringing his infant into the Covenant of Father Abraham. The congregation responds with a prayer for the child that "he might grow up and enter into the Law and the nuptial canopy (which means marriage) and good deeds." At this unction, another prayer is offered, namely, regarding the coming of the King-Messiah, that God might send the Anointed walking in His integrity to give good tidings and consolation to the people that are scattered and dispersed among the nations. "All-Merciful, send us the righteous High Priest, WHO REMAINS WITHDRAWN in concealment in Heaven, hidden until His throne, bright as the sun, and radiant as a diamond, shall be prepared for Him." At this solemn ceremony, father Eleazar and mother Gali dedicated their first-born son to God, with the prayer that he might become *"Godel B'Israel"* ("a great man among his people").

Having been born into a priestly family, little Isaac Levi was by divine order exempt from the *"Pidyon ha-ben"* or the "Redemption of the firstborn." The children of priests are in a special way separated or sanctified unto God, while all other firstborn children of Israel had to be redeemed by the payment of a price of five silver shekels, according to Numbers 3:11-15 and 45-50. There we read that God ordered that the firstborn children belong to Him because the firstborn children had been spared in Egypt under the protection of the blood of the Passover lambs.

The redemption of the children had to be carried out by an acknowledged priest in the Congregation of Israel. This procedure was (and still is today), likewise, a solemn service. At the age of one month, the child had to be presented by his father to the priest. The father and the mother would testify that the child is their first-born. God's ordinance of redemption was then recited from the Scriptures, and the father would be asked if he is willing to pay the redemption price for the child as commanded by the Lord. The father would say solemnly "Yes, I am willing to fulfill the behest of the Holy One; blessed be His name. I desire to pay the redemption price after the money of the Sanctuary" (the equivalent). Then the priest would answer "I take this money instead of thy son. This is the commutation for him. This is the price of his release. May this child enter into life, into the Law of the fear of God."

♈

Hebrew Schooling

♈

Little Leon started his schooling by learning the Hebrew language. The reason for this was that according to rabbinical tradition, the firstborn son who was dedicated from childhood to follow his father's rabbinical footsteps, should start by learning the holy language called *"Lashon ha-Kodesh."* (The Biblical Hebrew was not used then in everyday conversation). At the age of three, Leon had to say his first prayers in Hebrew. According to Talmudic tradition, Abraham first came to the knowledge of God at that age, therefore it was considered expedient to begin religious instruction of a child as early as possible.

The first grade in a Jewish elementary school is considered a "foundation laying" institution. What the pupil acquires there determines whether or not he is to proceed with rabbinical studies. Generally, the *"Melamed Tinoketh"* (the instructor), aware of the privilege and responsibility of laying the foundation for future rabbis, takes his position very seriously and watches over the children entrusted to him, to see that they make every possible progress in the short time under his care. Each pupil is cared for individually. The Hebrew alphabet is taught in the first few days, the teacher points to each letter with a little stylus to keep the pupil's attention to the form and shape of each letter, until he grasps it. To acquire the desired progress and fluency of reading, the child has to repeat every letter and every word aloud. The later studies in the rabbinical schools, such as *"Bet ha-Midrash,"* or Rabbinical Seminary, require excellent scholarship and superior intelligence.

Believing in the methods mentioned in the Bible, Leon's teacher followed the instruction of the wise King Solomon — not to withhold the "rod" from the child, because use of it is proof of love and will not kill the child. (Prov. 13:24) He used a lash, by use of which he made the little ones obey and learn — his maxim being "Ye must know." Progress had to be made at a rapid pace.

Leon's mother watched her son with delight as he learned to read his morning and evening prayers in Hebrew. The first thing he did in the morning was to chant, "I praise Thee, Living and Everlasting King, that Thou hast returned to me my soul, and this because of Thy great mercy and the abundance of Thy faithfulness. May it be pleasing to Thee for a minute, not to become a cause of Thy disfavor."

Again before going to bed he prayed, "Blessed art Thou, O Lord our God, King of the Universe, Who makest the bands of sleep to fall upon mine eyes, and slumber upon mine eyelids. May it be Thy will, O Lord my God, and the God of my fathers, to suffer me to lie down in peace and to let me rise up again in peace. Let not my thoughts trouble me, nor evil dreams, nor evil fancies, but let my rest be perfect before Thee. O lighten mine eyes, lest I sleep the sleep of death, for it is Thou O Lord, Who givest light to the whole world in Thy glory, God, faithful King. Hear, O Israel, the Lord our God, the Lord is One. Blessed be His Name, Whose glorious kingdom is forever and ever. In the Name of the Lord, the God of Israel, may Michael, the Angel be at my right hand; Gabriel, the Angel, at my left; before me, Uriel; behind me, Raphael, and above my head the Divine Presence (The *Shekinah* glory) of God."

Leon's parents truly did their best to assist him at home in his religious education, ceremonies and rituals of the feasts. But before all this came the learning of the Hebrew language.

Hebrew was the only acknowledged language to be used in approaching God and in studying the Holy Scriptures. That was the reason why the Jewish scribes in Judea did not acknowledge the translation of the Bible into Greek, the "Septuagint." To them Greek was a pagan language. They likewise rejected the Jewish religious writings which were written in Greek, and which they called "apocryphal" or "unauthenticated."

There are only three translations which were tolerated and are still used by religious Jews: the so-called *"Targumim,"* written in the Semitic language, namely, the Aramaic or Palestinian dialect, or the one mixed with the Syrian dialect. These *"Targumim"* are the ones of Jonathan Ben Usyel and of Uncaleth, who was himself a proselyte, and then, the "Jerusalem Targumim."

Those Jews who lived in Alexandria, Egypt, who had fled from Judea at the time of the siege of the Holy Land by King Nebuchadnezzar, of whom many became followers of the teachings of the philosopher Philo, using the Greek language, forgot the Hebrew, and needed to have a translation of the Scriptures in that language (Greek). Because of this, they were despised by the Palestinian Jews and were branded with the name "Grecians" *("Helenos")*. Many of these, when they returned to Judea and became again acquainted with Hebrew, were allowed to join the Hebrew Synagogues along with the other Jews. These were the Grecians mentioned in the New Testament, whom the Apostle Paul found in various places in the Jewish synagogues on Sabbath days where they gathered with the other Jews for worship. Having been quite broadminded and tolerant, they listened eagerly to the proclaiming of the Gospel by Paul. It is obvious that they were not heathen Greeks who as such would never have attended Jewish places of worship.

☙

Tzitzit and Huetel

☙

In the wardrobe of a rabbinical Jew there are two articles which old and young should always wear. One is the *"Arbah-Kanfot"* (four corners) — a garment worn next to his body, covering the breast and shoulders with *"Tzitzit"* (fringes) — one on each corner. This is in compliance with Num. 15:37-41. The significance of this little garment is to remind the wearer that he is bound always to be loyal to the God of his fathers, and to observe His statutes and commandments. The rabbis have made of this also a means of protection against evil spirits.

The other article is a typical Jewish skull-cap, *"huetel"* or *"yarmulkah."* Two reasons were given as to the kind and the necessity of a constant head covering. One — the Jew in his apparel should be different from all other nations, according to the command that "he should not walk in the way of the Gentiles." For the same reason the Jew keeps his head covered during prayer, because the Gentiles pray with their heads uncovered. The head covering is also considered a sign of mourning in compliance with 2nd Samuel 15:30-32. Here David is shown in his bereavement when dethroned and persecuted by his son Absalom, and the text states that David's faithful followers covered their heads. Now the Jew, who has lost his kingdom and his sanctuary, is being persecuted by the nations and mourns until God will restore him to his former position. For comfort during the night, the Jew uses another kind of cap — a soft one.

♕

Mezuzah (Hebrew: *Doorpost*)

♕

From childhood on, Leon's attention was drawn to the Mezuzah in his home, placed on the door post in fulfillment of God's commandment in Deut. 6:9: "Thou shalt write them (God's Commandments) upon the posts of thy house." Complying with the rabbinical interpretation of this command, each Jewish home has a kind of *"phylactery"* on each door post. This phylactery, called *"Mezuzah,"* is a little container with a scroll of parchment inside, on which a passage from Deut. 6:4-7, beginning with *"Shema Israel,"* is carefully written in Hebrew letters by an accredited *"sofer"* (scribe). It is to preserve the sacred writing on this scroll that it is placed in a metal case which has a small opening for the Hebrew letter *"Shin"* — ツ (first letter in one of the mystical names of God — *"Shaddai"* — Almighty). The Mezuzah is attached to the door post in the vertical position so as to be visible.

On entering and leaving the house, young and old touch the Mezuzah, and the finger which touches the letter *"Shin"* is kissed, while the words in Deut. 28:6: "Blessed shalt thou be when thou comest in and...when thou goest out," and the words of Ps. 121:8: "The Lord shall preserve thy going out and thy coming in..." are especially applied.

The Mezuzah is connected with Divine protection, as cited in the *"Machilta,"* one of the earliest rabbinical writings, where it is said to be placed as a memorial of the blood of the Passover lamb, sprinkled on the door posts of the houses of the Israelites on the night of the deliverance from death of their firstborn sons when the death angel passed over the land of Egypt. The Mezuzah, which embodied the name of the Lord no less then ten times, became a mystical amulet.

ψ

Channukah, Dedication Feast

ψ

National festivals and holy days were so precisely described and interpreted that they made an indelible impression upon little Leon. Once a year there was a special candlestick with eight arms set before the window for eight days. The arms of these peculiar candlesticks were filled with pure oil and were lighted — one on the first night, and one on each succeeding night — until all were lit by the eighth night. Hymns of praise were sung, especially the so-called *"Mouz Zur Iesimeti."* The story told on this occasion was about Antiochus Epiphanes IV, the Seleucidan tyrant, desecrating the Holy Temple, and victory given by the Almighty to the zealous priests, the Maccabees, who defeated the enemy and rededicated the Temple. The candles are in memory of the miracle when the golden candlestick could be lit again. These lights were considered sacred. They were not to be desecrated by using them for doing any kind of work while they were burning. They were for the worship of God as a memorial of the great miracle which He wrought for His people. A sealed jar, filled with sanctified, was found in a hidden place in the sanctuary. This enabled the priests to light the golden candlestick for eight days during the dedication. This memorial of dedication is referred to also in the New Testament (John 10:22).

ψ

Purim — the Feast
Described in the Book of Esther

ψ

The event recorded in the book of Esther concerning the miraculous deliverance of the children of Israel from the hand of the wicked Haman, was another glorious event for Leon, and was, indeed, an event of many thrills for young and old — the festival *"Purim"* bringing joy and merriment with songs of praises to God and hymns of victory. In memory of this glorious event, gifts were exchanged as a token of friendship, and help was administered to the poor, as in the days of old (Esther 9:22-23).

Lag B'Omer

This was a day set apart for enjoyment — to celebrate Spring outside the town in the fields, and was much appreciated by the youth, This celebration in those days was also in remembrance of the homeland and the Holy city of Jerusalem, when the Israelites, an agricultural people, had their harvests. According to Scripture, the next morning after Passover, the early fruits, the first gleanings, had to be brought as the wave offering to the Temple. From this day on Israel was ordered strictly to count each day during seven weeks until the day of the harvest of the first fruits, which was celebrated in the Temple as the Feast of the Seven Weeks — *"Shavuot"* (Lev. 23:9-22). Now that the Jews once again enjoy harvesting crops in the State of Israel this feast has acquired a renewed meaning after centuries of serving merely as a great encouragement to them.

On the day of *"Lag B'omer,"* or the 33rd day, long excursions were undertaken. Teachers and students from the grade schools and Rabbinical Seminaries marched into the fields to play all kinds of games with self-made bows and arrows, wooden saws etc., which symbolized the armies of Israel's kings in the days gone by — an exercise which appealed to and encouraged the oppressed, despised Jewish youth, to at least remember the glorious days of the past.

♈

Sabbath

♈

The weekly return of the Old Covenant Sabbath was strictly observed. It was not only a day of rest and a holy season of worship, but a pleasant family fellowship time as well. All the preparations for this holy day had to be finished before sunset. The food for the Sabbath meals was put in the hermetically sealed and specially heated oven to be cooked and kept warm until the next afternoon — no fire being allowed during the entire Sabbath — this is in accordance with Ex. 16:23 and Num. 15:32-36. The best foods had to be used for the three obligatory Sabbath meals, from which not even the poorest family was exempt.

As an exception, the Jewish married woman had her share in honoring the Sabbath. She had to light the candles for the festivity. This is one of the three commands she had to observe while the men married or unmarried alike — were strictly under the obligation of the entire Law, which contained not less than 613 precepts, regarding things that he should or should not do.

Leon's mother usually dedicated her candles early before sunset, using large ones to be sure they would last for the whole evening. Leon liked to see her encircling the candles with her hands as if she wanted to have the full blessing of them as she prayed to God for enlightenment. Then she prayed for her family, relatives and the nation.

The rabbis attached quite a few mystical applications to the observance of the Sabbath. It was then, and still is today, celebrated as a "queen," or a "bride," with a special order of worship and prayers. One hymn which is still sung in the synagogue on the eve of the Sabbath, became very popular. It is the *"Lechah-Dodi,"* composed by Rabbi Shelomoh Halevi Alkabez in the year 1540, and sung to some two thousand different musical settings in the synagogues and Jewish homes of the world. In it the Heavenly Father is invited to meet and greet Sabbath as the "bride," the "queen." *(Shabbat ha-Malkah* in Hebrew)

Returning from the synagogue with his father, upon entering the door, Leon was aware of the presence of the invisible holy angels, the messengers of God, sent to attend the festival. That is why they were welcomed by Leon and his father with a hymn, *"Shalom aleichem"* — "Peace be with you, you angels of peace, you serving messengers from the Most High King of Kings. O, Holy One, bless us with peace," etc.

At the head of the royally-decorated table were placed two emblems of great significance, namely, bread and wine. The special bread was home-baked of the finest flour. On the table were two loaves covered with a white napkin. They represented the two rows of the *"Lechem ha-panim"* — the shewbread in the sanctuary of old — which were set every Sabbath before God (Ex. 25:30 and Lev. 24:5-8.) With the bread there was wine prepared of grapes or raisins unfermented. There is a mystical significance attached to these emblems... one of these loaves being made of three strips, plaited together and baked into one loaf.

It was customary to invite strangers from other places who could not return to their cities to enjoy the observance of the Sabbath with their own families, to share in the celebration.

The first ceremony at the table on Friday evening was the blessing of the cup *(Kiddush* — sanctification) in which the final act of creation and the institution of the Sabbath was related by reciting Gen. 2:1-3. This was repeated by all male members of the family at the table, each holding in his hand the goblet filled with wine.

After the traditional washing of the hands, the father lifted the loaves, saying grace. Then the plain loaf, designated for the evening meal, was shared by all. During the meal songs of praise were sung, and hymns of remembrance of Jerusalem and of the King Messiah were chanted. The invited guests related their experiences which added to the merriment of the event.

Each meal of the Sabbath was dedicated by chanting the *"Athkeinu Saidatha"* from different aspects of the Deity — the first to the *"Atkins Kadisha,"* which suggests the Ancient One (meaning God, as we find the word used by Daniel in 7:13). Another is dedicated to the honor of *"Zair-Anpin,"* the *Shechinah* Glory, or the visible manifestation of God; and one, to the name of *"Kakal Tapuchin,"* or *"Malkah ha-Mashiach"* (the King Messiah).

The third meal of the Sabbath, the *"Shloa Seuda,"* ended with a ceremony of *"Havdalah,"* meaning separation. This separated the holy Sabbath from the approaching weekday, etc. To this, too, the rabbis attached a mystical significance, which was observed in Leon's home very strictly. It was linked with the fellowship meal at which a group of the caste to which Leon's father belonged, was present, bringing with them of the good things from their home meals to share together. The main object of their gathering was to listen to rabbinical discourses which Leon's father gave on such occasions.

After this fellowship meal, when the tablecloth was removed, a cup was filled to overflowing with wine to demonstrate gratitude to God for His bountiful blessings with the words of Psalm 23:5 — "My cup runneth over," — then, standing with the cup in his hand, Father recited the word from Isa. 12:2 — "Behold God is my salvation; I will trust and not be afraid: for the Lord Jehovah is my strength and my song; He also is my salvation." This benediction was uttered at the lighted candle, which in itself had mystical significance.

This candle was plaited of three thin paraffin tapers, each of different color — blue, red, and white. When lighted, the three flames merged into one. Little Leon was proud when given the privilege of holding the *"Havdalah"* candle, and he enjoyed seeing the three lights merging into one flame.

The singing at this third Sabbath meal — dedicated to the King Messiah — *"David Malkah Mashiach"* — was also mystical in nature. Father sang it in a minor tune very solemnly, the hymn *"Bene Hachlo"*: "Those of the inner court who desire with longing to see the radiance of the *"Zair Anpin"* (Shechinah Glory) behold these emblems as manifesting symbolically the countenance of the King." After this, another hymn was sung by all. This hymn was to honor Elijah, the prophet, asking him: "Will the Messiah, the Son of David, soon come to us?"

♼

Melava Malka

♼

The gathering of friends remained until after midnight to bid farewell to the "Queen" Sabbath — as well as to the *"Neshamah Yeterah"* — additional soul. Those mystics believe that God gives to His faithful ones for the duration of the Sabbath an additional soul to be able to observe this day in a worthy and holy manner.

♼

Succot

♼

Another pleasant holiday in the festive cycle of the seven Jewish feasts is the observance of the Tabernacles. In compliance with the command in Lev. 23:42-45, every Jew has to build a booth for his abode during the whole week. This is in remembrance of the nation's wandering in the desert after deliverance from Egypt.

Leon gladly joined his father, and enjoyed the meals even more than in the house. The booth was nicely decorated and offered an altogether pleasant change. The last day of this festival was celebrated to the honor of the Law, *"Simchat Torah,"* a really joyous event for old and young. The old folks rejoiced that they were enabled during the whole year on each Sabbath to read a portion in the Law, and that, as the last portion was read, they could roll the Scroll back to Genesis to start anew the reading of the Holy Law.

This was celebrated as a pageantry with a procession in all the synagogues, where all the Scrolls were taken out from the Ark and carried around. Those present, both young and old, were honored to carry one of the Scrolls, while the little boys were holding banners with burning candles attached to the top of the staffs. Prayers were chanted, hymns were sung, literally reenacting the scene when King David brought the Ark home (2 Sam. 6:16 and 1 Chron. 16:28,29) and danced for joy. How different was this feast from the two preceding ones — the solemn New Year and the Day of Atonement — which were accompanied by crying and fasting without any assurance of the required results.

ॷ

Passover Feast

ॷ

Most of all Leon liked the Passover Week, as this gave much pleasant excitement when everything in the house was turned upside down, receiving a thorough cleansing and ritual purifying. This included the careful gathering of crumbs of leavened bread on the eve of the 14th day of the month of Nissan before the morning of that day, with the dawn of which only unleavened bread was allowed in the house for the next seven days. (Ex. 12:19-20)

It was for this festival that every member of the family had to put on new clothing and new footwear, and the whole setup, even the food, was different — not only the *Matzoth,* which were exceptionally unleavened — but most of the dishes were different also.

The *Matzoth* were prepared of carefully selected wheat meal and water — without salt or any other substance. The wheat, from the very day of harvesting and during the process of milling, was strictly guarded from every mixture and any by-products. Even the water which was used for preparing the dough, had to be drawn from a spring, and was carefully protected. Any other element, even microscopic, would defile its purity. Those *Matzoth* were baked in specially prepared ovens or, if in a bakery oven which was normally used for preparing leavened bread, it was purified by red-hot heat before being used for the baking of the Matzoth.

Father was dressed in a white linen garment with an embroidered or velvet skull-cap upon his head, and before him was set a large plate with three Matzoth, unleavened cakes, baked by the men of the *"Chasidim"* sect themselves, to be sure of the strictest observance in their ritual preparation, hence the name *"Matzoth Shmura."* These Matzoth were wrapped under one cover and put on the Seder plates.

On a separate special plate there were five other symbols: a roast shank-bone of a lamb, a hard-boiled egg, bitter herbs (horse radish), parsley and charoseth, the latter made of crushed almonds and other nuts mixed with wine to look like miry clay. A dish with salt water was set in front of the Seder plate. All of these symbols were reminders of the experiences of Israel in Egypt, including the night of their hasty, miraculous deliverance and the crossing of the salty Red Sea.

The reason why the Jew today has not the Passover lamb, only a shank-bone, is according to God's commandment in Deut. 16:2, 5 and 6: "Thou shalt therefore sacrifice the Passover unto the Lord thy God of the flock and the herd, in the place which the Lord shall choose to place His name there... Thou mayest not sacrifice the Passover within any of thy gates, which the Lord thy God giveth thee, but at the place which the Lord thy God shall choose to place His name in, there thou shall sacrifice the Passover at even..."

Therefore, the shank-bone is only a memorial, a symbol, of the Passover Lamb. Likewise, the egg is a symbol of the *"Korban Chagiga"* — the usual festive offering — which is also forbidden to be sacrificed outside of the sanctuary. These two memorial symbols are only a reminder, and not to be eaten like the others.

At this *Seder* evening Leon had to ask his father four questions. While usually Jewish children are not allowed to question things regarding religion, at the Passover festival the Rabbis allowed their questions to be asked in accordance with Ex. 12:26. Those four questions concerning the procedure and the whole setup for the Passover celebration, are answered by the father and by all those present at the table by reading the history of Israel's experiences in the land of oppression and the miraculous deliverance out of Egypt.

Leon would have really appreciated hearing the whole story out of the Word of God in two or three verses, but the rabbis prescribed telling it in great detail, which was very tiresome for little Leon, who was hungry and sleepy, but was obliged to wait until the end, when mother would finally be allowed to serve the good meal.

One procedure of the Passover night scared Leon, when father ordered the door to be opened, and everyone turned in anticipation of the appearance of the prophet Elijah, for whom a silver cup of wine was placed in the center of the table...

This was a very meaningful and festive part of the Passover Meal. Being just a little boy, Leon did not yet grasp the whole significance of this part in the evening, but later these things became much clearer to him and he could see that all symbols of the Passover meal, and especially this last one at the close of the meal, were pointing to the ultimate Deliverer of Israel — their Messiah.

For many years to come, as this little boy grew and matured, he remembered the words his father read from the Holy Scriptures, that this was a special night, "A NIGHT OF THE LORD TO BE OBSERVED OF ALL THE CHILDREN OF ISRAEL IN THEIR GENERATIONS." (Exodus 12:42). Sensing the importance of this solemn occasion, Leon cherished the Jewish tradition which, accordingly, to this day includes at this stage of the Passover meal preparations to welcome Elijah, the ever-living Prophet, who is to be the harbinger of the Messiah. To this day it is customary to fill a SPECIAL GOBLET of wine in his honor — THE CUP OF ELIJAH, especially adorned with scenes from the Prophet's career, as for example, the occasion when he fearlessly reproved King Ahab (1 Kings 18:17-22), as well as several others. Tradition also prescribes that while the cup is filled, the door is opened without fear (for is this not

a night of watching for the Lord?) so that the PROPHET
OF REDEMPTION may enter."

ψ

Fear of the Cross

ψ

All of this and much more was being stored deep in the
heart of Leon and became clear only years later, but
meanwhile, the little Jewish boy was growing up in the
constant fear of the Cross. He avoided all contacts with
Christians. The so-called "Christians" around Leon had
neither influence nor attraction for him. As a rule, the
Gentiles in the place where he lived were hostile to the
Jews. Gentile boys poked and kicked Jewish children
they approached. From the window of his parental home
facing the street, Leon saw a big crucifix, which to him
was a symbol of fear and trembling. On Sundays and
holidays, when the peasants from the surrounding countryside came into town, they first assembled around this
crucifix on the crossway, kneeling before it and chanting, and woe to the Jew who happened to pass by at
such a time.

It happened more than once to Leon, that on his way
to school he was attacked by one or another of those
worshipers of the crucifix. After being repeatedly mis-
treated, Leon went with his sorrow to his parents but
always received one answer: "Little boy, we cannot help
you. We are Jews in exile and are in the hands of the
uncircumcised. The Gentiles are always persecuting us
Jews, because we are different and believe in the living
God." On these occasions they would also tell Leon of
crusades of persecution, of martyrdom and of wild leg-
ends and falsehoods spread against the Jew, such as —

"The Jews use Christian blood in their Passover bread, the Matzoth." As a result many Jews were massacred during the celebration of the Christian Easter.

Such stories naturally filled Leon's heart with sorrow and indignation, for he knew that the Passover bread was prepared with painstaking care as to its purity. He also knew the strictness of the Divine Law with regard to the use of blood, that the Jew is obliged to abstain from any kind of blood in his food (Lev. 7:26-37 and 17:10-14). When he asked the question "Why should the Jew be so hated and persecuted by the Gentiles?" he never received a satisfactory answer, but was warned to keep himself away from the crucifix and the Christians.

ψ

A Youthful Prank

ψ

The studies to which the ambitious and persevering Leon was deeply devoted, were very strenuous. Being a lively boy and full of energy, he felt a desire from time to time to enjoy a little freedom. The monotony of confinement to the stuffy school room was sometimes too much. Too little liberty was given for "free breathing" as the boys liked to say. Festive days were no vacations at all. Services in the synagogue, with chanting of long prayers, required much time. The only pleasure to be had was the enjoyment of the good festival meals, prepared by the loving hands of Leon's mother and eaten in the company of the whole family. Between meals and worship hours on Sabbath days and other holidays, there were additional religious exercises, such as reciting of

Psalms from memory, the study of the *"Pirke Abot"* (Aphorisms of the Fathers), the Bible Book "Song of Songs," and customary visiting of relatives.

One time something happened to the teacher and studies were interrupted for the day. Leon, with a few other boys who were just as lively and impulsive as he, took advantage of the occasion and used the unexpected free time to play some pranks. Among other games they played was the so-called "horse racing." Three boys joined hands and racing with three other boys across the street dashed blindly into an elderly woman, throwing her to the pavement and injuring her. This unpleasant incident was reported to the supervisor of the school. As a warning for the future, the teacher inflicted a severe disciplinary punishment upon Leon, who was the instigator of the game. The entire class was mobilized to take part in the punishment. Leon was disguised, dressed as a hussar, his clothing rolled up above his shoulders representing a soldier's kit. A military top hat was made of cardboard. Thus disguised, he was obliged to "run the gauntlet," while the fellow students "applied the rod." Later these boys who did this with great pleasure received their portion in return.

In general, Leon did not have a sunny boyhood. There was no time for carefree play and other recreation such as Gentile boys of his age enjoyed. From his earliest days the yoke of Rabbinical Law was placed upon his slight shoulders. The misinterpretation of the exhortation in Hosea 9:1 — "Israel, thou shalt not rejoice like other people," did not exclude children. Leon was brought up literally "in the fear of God," not in a sense of awe toward God, but in real fear of Him.

♈ Preparatory Studies ♈

The preparatory studies of the Hebrew language had to proceed with much speed. The first milestone was reached by Leon in record time, and he learned to read Hebrew fluently. Now he could advance to a higher grade, becoming a student of the Holy *Torah* (Pentateuch). Leon was considered a very bright student with brilliant intellect. He was thus spared some of the lashes of the teacher's whip.

The study of the Bible did not begin with the first book, Genesis, but with the third book, Leviticus, the so-called *"Torath Kohanim."* This was done that he might first of all become familiar with the priestly service as it was practiced in the sanctuary.

The beginning of these studies was joyfully anticipated by the parents and grandparents, and no less by Leon himself. It was celebrated by a grand feast given in his honor. A shower of gifts from parents and friends was the reward of progress made. Praises and encouragement stimulated pride in the heart of the "hero" of the day, and increased his zeal for further contests with the boys of the intermediate school. The ambitions of the teachers in spurring Leon to make steady progress in his study were fulfilled.

Hence Leon was obliged to be in school every day from early morning until late in the evening. The meals were sent or brought to the school. Light and ventilation were very poor. For the evening hours the parents supplied the teachers with candles, which in those days were made of tallow. However, these were advantageous to the tired boys, as they invented various tricks for curtailing or shortening the length of time for burning. Sometimes a little sand was sprinkled around the wick, and the candle would begin to drip.

Memories of the early school, the cold and frosty days, long winter evenings with blizzards and icy streets were indelibly imprinted upon the mind of Leon.

His teachers were particularly strict in their demands of him to learn as much as possible by heart. They often said, "Nobody knows what might happen to us as a people, being surrounded as we are by enemies. They might again forbid the study of our holy books, as happened time and time again, so it will be necessary to learn them by heart that the Law may not fall into oblivion in Israel.

♈

Self-Respect

♈

Leon's father, Eleazar, was very strict and austere. This, among the Jews, was considered characteristic of the very pious priests. He took everything most seriously. He would not tolerate omissions in the life of his first-born son which other parents might overlook. He always stressed the importance of self-respect, saying "Never forget whose son you are or the high calling to which you were assigned and dedicated." Such repeated admonitions were not always pleasant, yet they served as a real preventative, and in later years Leon expressed his appreciation to his father for this strictness.

His mother, Gali, on the contrary, was lenient and sweet, and balanced the strictness of her husband with regard to her darling. She acted as a "guardian angel" with great tactfulness whenever father's severity was too much for the little boy. This was most comforting to

Leon. The maternal influence was very great in Leon's life, his mother helping him in every way, so that his mind might be thoroughly imbued with the sacred things related to the Holy Scriptures.

Five other children were born into the family — three boys and two girls. One of the boys died early.

♼

The First And The Last Cigarette

♼

Smoking is contagious among youngsters, especially among Jewish boys of all classes. They learned from their fathers and grandfathers even from their teachers and rabbis — who smoked at home as well as at the places of worship. In the rabbinical seminaries students could also see their dean and all the supervisors smoking their pipes. Even the famous *"Tzaddikim"* did the same. No wonder that the Jewish people became slaves to this vice early in life. Leon too was tempted, because he wanted to become a big man. He envied those of his pals who soon learned to inhale the cigarette smoke and then exhale it from their nostrils and mouths. However when Leon tried it for the first time, he turned green and became nauseated, so he never touched tobacco again as long as he lived.

♼

Chapter 2

GREATER RESPONSIBILITIES FEARS AND QUESTS

♆

Bar Mitzvah

♆

*T*he age thirteen, at which time a Jewish boy becomes, according to tradition, a son of the Commandments, was a great milestone in Leon's life, for at this age he entered upon his religious duties and responsibilities. Circumcision, to which each Jewish boy is subjected on the eighth day after his birth, grants him only the privilege to be included in the Abrahamic Covenant, which God made with the Patriarch long before the giving of the Law. Since the responsibilities in regard to God's commandments are very important, it is natural that Leon had to undergo a special course of instruction to be able to acknowledge the authority of the Holy Torah with a personal conviction. The age of thirteen, set by rabbis as the age of spiritual maturity, corresponds with the number of articles (13) in the religious creed, which was beautifully expressed by Daniel ben Judah, a poet of Rome, in his poem *"Yagdal."* It also received a number of musical settings and became one of the noblest hymns in the liturgy of the synagogue.

As a *"Bar Mitzvah,"* Leon received the phylacteries *(tefillin),* to put on each weekday morning for prayer, symbolizing tangibly the fact that he was bound to the

Law. Becoming a member of the synagogue, he was then included in public congregational worship by joining the *"Minyan,"* at which not less than ten men had to be present, the number ten being necessary, the rabbis say, because of God's promise to Abraham when he pleaded for Sodom to be saved if there were to be found ten just persons (Gen. 18:32). For this purpose the Jewish congregations support ten elderly men always to be present in their synagogues.

Nothing is said in the Bible about phylacteries, but the rabbis stressed vainly the letter of Deut. 6:8, which they interpreted in their own way. There it is recorded: "Thou shalt bind them for a sign upon thy hand, and it shall be as frontlets between thine eyes," which means to keep God's Law in mind constantly, and to act accordingly.

To implement this, the rabbis invented two little boxes from two to four inches square, made from the hide of a clean animal. There were four divisions in each, wherein were placed four passages of Scripture: Deut. 6:4-7 and 15-21, Ex. 13:2-10 and 12:16. Another respected rabbi, Jacob ben Meir (Tam), suggested a reverse order of these passages — therefore rabbinical Jews put on both.

These Scriptures are written on parchment by a *sofer* (scribe) and hidden inside so that the average Jew does not even know their contents. The phylacteries are fastened by means of leather straps, one to the forehead and one on the upper left arm near the heart. The one for the forehead has the first letter of *"Shaddai"* — God the Almighty — embossed upon it in one Hebrew character — *"Shin."* The knot of the *"Retsuah"* straps which fastens the phylacteries is made in the shape of the two other letters of the same divine attribute. The strap being wound around the left arm seven times symbolizes the words in Deut. 4:4: "But ye that did cleave unto the Lord your God are alive every one of you this day," according to the Hebrew text. With the same *"Retsuah"* the third finger is wound three times, and each time the words are chanted": I will betroth thee unto Me forever. I will betroth thee unto Me in righteousness and judgment and in loving kindness. I will betroth thee unto Me in faithfulness and thou shall know the Lord" (Hosea 2:19,20).

As *"Bar Mitzvah,"* Leon was summoned to read the Torah on the first Sabbath, which is considered a great honor. At the beginning of the reading he pronounced the following benediction: "Blessed art Thou, our God, Who has chosen us out from all other nations, and Who has given us His Commandments. Blessed art Thou, our God, the Giver of the Torah" After finishing the reading, he said, "Blessed art Thou, Jehovah, our God, Who has given us the true Torah, and planted among us the everlasting life."

With these privileges as a *"Bar Mitzvah,"* Leon fully realized the solemnity of his responsibility before God and his nation. The sins for which his father had been responsible, were now on his own account. It made a lasting impression on Leon when his father pronounced before the unrolled Torah: "I thank Thee, God, that Thou hast released me from the responsibility for the sins of this, my son."

After this, Leon said the following prayers "O my God, and the God of my fathers, on this solemn and sacred day, which marks my passage from boyhood to manhood, I humbly raise my eyes unto Thee, and declare with sincerity and truth, that henceforth I will keep Thy Commandments and undertake to bear the responsibility of mine actions towards Thee. In my earliest infancy I was brought within Thy sacred Covenant with Israel, and today I again enter as an active, responsible member of Thine elect congregation, in the midst of which I will never cease to proclaim Thy Holy Name in the face of all nations."

This day was celebrated in a special way in the presence of relatives and friends. Leon again received a shower of gifts as a reward for his Talmudic discourse — the "Derashah." The speeches, made by some of his rabbinical teachers on this occasion, emphasized the importance of religious maturity, and the solemnity of such a responsibility, burdened his heart the more. He knew too well that besides the six hundred and thirteen Biblical commandments (mitzvoth) contained in the Torah, according to rabbinical estimate, there were also innumerable precepts and bylaws, added by the rabbis, which were to be strictly observed, since it is demanded that their precepts be exercised more carefully than the great commandments of the Torah.

The burden, the heavy yoke, which was laid upon Leon's shoulders, can be fully appreciated by those who were in the same line. To live up to such a standard was impossible. Even prayer, although considered essential, was a heavy burden. It was compulsory three times on weekdays to offer long prayers, recited in the morning, afternoon and evening, as written in the old prayer books. Still longer were the prayers on Sabbath and holy day devotions, not to speak of the solemn season of repentance, the so-called "Yamim Noroim," including "Rosh Hashanah" and "Yom Kippur" (New Year and Day of Atonement). As a religious Jew, Leon solemnly repeated daily the creed containing the confession of his belief in the coming of the Redeemer, the Messiah — "I believe with perfect faith in the coming of the Messiah. If He tarries, nevertheless I am daily expecting His coming."

In addition to daily prayers, Leon was obliged to honor God with the hundred benedictions each day, the so-called *"Meah Berachoth."* The short benedictions he had to know by heart to be ready at any event. Drinking a little water or eating a snack of fruit, he had to use different kinds of benediction. Also for regular or irregular occasions of life, pleasant or unpleasant, for lightning, thunder, storm, accident, etc. Prayer is also considered a substitute for sacrifices, which no Jew is allowed to bring except in the sanctuary, where they plead with God: "May the utterance of my lips be acceptable to Thee, our God, as if I actually brought a burnt offering, a sin offering" etc. This is based upon the words of the prophet, "Take with you words and turn to the Lord, say unto Him, take away all iniquity, and receive us graciously; so will we render the sacrifice (calves) of our lips" (Hosea 14:2-3).

Very earnestly Leon Isaac emphasized in his daily prayers the confession of sins, even evil inclinations *(Yetzer ha-Rah)* by beating his breast and emphatically pronouncing each sin written — even such as he never committed. The only bright spot in all the religious exercises and the reciting of long prayers was, when the passages dealt with the coming of the Messiah, the restoration of the Temple, the rebuilding of Jerusalem and the return to the Holy Land.

Leon loved to sing the songs of Zion and to chant the *"Shemoneh Esreh"* (Eighteen Benedictions): "Sound the great trumpet to our deliverance and set us free.

Lift the banner to gather us from our exile. Assemble us together from all the corners of the world, and bring us into our land; return to the city, the city of Jerusalem, to dwell in her as Thou hast promised. Build her in our days as an everlasting building, and establish the throne of David, thy servant. Speedily cause the offspring of David, thy Servant, to flourish and let his horn be exalted by thy salvation, because we call for thy salvation all day long and hope for deliverance."

However, all the religious exercises failed to give Leon any real satisfaction. Most of them stimulated remorse, penitence, lamentation over the destruction of the Sanctuary and crying over the Shechinah Glory, which lost its habitation because of the sins of the people. It made a deep impression upon Leon, when he listened to the cries of his father during the midnight prayer: "Woe unto me for the desolation of the Holy Temple. Woe unto me for the Holy Torah which was burned with my Sanctuary. Woe unto me for the slaughter of those righteous martyrs — that His great Name and that His holy commands were dishonored. Woe unto me for the sake of the sufferings during all the generations — for the afflictions of saintly fathers and mothers — for the prophets and the just — those who are in paradise. Woe unto me for the sufferings of the Messiah, for our sins have caused Him that, and our transgressions lengthen the time of our redemption. Our iniquities are withholding the good from us. Woe to the children who are driven away from the Father's table. Although it was centuries ago that the Temple was destroyed, I consider it as though it happened in my day."

Ψ

The Talmud Student

Ψ

In accordance with a decree of the pillars of the rabbinical authorities of old, regarding the study of Holy Writ, as a rabbinical student, Leon was obliged to give one third of his time to the study of the *"Chumsah"* (Pentateuch), one third to the *"Mishna"* (Earliest Rabbinical Commentary), one third to the study of *"Gemara"* including *"Halachah"* and *"Agada"* (Talmudic classics). This literature is so vast and deep that the rabbis call it *"Yam ha-Talmud"* (Talmudic ocean). Into this stormy ocean Leon was thrown because of the goal set for him to become well-equipped and learned in all the strict rules and rituals. All the above-mentioned studies were in the original languages — the Bible in ancient Hebrew, the Targumim in Aramaic and the Talmudic books in Chaldean.

His Talmud teachers were very zealous, for they were of the old school, and it was not easy to satisfy their ambitions; but progress had to be made. Every Saturday afternoon an examination was held before father; or in his absence, before his appointee. Leon had to satisfy the whims and fancies of the examiners and to endure their sophistry — both quizzes and queries. The piercing eye of the ambitious teacher watched every procedure during these examinations, and woe if there was a slip on the part of his pupil. Besides reproach, a heavier and more intense drive was imposed.

One incident, which Leon would not forget, was an examination before the aged and very famous Rabbi Schmuel. This dear old man failed to consider that the student before him was only a young boy but expected him to be able to answer all his queries. The teacher who was present, felt humiliated because his promising student did not come up to his expectations. On the following week he laid a heavier burden upon the youthful shoulders.

Leon's studies had to begin daily before dawn, when night and day were still blended, in order to fulfill literally the Scripture "You shall meditate on it day and night." Since rising early in the morning to study was not easy for young people, Leon arranged with the town watchman on a monthly basis to awaken him before sunrise, and to avoid disturbing his parents invented a little trick. The watchman pulled a string, one end of which was attached outside the house, and the other end tied around Leon's big toe. This method was effective for he was able to leave his home quietly.

ψ

Enthralled by Superstition

ψ

The Jew in his dispersion — away from the homeland, the base of his religious obligation — has no means of observing God's commandments according to the Law. Since the Temple is destroyed, he is entirely subject to his rabbis and their interpretation of the Holy Writ. Of the Divine Law given to Moses only a "shell" was left, and even this was filled with rabbinical "stuffing" made of all kinds of substitutes, wherefore the Lord said "Their fear toward Me is taught by the precepts of men" (Is. 29:13). Over this pitiful condition another prophet lamented in the Name of God: "...they have hewed them out broken cisterns that can hold no water" (Jer. 2:13). SELF-righteousness was established instead of GOD'S righteousness; tradition and superstition instead of biblical truth, instead of love to God and reverential adoration, there is slavery: dread of Him, fear in life and fear of death. This results also in pangs of fear of the dead and of all kinds of spirits. Superstition prevails chiefly among the rabbinical Orthodox Jews.

In the evenings and by night the mind is more affected by it. After midnight, synagogues stimulate trepidation in the hearts of those who pass by in the early hours. Many ghost stories are told in connection with the synagogues, as if the souls of the departed, who during life neglected their observance of religion, gather there in groups for prayer and exercise of such rites and ceremonies. In case these dead should not have the required number for congregational prayer and the reading from the Scroll, they might cause sudden death to some passerby just to reach the full number. It makes it especially gruesome for a priest, whose presence might be indispensable for the reading of the Scroll for the congregated spirits.

Many a time, Leon, being a young priest, endured such horrors of fear when he was obliged to pass a main synagogue. To protect himself from such an eventuality, his grandfather advised him to use a cabalistic formula on his way home, as well as to recite the 92nd Psalm and Psalm 107:13-14. As another means of protection, he was advised to construct a lantern with five panes of glass, and to paint on each pane a star of David.

ψ

Intensive Secular Studies

ψ

Having been well-grounded in rabbinical studies, Leon could allow himself more time for the advanced secular studies; his keen intellect and diligence helped him not only to keep pace with the other students in the Rabbinical Seminary, but promoted speedy progress in other subjects. Leon liked history, geography and physics, and became much interested also in foreign languages. Naturally, these studies caused the sacrifice of many precious hours of sleep which were already much curtailed. "Toil with perseverance" became more and more his slogan.

ॐ

Questions

ॐ

The rabbis knew well the reason why they forbade certain questions on Bible subjects. The more one tries to exercise the ceremonial law according to Holy Scriptures, the greater the difficulties become, and less the spiritual satisfaction; the ceremonial substitutes become shallow and empty. The zeal for God, the longing to please Him with much prayer, fasting, good works and many other means of pleasing Him, leave the soul famished, the thirst unquenched — the hunger unsatisfied. The whole Jewish religion is based on past glory, with nothing to calm and assuage the anguish of the present. The poor religious Jew is deprived of the gist of his Messianic hopes.

Many questions became of earnest concern to Leon. Why would the Jew suffer as a nation without exception? Should not the righteous, the *"Tzadikim,"* the *"Chasidim"* be exempt and spared tribulation? Even the nation in its majority, in comparison with the time of the prophets of the temple, is more loyal to God than ever before. There is no actual idolatry in Israel. Why does the present dispersion of the Jewish people last longer than the previous ones? To these and similar questions Leon did not find an answer, neither from his rabbis, his father, nor from available rabbinical literature. The only reason given was: "We have sinned against God, and therefore we lost our homeland and our Sanctuary, and God is waiting until we become better Jews." This is repeatedly expressed in the popular prayers of the *"Umiphney Chalucinu"* at the solemn festivals on New Year's Day and on the Day of Atonement.

One day Mr. B., Leon's seminary colleague, entrusted to him the secret that he was studying the writings of the *"Kuri,"* the *"More Nerochim,"* and other similar religious philosophical books, which to him were eye-openers, revealing different aspects and giving more satisfaction. He invited Leon to join him. He urged him to study with him especially the Prophets.

While one could understand why the "pillars" of the Orthodox Jewry decreed to keep away from such books as were just mentioned, calling them *"Sforim Chitzoim,"* because they are of different nature, Leon could not understand why the prophetic books should be neglected or avoided. There is a warning not to meditate upon them because they DRAW — and to this warning Rabbi Solomon ben Yitzchak Rashi added the word M I N U T H — the Hebrew abbreviation of the words indicating that such meditation draweth towards the acceptance of the belief in Jesus, the Nazarene.

Knowing his colleague's piety, his complacent nature and deep knowledge of the Talmud, Leon finally joined him in the studies, in which he found a new field of thought. Soon he absorbed the study of Prophets and the Messianic predictions, which flooded his mind with more and more questions.

A Mysterious Book

One of Leon's non-rabbinical teachers took a great fancy
to him and became his friend. Time and time again he
spoke to him of modern ideas — of a destiny more pro-
ductive and beneficial than that of becoming an Orthodox rabbi; but for some reason he never made a definite
suggestion. When this teacher left, the first thing Leon
received from him in the mail was a book in Hebrew, in
a very attractive binding. In the enclosed little note this
teacher advised him to read the book in secrecy and to
let no one know about it. No further explanation was
given.

The title of the book was *"Brit Ha-Dasha"* — the
New Testament. It was new to Leon. Reading the first
page, he was puzzled by the secrecy of which the sender
spoke, wondering why such precautions were necessary.
The statement "Abraham begat Isaac and Isaac begat
Jacob" was an old story, well known to him from childhood. Thinking his teacher friend was playing a joke on
him in presenting him a religious book, as for a child,
Leon went to his colleague B. and showed it to him.

Well-read as B. was, to him also this book was a
riddle, and he paid little attention to it. In those days the
real name of Christ was never mentioned among Jews
nor in rabbinical literature. The few pamphlets in circulation spoke of *"Ishu,"* using a more blasphemous expression in reference to a *"Toli"* (the hanged one). The
New Testament was never in circulation among the Jews,
therefore it was obvious why the name of the book and
the beginning of the story did not mean much to them.

A New Discovery

Leon became more curious as to the book he received from his teacher friend, and the advice to keep it secret. When he opened it, turning the pages to have a glimpse here and there, his attention was arrested by a portion of Paul's letter to the Romans, the fifth chapter. Strange words hit his eye, like a ton of bricks: "justification by faith," "peace with God," "access into Grace," "joy," "hope," "glory." Having made this discovery, he ran to his colleague B. The reading of the first eight chapters in Romans opened a world of controversy and inner conflict. How different it sounded than the talmudic teaching of the rabbis!

The content of this book, being so interesting and new, stimulated an earnest desire for further study. Suddenly Leon fully understood why it should be treated with great precaution, and he set aside a special late hour, once a week, for the study of it. From chapter seven he learned that the writer speaks to students of the Torah as it is known in the Hebrew wording.

A Storm of Persecution

Soon rumors spread with lightning rapidity throughout the town, that the most dangerous book of the *"Toli"* was circulating among the rabbinical youth. An order was issued by the chief Rabbi S. to announce from pulpits of various synagogues, as well as in the Talmudic Schools, demanding that the book, which he called *"Treife Possul,"* be delivered to him immediately. Leon suspected that the warning was against his book and wondered: how did the rabbis find out about it?

Since the title of the book was not mentioned, and no further reference to the matter was made, he waited to see how things would develop. However, when days passed by and no one had responded to the rabbi's demand, he repeated it with more earnestness and said, it was certain that those who read this book will fall into the *"shmad,"* (a description used for becoming an impostor or a heathen).

The entire population was panic-stricken. The rabbi demanded to bring to him all *"Sfurim Kitzonim"* (books which have no rabbinical application). Some of the parents, not knowing the difference, brought rabbinical and other school books to him. However, the book he wanted was not found.

When questioned as to where he got his information, the rabbi said, he received a letter, informing him, that the most dangerous book, used by the *"Meshamudim,"* was sent to one of the young people of the congregation, but he did not know exactly the name of the book, nor to whom it was sent.

By that time Leon and his colleague B. had learned unmistakably, that the book wanted, was the one in their possession. They did not know what to do about it. It was not a simple matter to hand it to the rabbi, as this would mean exposing oneself to the pillory. To destroy the book would mean that the terror of panic, which affected many innocent people, would increase, and to send it to the rabbi, would extend the suspicion to others, not guilty of having it, and would also be cowardly.

The rabbi threatened that if the accursed book were not delivered to him, the wrath of God would visit the whole congregation; expectant young mothers and innocent children would perish. "I will not rest," he said, "until the book is destroyed in my presence."

Nothing else could be done toward appeasement of weeping mothers, embarrassed fathers, the indignant, zealous rabbi and the elders of the congregation, so Leon and his colleague decided to deliver the book and tell how it came into their possession — that the content was still strange to them even though they read a little here and there.

Pursuing this course, Leon and his colleague ran into great trouble. No chance was given for explanation and vindication. In his fury, the rabbi ordered a fire to be kindled immediately, not permitting anyone to touch the book, lest he become defiled. He demanded that the book be thrown into the blaze, while he solemnly recited the words of Deut. 13:5: "...so shalt thou put the evil away from the midst of thee."

B. wished to save the nice cover of the book, endeavoring to rip it from the pages, but was slapped in the face by the valet of the rabbi, and so the entire book was destroyed in the blaze. This triumph over the book was announced to all the synagogues without delay. However, the excitement continued, because those who had had this forbidden, dangerous book were still part of the congregation, and a storm of persecution broke over the heads of Leon and B.

♉

Strange Interference

♉

In spite of the great respect and reverence towards Leon's parents, it was voted that Leon be excommunicated from the *"Stebel"* (special place of worship used by the pious Chasidim), to whom he and his father belonged as members. The sin committed by Leon was considered a disgrace to the entire clan. None of those, who otherwise would have done anything for Leon, whom they loved, dared to interfere or to protect him against this severe measure; but something unexpected happened. One Sabbath morning, as the congregation gathered for worship, a group of Jewish men, 'who did not belong to the caste, came and strongly demanded that this ban be removed, declaring: "We will not leave this place, and we will not let you take the Scroll out for reading, unless you exonerate Rebb Eleazar's son."

The leader of the group, being a man of influence, succeeded in his demand, and the ban was lifted from both. They were again admitted to the synagogue. Nevertheless, the more zealous among the rabbinical students continued expressing their opposition against Leon and B., and both had to endure shame, reproach and severe persecution.

Leon's mother suffered much because of the reproach brought upon the family, yet remained unchanged in her devotion to the son of her hope, which was a great consolation to him. To Leon's surprise, the rebuke of his austere father, when he was summoned home, was much less than he had anticipated. Very wisely he took a different attitude toward the episode with the book, minimizing its significance.

Instead, he manifested his indignation and protest to all who dared to humiliate him, by misjudging and ill-treating his son. This was wise of him and Leon was really thankful for that.

For the sake of the future of his son, Leon's father decided to move to a distant place. By moving the entire family, he not only took Leon away from his current environment, but also established a new home for all of his loved ones. In this new place Leon found a better opportunity for proceeding with his studies, both rabbinical and secular. The progress he had made thus far spurred his ambitions for more and speedier advancements. The vigilance of the father, however, who watched his son closely, was sometimes too much for Leon. Father wanted to know all associates and colleagues his son had made in the new town. It looked a lot like distrust, and Leon became resentful.

His resentment was typical of all young men under parental scrutiny. There was ample reason for distrust, because Leon secretly, through correspondence, maintained his friendship with B., from whom he learned, to his dismay, that after B. obtained his rabbinical diploma, he decided not to accept any call from any congregation, because this move would not comply with his present views. Leon understood that his friend's interest in the "forbidden book" was more than mere curiosity.

Ψ

New Friendship

Ψ

Among the rabbinical students in W. was a young man named Samuel, of respectable parents, who was a little older than Leon, and an exceptionally gifted student. He was well-read, very intelligent, and more progressive than was generally known. Leon found in him a colleague after his own heart and, this with full approval of his father. Both also found pleasure in playing the violin together; but it was in their mutual studies that Leon discovered that Samuel was of the same mind as his colleague B., who spent much time studying other things... This bound them closer to one another.

Once, in talking about books, Leon related, in part, his last experience with a "unique book." To this Samuel remarked that he too owned one "very rare book." This aroused Leon's curiosity, and he begged his friend to show it to him. Samuel did not easily yield to this request, but finally it was arranged to bring the book to their next walk in the forest. Holding it under his coat, Samuel exposed it and allowed Leon a glimpse. This was sufficient. He recognized it at once as being the *"Brit Ha-Dasha."* The expression on Leon's face revealed that he knew the book, and both friends wished to share the secret as to how they came into contact with it. First Leon told his whole story, which made a deep impression on Samuel, but the fact that this book was once more put before him, caused Leon's heart to tremble with fear. Something was happening quite out of his control...

More exciting was the story which Samuel had to tell about his *"Brit Ha-Dasha":* "A friend of mine," he said, "while traveling by train, had met a Jewish gentleman, who during conversation revealed himself a believer in Him, whom we call the *'Toli,'* as being the Messiah of Israel. In the course of their conversation he brought such convincing arguments and unfailing evidences from the Prophets, that being sincere, very religious and well-read in rabbinical theology, my friend became really interested in the subject and in the study of the book, so this stranger gave it to him. He began comparing it with the Bible, the Messianic promises and history, and became persuaded that this man presented to him the truth.

"My friend shared with me his new convictions, saying that we, as Jews, made an ominous mistake in rejecting Him who was the promised Messiah, by name

Yeshuah, whom the zealous leaders of our people delivered up because of envy, into the bands of the Gentiles, and this was how He became the *'Toli.'"*

Suddenly tears came to Samuel's eyes. He paused, and with enhanced emotion told what happened to his friend: "His father, noticing a change in his son, made life miserable for him, trying to destroy the book which my friend defended. The book was torn and lost its cover. My friend ran away and no one knew were he went. After several months he sent me a letter from a city in England and a little parcel containing this book. In the letter he wrote among other things: 'I treasure this book as my 'eye-opener': It helped me to find our Savior, and I send it to you.'"

For some reason, Samuel urged Leon not to mention this book to him again. He treasured it as a relic from his friend and kept it secret. Although he was quite familiar with its contents, it did not affect him as one would suppose.

Leon was eager to read the book, since the little he had read before in the Letter to the Romans, had provoked him to try to find one, but all was in vain. There was no way for Leon to procure a copy of the book in those days when the work of Jewish Missions, particularly in the Russian Empire, was in its infancy.

ψ

New Paths

ψ

By and by, a new light began to break through in Leon's life. From the correspondence with his friend B. he learned a little more of the reasons why he had decided to give up his rabbinical career. They became of great concern to Leon, but he continued in his own rabbinical studies, although in his new environment he found that more than one of his colleagues were disappointed and regretted spending so much time in that kind of study.

Through his colleague Samuel, Leon was introduced to a group of friends who were *"Maskilim"* (progressive intellectuals) and *"Chovevei Tziyon"* (lovers of Zion). As harmless as their activities were, since they were only educational, endeavoring to revive the Hebrew language and the repatriation of Jewish people to the Holy Land of the fathers, the opposition on the part of the zealous rabbinical fanatics was very strong everywhere. They tried everything to uproot this young movement.

The President of the Society was a certain P., a medical doctor and a great scholar; so also was Dr. B., the Secretary. The members were a select group of earnest intelligent people really devoted to the cause. One of the aims was to maintain an educational center with free college courses for Jewish students, to prepare them for the university. In Russia such an effort was of immeasurable importance for assiduous young men, who were handicapped because of restrictions.

Leon's linguistic preparation with a good knowledge of Hebrew was welcome in this society, and he soon became one of the staff in editing an hectographed local Hebrew paper, *"THE DAWN."*

Encouraged by Dr. P., the President, and other members of the Society, Leon began to prepare himself for pharmacology. He too became convinced that he should give up the rabbinical career, although it was very promising for him. This decision caused great dismay and disappointment to his parents, relatives and friends. After some unpleasant arguments at home, it became necessary for him to leave his parental home.

The most promising place to reach the new goal before him was the city of Warsaw, formerly Poland (and now again Poland), but then the capital of the general government, included in the empire of the Russian Czar. Although under the domination of Russia, it had some autonomic privileges, with less restrictions for Jews. This was the only part of Russia where Jews were permitted to settle in large numbers. There also was more opportunity for Jews, at least, to study some free professions at the local university.

Leaving the cozy atmosphere of home, being without cares and responsibilities to anyone, proved not easy for Leon, but the foresight and friendly advice of his friends helped him to handle this new phase in his life. He was advised to take a course in bookkeeping in a business college, which enabled him, after obtaining some of the skills, to earn enough money to take care of himself. Still, the conditions and strange environment demanded of him new adjustments. Regulations and restrictions in this place proved also a great handicap for him. The struggle was much harder than he had anticipated.

ψ

Chapter 3

GOD'S DISPOSALS

*T*he proverb "Man proposes and God disposes" was confirmed time and time again in Leon's life. It became evident that after his plans in the realm of rabbinical ambitions were dashed by God's providential interference, the action of God's providence in his new endeavors became even more evident. Twice Leon came into direct contact with the New Testament, without recognizing or understanding God's leading. His new ambitions had put his remarkable experiences of the past into the background, and he pressed on with great determination to reach his new goals.

One day, the son of the house where Leon was rooming, came in, and began to describe excitedly an unusual occurrence he had just witnessed. A Jewish man had distributed books and leaflets in Hebrew and Yiddish and caused a great stir among the Jews. The street was littered with the torn leaflets and books, and the man, after being severely attacked, had barely escaped.

Leon could not resist the inner urge to go and see for himself what had happened. It was obvious that this was something unusual. Why should a Jewish man be attacked for distributing Hebrew and Yiddish literature, and why would his books be destroyed? Leon immediately realized that this event might be of great interest to him. He rushed to the scene where the trouble occurred, and on the way there met a Jew with a flushed face, holding in his hand a few of the torn leaflets. Leon asked if he too witnessed the commotion. "Yes," the man replied, "I myself gave him plenty of trouble." The *"Meshamud"* will never again dare to deceive us with the *"Apikorahishe"* books.

When Leon approached the area, he found groups of Jews still excitedly discussing the incident, and in many places the torn pieces of literature were still littering the street. He cautiously picked up some of the leaflets which were not in Hebrew but in Yiddish. He was disappointed, being more interested in Hebrew literature than in Yiddish — the common language of the unlearned. Throwing them away, he picked up others, and glancing through them, discovered a rubber-stamped address of the place where literature in different languages could be obtained.

In spite of an inner warning, reminding him of his previous experience with the forbidden book, he was moved to visit the place. However, realizing the necessity for precaution, he waited until evening. When he entered the place, a man welcomed him with a smile, and the usual Hebrew greeting *"Shalom Aleichem"* was extended to him.

It was the right place, but because of the man looking too typically Jewish, with a black beard, Leon asked him if he could advise him where to buy a copy of the *"Brit Ha-Dasha."* "But, of course, you'll find it right here," replied the man, and began to ask questions to make his customer stay a little longer and gain time to talk to him. He wished to know how and why Leon became interested in this particular book. Standing in front of this man as if on fiery coals, Leon tried to evade a parley. He was in a hurry to get the book and leave the place. The man, however, introducing himself as

Mr. Silberstein, was not in a hurry to wrap the book and hand it to Leon. More questions on a subject of an irritating nature led to a heated argument.

ψ

A Trodden Treasure

ψ

Mr. Silberstein wanted to know whether Leon was present at the scene when he was attacked on the street. Answering the question, Leon could not resist asking why the man wasted so much of his literature by giving it away to be destroyed by fanatics. Mr. Silberstein replied with sadness in his voice, "If our people could only know that they have been treading upon a treasure in destroying the Word of Life, they would certainly not have done it. It was because of spiritual blindness that they rejected the Messiah, of Whom my literature speaks. I am 'casting bread upon the waters,' and it will yield its fruit in due time.

Leon was stunned to hear him call Jews "our people," in spite of their attitude towards him. He referred to a passage in the Gospel, relating to the Messiah's compassion towards His scattered Jewish people, the lost sheep of Israel, and Mr. Silberstein added: "He commanded us to love and to pray for those who hate us without cause."

The sincerity of Mr. S.'s testimony impressed Leon very much, and called forth more arguments. It was the first time in his life that he stood face to face with a man who believed in Jesus as the Messiah, and who propagated His teaching so openly and fearlessly. This was too much for Leon, and he considered it his duty to contradict. Rabbinical traditions, Talmudic scholasticism linked with modern knowledge and views, were the weapons Leon used, while Mr. S. humbly, but bravely, used the double-edged sword of the Word of God, quoting one Scripture after another. The discussion became more heated than was really intended, particularly on the part of Leon.

Mr. Silberstein manifested great understanding of Leon's opposing arguments. However, the quotations from the New Testament, 2nd Corinthians 3:13-17, regarding the veil of Moses which covers the Jewish eyes and heart, and from his Torah, were like oil poured onto a flame. Leon asked again for the book for which he came, that he might leave the place, which was uncomfortably hot for him; but Mr. Silberstein explained to Leon that he had nothing to fear, for if anyone should come in, this person would be either a seeker after the truth or a secret believer.

♼

Inner Conflict

♼

The evidence from the Tanach, the complete Hebrew Bible, which Mr. Silberstein called "the identification documents" to prove Jesus of Nazareth the messiah, was indeed striking. Although Leon knew by heart almost all of these quotations, as well as many other passages, he had never seen in them any reference to Jesus. He could not see the link between the expected Messiah of Israel and the Jesus of the Gentiles. This was the greatest stumbling-block for Leon, and provoked him to real controversy with this man, whom he considered an impostor — a man who had fallen into the heresy, or the *"Neshome."*

Leon felt it his duty, and also considered it would be a great triumph, to win this poor soul back into the

Jewish faith. Time and again, however, one or another of Mr. Silberstein's arguments with quotations from the Scriptures, stirred Leon's mind and increased his inner conflict.

After a number of weeks, he again visited Mr. Silberstein and the debate, which started on the first visit, was taken up once more. Noticing that Mr. Silberstein was not so well equipped with rabbinical or modern arguments, Leon made it hard for his opponent by using his own knowledge of the Old Testament Scripture texts and mixing them with sophistry, ingenuity and sagacity of the interpretations of the rabbis.

By and by Mr. Silberstein took a special fancy to his opponent and invited him to visit him at his home as often as possible. Leon, on his part, although busy, became more and more interested, spending increasingly more of his time in these arguments. When, gradually, a gleam of the truth about the unfailing predictions in the Bible concerning the Messiah began to enlighten Leon's mind, it caused a very serious reaction, which even more than before deepened his inner conflict. "It cannot be true," he said to himself, "If Jesus was the Messiah, then the entire Jewish nation is in a predicament, because of rejection of Him. Then everything is lost, there is no use to hope any more." And so he understood the Scripture, recorded by Jeremiah and applied by Apostle Paul to Jesus as the Messiah in Acts 17:25: "The breath of our nostrils, the anointed of the Lord, was taken in their pits, of whom we said, 'Under His shadow we shall live among the nations." (Lam. 4:20).

Leon's perplexity grew. The thought of the destiny of his nation, which he loved so dearly, was overwhelming. Judging by the attitude of the Jews he knew and how yearningly they expected their Messiah, he could not imagine that there could have been a time in Israel's history, when the same nation would reject the One they had been waiting for, although He was able to prove to them that He was the Messiah, the promised One, and would thereby satisfy their anticipation and longing.

Unwittingly, Leon had the same thought which Paul expressed in an epistle to the Corinthians, dealing with the rejection of Jesus, that "if they would have recognized in Him the Prince of Glory, they would not have crucified Him" (1 Cor. 2:8), as well as what he said to the Jews in the synagogue in Antioch — that "the citizens of Jerusalem and their elders rejected Jesus because they did not recognize in Him the Promised One." (Acts 13:27)

Leon was about to give up the whole thing as a matter belonging to the past. If the rejection of Christ was a national mistake, then it could never be made good again.

Several weeks passed. Leon shunned the place and refused to visit the home of Mr. Silberstein to which he was repeatedly invited for more private talks.

♍

"Coincidence"

♍

Not paying attention to the fact that it could be providential, Leon considered it a mere coincidence when Mr. Silberstein approached him on the street and urged him to visit a friend from England with him. Leon could not resist such a friendly invitation, and besides, he was quite curious. The man to whom he was introduced was older than Mr. Silberstein and was also a missionary. It wasn't long before they were in an argument. Here was a new challenge for Leon. The new friend had more skill than Mr. Silberstein, and found much pleasure in arguing. With much determination he rather imposed his arguments and had very little patience.

The Argument About Trinity vs. Monotheism

After becoming a Christian, Leon often regretted the embarrassment he caused the missionary from England, who eventually became a real personal friend, but it was his own fault because he acted so over-zealous. There were many obstacles to be removed from Leon's path. He was an ambitious young Jew who loved his nation and was loyal to the God of his fathers, and so, the Holy Trinity, a basic dogma of Christian faith, was the greatest obstacle for Leon, due to the fact that the basis for his religion was monotheism — belief in one God. Leon firmly believed that there is only one God, and that there can be none other equal to or besides Jehovah.

The argument, started by the missionary with attempts to prove to Leon that the word *"Elohim,"* in the book of Genesis, indicates that the God of creation is a plural God, met with a counter-argument. While Leon admitted that *"Elohim"* is indeed plural form, derived from the word *"El"* (meaning the Mighty or the Supreme One), yet it does not necessarily indicate a plurality of persons, not to speak of *"pluralistic majestus."* Leon further argued, that in many places in the Bible, even in the same book of Genesis, in the record of creation, *"Elohim"* is used together with *"Jehovah."* If the word *"Elohim,"* in itself, would suggest the Trinity, then certainly Jehovah would be a fourth deity besides the Trinity. Furthermore, he argued, the term *"Elohim"* is used in the Bible in reference to men as well as to idols, God said to Moses: "I will make thee an *"Elohim"* to the Pharaoh, and Aaron to be thy prophet."

"Elohim" is applied to men in general in Ps. 82:6 and in the Epistle to the Hebrews: "I have said you are *'Elohim'* — 'gods' — and children of the Most High." In many places in the Bible the heathen idols are also called *"Elohim."* This suggests that the word "Elohim" in itself is not the highest attribute of Deity, and cannot always be interpreted as plurality. Moses was only one person.

The strongest argument for Leon, however, was that in the Decalogue, in the first commandment God gave to Israel on Mount Sinai, He emphatically introduced Himself in singular form, as *"Jehovah El"* The same form is repeated in the Ten Commandments in Exodus 20, not less than five times, in verses: 1,5,7,10,12. Furthermore, in the Decalogue, God warned Israel not to have other *"Elohim,"* besides Himself, (v.3). In Deut. 13:5-12 God decrees the severest punishment of death upon any person who would teach or believe in another God than Jehovah. Monotheism is the bulwark of Rabbinical Judaism and is not easily defeated. It is a basic dogma in its creed *"Ani-Maanim,"* which it repeated daily in the Jewish rituals.

The conversation was revived another time and again the subject of *"Elohim"* was tackled. The debaters were shocked when Leon cited from Exodus 22:20 "He who sacrifices to *'Elohim,'* except to Jehovah, shall be destroyed." Also in the *"Shema Israel"* (which is very popular in the Jewish religion) God is spoken of as Jehovah, the One God of Israel. This argument, however, was repudiated by the missionary from the very verse which Leon quoted, "Hear, Israel, Jehovah our God is one God." To verify his point of the view that this rather suggests very strongly the Trinity, because the name of God is used three times, as an *"echod,"* which means a unity, and not a *"yochid,"* which would suggest a strict singular.

(The Rabbi's interpretation can be found in the 13 articles of the Jewish Faith — called *"Ani Maanim"* (composed by a Jewish Rabbi, Moses Ben Maimon, known as the Rambam, 12 century scholar). These articles blatantly distort the meaning of the passage "Hear, Israel, Jehovah our God is one God," by stating: "I believe with a perfect faith that the Creator, blessed be He, is *'YOCHID'* literally single." Though the Bible says *"Echod,"* they say *"Yochid"!)*

These arguments according to the Hebrew texts of the Bible, were indeed striking and powerful. The missionary had other proofs, yet nothing was convincing to Leon. His eyes were still blinded. What the missionary said did not fit in the rabbinical interpretations. This time, Leon argued that while it is true that God is used three times, yet there Jehovah is mentioned twice, and not as three different deities. The Hebrew wording is: *"Jehovah — Elohim — Jehovah Echod."*

The missionary made again an issue of the word *"Echod,"* quoting Genesis 2:24, where the word *"Echod"* is applied to Adam and Eve. "They being two different persons, became one flesh — *"Bosor Echod."* Repudiating this statement, Leon replied that Adam and Eve became one flesh in the purpose of marriage, but not one person which is indicated in the next verse Gen. 3, where they are spoken of as two and not as one; namely, that both were naked.

At the end of this debate, Leon quoted Mal. 2:10, where the word *"Echod"* is applied to God in singular form, namely, *"El-Echod,"* and of *"Av Echad"* — one Father and that the word *"Echod"* is in compliance with the Hebrew grammar used to express the Hebrew "one" — like in *"Bet Echod"* — one house, *"Adam Echod"* — one man, etc.

This subject, however, engrossed him more than he ever dreamed, and he began to search the Scriptures more diligently. It amazed him when he began to discover verses as if he had never seen them before, though he had known them by heart. The revelation of God to Abraham in three persons (Gen. 18) was certainly not new to him, but it was wrapped in rabbinical commentation.

Also, in the record of the creation of Adam, God Elohim said, "Let us make man after our image and our form..." (Gen. 1:26); and after Adam had sinned, God said, "Behold Adam became as one of us..." (Gen. 3:22).

At the building of the tower of Babel, God said, "Let us go down and see..." (Gen. 11:7).

Joshua, in speaking of God, said that He is the *"Elohim Kadoshim,"* which means Holy *Ones* (plural) and not the Holy *One* (singular).

All of these Scriptures are interpreted by the rabbis as to appeal to the carnal mind and to fit their position.

After these discoveries, the subject regarding deity was discussed more calmly. Leon appreciated that other Scriptures, which he had not noticed before, were shown to him, such as Gen. 1:2 where God and God's Spirit are mentioned together, and Isa. 6:8, where God asks the Prophet, "who will go for us?" and Isa. 48:16 which speaks of God Jehovah and His Spirit as Those Who sent the Messiah. Hence there was no further need for stressing words of proof that the Bible speaks not only of one God, but also of God in the plural form.

In this new light, Leon's attention was drawn to portions and expressions in the mystical books of the most exclusive rabbinical teachers. *"Zohar and Cabbala,"* and other books, speak of God not only in terms of plurality but distinctly of Divine Unity, consisting of three in One, as the *"Tlath Kishra Dimhainmitra"* (Deity knitted together as a Trinity). There are also comparisons of deity with a human being consisting of body, soul and spirit — *"Guf, Nefesh, and Ruach"* — and these are being three in one.

Another comparison is the *"Mishkan"* (sanctuary), which had three distinct divisions and yet it was one sanctuary.

In a Sabbath hymnal, the *"Kegavno"* speaks emphatically of the unity of Deity in Heaven which should inspire the unity of the family and of the nation on earth as one.

There are quite a few *"Leshem Echods"* where God and the Shechinah Glory and the *"Tomir Venelom,"* as a three-fold united Holy Deity, are worshipped equally as Trinity.

Symbolically the figure three applies to Deity, if given with the first letter 'Shin' in 'Shema Yisrael,' which is Israel's confession. This single Hebrew letter shows distinctly three equal characters having one root. The significance of this letter is evident. It is embossed on the right side of the phylactery for the head and on the mezuzah for the door, as mentioned before.

As convincing as these evidences are concerning Deity, to Leon they proved thus far that God cannot be

measured by human figures to limit Him in His Being
and Revelation. According to rabbinical assertions, God,
the Torah and Israel are an inseparable unity as an Echod.

With all these arguments Leon came only one step
nearer in his approach to Christ.

ψ

A *Stumbling Block*

ψ

In Leon's mind it was still irreconcilable to align Jesus
with Deity. As plain as the predictions of the incarnation of the Messiah were in Isaiah 7:14, 9:6-7 and Micah
5:2, to Leon they still gave much material for argument.
Again rabbinical interpretations interfered with his reasoning. Their hairsplitting sophistry deprived these Scriptures of their real meaning. Also Isa. 53, which is the
most wonderful photographic picture of the Messiah, is
recklessly interpreted in their own way. It was not easy
to come out of such an entanglement.

The rabbinical interpretations aside, Leon's loyalty
to the God of his fathers and the direct commandments
of the Bible, concerning other gods — other religions —
stood in his way. "You shall not have other gods before
Me" — rang in his ears. From Deut. 13 he knew God's
command regarding prophets, whose predictions came
to pass and who gave real signs and performed real
miracles in evidence of their being true prophets, that
even if such a prophet would dare to proclaim another
god, he should die.

The same severe punishment is to be carried out
upon any man, any relative, or the closest friend, who
would dare to entice one secretly to serve other gods
(Deut. 13:6-10). Leon knew that it was because of his

nation's turning from God and accepting the gods of their non-Jewish neighbors, that they were severely punished by being taken into captivity to Babylon. The Prophet Jeremiah gave them one text to always remember and to use against the Babylonians when they enticed them to worship their gods, namely, — "The gods that have not made the heavens and the earth, even they shall perish from the earth, and from under these heavens" (Jer. 10:11). This text Jeremiah gave in the Chaldean language, and it is the only one in the book of his prophecies. Before giving it to his people, he exhorted them not to walk in the ways of the Gentiles, and not to learn from them. He put before them the nature of the heathen gods (Jer. 10:1-5), and solemnly exclaimed: "None other unto Thee, O Lord; Thou art great, and Thy name is great in might" (vs. 6). "Jehovah (the Lord) is the true God, He is the living God, and an everlasting King" (v. 10). These three prayers — (1) *Yagdal,* (2) *Adon Olam* and (3) *Olenu,* pages 2, 57[b] in the Prayer Book, constituted the Creed of Israel then and are still part of it today.

With all this in mind, it was not easy for Leon to believe in the divinity of Jesus. The predictions in the Prophetic Books concerning the Messiah can only be conceived and believed by those to whom the arm of the Lord is revealed. This the Prophet Isaiah exclaimed in the introduction to his great vision in Isaiah 53:1. Books are sealed even to scribes and teachers of Israel and this is solemnly stated in Is. 29:11-12: "And the vision of all is become unto you as the words of a book that is sealed, which men deliver to one that is learned, saying, 'Read this, I pray thee: and he saith, I cannot; for it is sealed...'"

There were also other obstacles, namely, the misrepresentations in the lives of those who, while professing to be followers of Jesus, the Messiah of the Bible, showed forth a very unappealing brand of Christianity. No wonder that, in defense of his Judaism, which he still thought to be the right — or at least the best — religion, a rabbinical scholar like Leon tried to protect himself against any attempt to undermine his belief. How solemnly he used to confess at the open shrine, or the ark, in the synagogue before the scroll of the Law was taken out for the congregational reading, chanting the *'Baruch Schamey'* — "Blessed be the name of the Lord of the universe, Who is the only true God, and Whose law is the only true one. In Him alone we trust, and we do not trust any *'Bar Elohim'* (any Son of God). Leon was more ready to pay tribute to Jesus as a great reformer for the Gentiles — a prophet — yet not as the Messiah of Israel. He argued that Jesus did not fulfill the promises given by the prophets, namely, that Israel was to be delivered from her enemies, restored to her kingdom, etc. Even less was Leon prepared to believe in the omnipotence of Jesus, who lived as a human being, who was subject to suffering and died a violent death without defending Himself. In the course of the discussions, the missionaries emphasized the supremacy of Jesus, putting Him higher than the prophets, even greater than Moses. This was too much for Leon who then understood, as an eternal axiom, God's statement: "There arose not a prophet since in Israel like unto Moses, whom the Lord knew face to face." (Deut. 34:10) Also Num. 12:6-7, where God compares other prophets with Moses and emphasizes his prominence above all the others. This was inbred in Leon from childhood and could not be changed now or ever...or so he thought.

Nevertheless, gradually the scales began to fall from Leon's eyes. He became more willing to listen and to learn. His hunger for the 'truth' became more and more evident, and he spent many sleepless nights reading, searching, studying. If he could only believe in the miracle of the incarnation of Jesus, he thought, then other difficulties regarding His Deity would be more easily overcome.

Once Mr. Silberstein asked Leon whether he really believed that God is the Creator of the universe. "Yes," he replied. Then — "Is there anything impossible with God?" "Of course not," Leon answered. "If not, why is it considered impossible for Him, Who is the wonder-working God, to let the Redeemer of mankind be born in a supernatural way?" Not waiting for an answer, Mr. Silberstein continued, "Every true Jew believes that Adam was created and that Eve came from Adam in a very supernatural way. The necessity for the Redeemer to be born in a human body was predicted in the garden of Eden (Gen. 3:15) and later through the prophets."

By the time Mr. Silberstein finished talking, Leon was more prepared for these statements than he ever had been before. There was no doubt any longer as to the violation committed by the rabbis in their interpretations of words and verses in the Bible to overshadow Messianic promises in order to justify their antagonistic attitude towards Jesus. Leon could now see that they wrongly interpreted Isa. 7:14. *"Almah"* in Hebrew never meant a married woman, for such are called *"Isha"* or *"Nekevah."* A female child is a *"iolda"* — a young girl is *"bethulah"* or *"narah."* A mature girl is *"Almah."* The last is the feminine form of *"Alam,"* which means a young, unmarried man.

The incarnation of the Messiah was suggested in a commentary of the famous rabbi, Jacob Emden, in the Prayer Book after his name, *"Beth Jacob,"* used by the strictest caste of the *"Chasidim."* He says on page 390, regarding the Messiah, that "He is the Head of the first One, and that He originated in the *"Ruach ha Kodesh"* (Holy Spirit)."

Leon's previous argument, based on rabbinical interpretation of Ps. 2:12, that the word *"Bar,"* in the Hebrew text *"Nashku Bar,"* did not mean "kiss the Son" — as the usual term for son is *"ben"* and not *"bar,"* was soon annulled. The word *"bar,"* as "son," is used by the prophet Daniel more than once (Dan. 3:25), *"Bar Elohim"* (Son of God) and Daniel 7:13 — *"Bar Anash"* (Son of Man). In the *"Baruch Shamai,"* which is chanted as a protest against belief in the Son of God, the term used, strangely is: *"Bar Elohim."*

Concerning the two lines of Messianic predictions of glory and suffering, there is some confusion in the commentaries of the rabbis of the oldest School. It is a most commonly accepted suggestion, that the prophets spoke of two persons as Messiah: the Son of Joseph, who is the Suffering One, and the Son of David — the Glorified One.

Other authorities contradict themselves in commenting on Messianic prophecies. The Is. 52:13-15 passage, which relates to the Servant of Jehovah, is understood to be the Messiah as the Servant in His humility, yet exalted and extolled above Abraham, Moses and the Angels.

In the Talmud, tract Sanhedrin 98, col. 1, it is told about the rabbi, Yeshua ben Levi, who had a conversation with the prophet Elijah concerning the Messiah, asking him where he is and when He will come. In response, he was directed to the gates of Rome where he found the Messiah amongst the poor and the sick, looking at His own wounds and binding them one by one. The rabbi asked: "When will my Lord come?" The Messiah answered: "Today," alluding to the words in Psalm 95:6-11.

On the most solemn Day of Atonement, there is a confession made that Messiah came and turned away — the *"Pinu Menu Mashiach Tzidkenu"* — the Messiah our Righteous One has turned from us. There He is called the Sin Bearer — the Wounded One. At the end of this confession they plead with God to send Him soon again.

In spite of such clear indications (whether or not the authors of such striking assertions or statements have acknowledged the fact that it was Jesus whom they had in mind), the rabbis of today and the Jews in general do not know what they are reading about.

For Leon it was no longer difficult to apply these and other Messianic predictions and statements to Jesus. Suddenly he could clearly see that the Messiah was rejected, because of spiritual blindness of the nation of Israel, misled by their blind leaders. It saddened his heart and he exclaimed with the prophet:

> *The crown is fallen*
> *from our head:*
> *Woe unto us,*
> *that we have sinned!*
> *(Lamentation 5:16)*

With this, all resistance came to an end. The conviction Leon gained, gave him much satisfaction and peace of mind. Much of the rubbish of a controversial nature was brushed away, and yet, the historical fact that the coming of the Messiah had already occurred, did not have any effect on his spiritual life. Alas, his conviction was only an intellectual one, leaving the heart untouched.

The enemy successfully intervened, and Leon did not make any further effort to find out about the "one thing needful." So he went on with his study and work routines, according to schedule.

ψ

New Struggles

ψ

One day, while visiting an uncle with his family, Leon discovered with great amazement, that the eldest daughter of the house, who used to be his childhood playmate and in his memory still just a little girl, had blossomed into a charming young lady. The uncle was a strict Orthodox type and the aunt was also a very religious Jewess. Both were disappointed in their nephew, seeing that he had given up his career and had changed his way of life, dressing himself as the Gentiles transgressing the Law set forth in Lev. 20:23, and they scorned him because of his short coat and a derby hat.

Orthodox Jews observe Lev. 20:23 literally: "Ye shall not walk in the manner of the nations around you...," etc. therefore, the Jewish apparel is always different. Instead of a jacket, a long coat is worn, made either of wool, or of cotton, and never of mixed fabrics.

Leon's cousin Frymet (Fanny), was astonished to see before her a nice young man whom she remembered as a boy, whose pranks, while playing together, caused her some unpleasant experiences. She was favorably impressed with his present appearance and his goal in life. The pals of childhood quickly became devoted friends.

Leon's cousin was a progressive girl in spite of the fact that she was brought up in a strict religious environment. She was exceptionally well educated and well mannered.

Realizing that there would be a gulf between them because of his new convictions, Leon kept them secret from Fanny for as long as he could. However, by and by, he felt he must risk revealing his views to her. As he expected, she disapproved and rebuked him for what she called "crazy ideas" of religious fanaticism. Although he anticipated opposition on her part, he was disappointed to find that his beloved friend, in spite of her liberal education, was still in the grip of prejudice. Under ordinary circumstances, this discovery on the part of both would easily have led to a "break," but the love ruling in both hearts was deep. She tried hard to persuade him that he was wrong. On every occasion she came with her arguments, which gave Leon new opportunities to talk about his favored subject.

Much like Leon, Fanny too had an exceptionally good knowledge of the Old Testament Scriptures, which generally was not the case with Jewish girls; besides, she was well-read in other literature. This again gave ample material for the discussion of other question-raising matters. It was not difficult for Leon to show her that the other things — as interesting as they were, and the progressive literature which she cherished, would not give satisfaction for the yearning of her religious soul. While she was willing to listen to quotations from the Old Testament, she strongly opposed considering the New Testament. However, in spite of the differences in their opinions, their mutual affection was not diminished. However, because of Leon's Christian convictions there could be no thought of an imminent engagement.

ψ

An Ominous Decision

ψ

At a crucial moment, when Leon was earnestly weighing his convictions when he first came into contact with the New Testament against the opposition he met on the part of his beloved friend, his experience of the past came again to his mind as a warning signal. The subtle enemy brought before him the sorrow he caused his beloved mother by leaving the parental home yielding to a decision so contrary to her cherished hopes. An inner voice kept saying: "You nearly broke her heart then, and now your new convictions will certainly be the blow which may jeopardize her very life."

He knew that anything could be forgiven a Jew except the step toward Christianity. This was, and still is today, considered the most unpardonable of sins. Christianity has always caused a permanent, even an eternal, break within the Jewish family. If a member of a Jewish family should choose to confess faith in Christ, he would be considered a *"Meshamud"* (an outcast by God and man). In rabbinical circles, to which Leon's parents belonged, it was strongly believed that this sin, if committed by one member of the family, excluded them all from the resurrection which was to take place at the coming of the Messiah; their souls would remain forever doomed in the grave under a special black cover.

The accusing voice continued to torture Leon's heart: "How can you do this to your beloved mother?" Leon remembered the heroic decision of Abraham, who changed his religious convictions and confessed them, when he became a believer in the Living God. Abraham left his home and his land, and separated himself from his loved ones. But again came this warning: "Your case is different. You are turning away from the faith of your fathers, who believed in the God of Abraham, Isaac and Jacob. You intend to become a Christian and to believe in the religion of the Gentiles."

This was indeed an inner conflict. Leon was then reminded of another Scripture in Deut. 33:8-9, regarding the event on Mount Sinai, when the whole tribe of Levi, from which Leon descended, courageously stepped out, separating themselves from the other tribes who became disloyal to God. They were honored and their heroic act was related in Deut.: "Let the Thummim and the Urim be with thy Holy One, whom thou didst prove at Massah, and with whom thou didst strive at the waters of Meribah; who said unto his father and to his mother, I have not seen him; neither did he acknowledge his brethren, nor knew his own children, for they have observed thy word and kept thy covenant." The question arose in Leon's mind, should he not act likewise, giving honor to God according to the truth, not participating in the man-made religion, which was now void of its original significance and had become a religion of ceremonies not according to God's Commandments.

His mother meant more than anything in the world to him, and he decided not to cause her any more sorrow, particularly by such a reproach! At that moment he vowed that as long as his mother lived, he would not make any public confessions. This was indeed an ominous decision with very sad consequences.

ψ

God's Peculiar Ways

ψ

Weeks elapsed after Leon's vow to keep his convictions secret because of his mother. While his inward attitude remained unchanged, he gradually lost his zeal for studying the Word of God and no longer discussed religion with Fanny. This was what the enemy wanted. Leon's faith became indeed a private matter.

At that stage in his spiritual life Leon was not yet familiar with the words of the Savior in Matthew 8:22 in response to a request by one of His would-be followers, "Lord, suffer me first to go and bury my father." Jesus said to this 'almost disciple': "Follow Me, and let the dead bury their dead."

Not too long afterward, Leon received a telegram from home informing him that his mother was seriously ill after giving birth to her last child, a girl. Leon took the next train home. Arriving there, he found his beloved mother dying. She was unconscious for two days following his arrival, and he had no opportunity to talk with her, nor to hear her voice. She died at the age of forty, leaving her husband with four children, besides Leon, of whom the youngest was five weeks old.

This sudden severe loss was a heavy blow. The powers of darkness, often at work in such circumstances, again caused questions and queries in the heart of young Leon and, consequently, his faith in God was shaken. Again and again he asked himself: "Is there any justice with God? Why should his mother die so young?" Particularly, he began to doubt the doctrine of the New Testament concerning God being love — a typical reaction of one in trouble when the character of God is yet unknown and His ways inexperienced.

A Shocking Procedure

♅

The funeral and the burial of the mother made a shocking impression upon Leon. Belonging to the priestly cast, the family strictly observed the command in Lev. 21:1. Leon had never before attended a funeral, as priests could not defile themselves with the presence of the dead. However, in the case of a close relative father, mother, son, daughter, brother or unmarried sister — an exception was made as related in the same chapter, verses 2 and 3. The funeral was conducted according to strict religious rituals. The entire procedure was very depressing. Witnessing all the ceremonies was more than heartbreaking for Leon; to him it seemed downright gruesome.

Immediately following the pronunciation of his mother's death by the doctor, the undertakers were called. They were members of the *"Chebrah Kiddushah,"* or the "Holy Brotherhood," which served to comfort the mourners in every sizable Jewish congregation since Talmudic times. These men took the corpse and laid it on the bare floor with feet towards the door. Then a black blanket went over the body, covering it completely, and two black candles were placed at the head. Next the purification ceremony began, which was not a mere washing, but a religious rite, called *"Tahara."* Not less than nine buckets of pure water, substituting for immersion, were poured upon the corpse, while special prayers were chanted. The words of Ezekiel 36:25, "Then I will sprinkle clean water upon you and you shall be clean from thy filthiness," and many other passages were recited.

After the purification two fragments of broken earthenware were placed on the eyes of the dead woman to cover them, and the body was wrapped in "death cloth," the shroud, called *"Tash-richim"* (A white linen sheet, used for the rich and poor alike to symbolize equality of all humanity in death). This group of men customarily went calling on every family, saddened by death, and provided, in addition to the above mentioned service, modest tokens of condolence in the form of tempting delicacies of food and drink in wake of the funeral. No family member was ever allowed to prepare the post-funeral meal. Friends and neighbors were the ones who provided meals for the grieving family.

Shortly before the burial, while the body still lay on the board, Leon had to lean over the corpse of his beloved mother and, as a sign of mourning, rent his coat after it had been cut at the lapel by one of the undertakers. All other members of the family did likewise. All present asked the dead for *"Machula"* — forgiveness for every possible grievance. The funeral itself took place the same day the death occurred. In compliance with the Scriptures, the dead were not to remain unburied overnight. They were carried to the cemetery on a bier. According to the strictest religious customs, no coffin was ever used. As an exception, because Leon's mother was the wife of a priest, her body was laid in the ground on two boards. Other dead were simply buried in the ground. Following the funeral, Leon and his brothers said the *"Kaddish"* — prayer for the dead.

According to Jewish belief, the soul of every deceased person, without exception, did not ascend into heaven until a period of nine months had elapsed. The traditional belief was that the *"Kaddish,"* chanted three times daily at the synagogue during congregational services, lessened the suffering of the deceased in the grave. Through the merits of this prayer by the sons, the soul was elevated gradually until it reached its destination.

After the burial, the *"shevah,"* or the seven days of mourning, were observed. The whole family removed their shoes and were seated on footstools. The only book of the Bible allowed to be read was the book of Job.

The death of Leon's mother put a pall over his life, causing many changes. Before returning to his city of W., he gave expression to his feelings in a poem which was then used on the tombstone on his mother's grave. This poem was the outpouring of his despair and desolation. With the loss of his beloved mother, all prospective aspirations fled and the future looked dark. Again and again he was tormented by the inner voice "How can you now believe there is a loving and just God?" Consequently this led to an open rebellion.

Returning to W., Leon vainly endeavored to continue with his usual routine, but lost all interest in life. His friends noticed a great change in him. Even his violin, which he cherished, failed to attract him. Fanny, manifesting her sympathy for her beloved, could not hide her satisfaction in the change which took place in his religious life. She preferred his rebellious unbelief to his belief in Christ. Disagreeing with his agnostic views, she remained unshaken in her belief in the Jewish religion, and was very sorry that God punished Leon so severely for his foolish ideas. She did all she could to comfort him, urging him to go with her to operas and other places of amusement which she thought would reanimate him. Leon, however, found no pleasure in these things. But with the only obstacle in the way of their engagement now fully removed, Leon and Fanny made their future plans official and proceeded with the formal betrothal ceremony.

☙

Marriage

☙

After the betrothal of Leon and Fanny, the preparations for the wedding began, and as usual, it took several months to prepare the bride for the blessed event. The wedding ceremony itself had a solemn and mystic significance. Some hints regarding these ceremonies are given even in the New Testament, in the parable of ten Virgins, in Matthew 25, and in the fifth chapter of the Epistle to the Ephesians. Since Leon was married under the Jewish law and customs, he too was dressed in a white robe *(Kittel)* and led in a procession of friends and relatives with the typical triple-plaited candles *(Havdalah)* in their hands. The procession was headed by a band and led to the nuptial canopy, the *"Chuppa,"* and the groom was placed under it. (This ritual is to this day strictly observed by Jewry at large.) Once placed under the canopy, Leon was greeted by his friends and the officiating rabbi, who had gathered around it, with a traditional blessing *"Baruch Habah"* — "Blessed is he who cometh in the name of the Lord"! After the greeting, the groom stood under the *"Chuppa"* awaiting the arrival of his bride.

In the meantime, the bride was led towards the canopy by another procession. Prepared to meet her beloved, she was beautifully dressed in pure white. On approaching the canopy, she was led by her friends three times around her groom, and then placed at his right hand. The officiating rabbi read a written contract, the contents of which are traditional and fixed for all time for rich and poor alike.

The wedding ceremony was threefold. First the groom placed a ring on the index finger of the right hand of the bride with these words: "Thou shall be sanctified to me with this ring according to the Law of Moses and Israel." If the groom was a learned man, as in the case of Leon, he was expected to be able to recite by heart the threefold vows of the betrothal from Hosea 2:19-20: "I will betroth thee unto me for ever; yea, I will betroth thee unto Me in righteousness and in judgment, and in loving kindness, and in mercies. I will even betroth thee unto me in faithfulness; and thou shalt know the Lord." The second ceremony is the benediction of a cup filled with wine which the rabbi blesses and shares with the married couple. The cup must be of glass which is important for the third ceremony in which this cup is laid at the feet of the bridegroom and is broken by him. This breaking of the glass is a solemn reminder of the destruction of the Temple.

After the ceremony, the married couple is led home by the rejoicing friends and relatives, of both the bride and the groom, to the marriage feast which is always celebrated joyfully and with much entertainment. The learned groom has to give a discourse for which he is rewarded with wedding gifts. (Gifts are presented to the groom even if he has nothing to say). In rabbinical homes the feast continues for a whole week, and on each day the married couple is blessed with a seven-fold benediction.

After both Leon and his wife Fanny, became Christians, they received a formal blessing of the Church in the customary way for Christian wedlock. If someone had told them at their Jewish wedding that such a thing would ever take place, they would have dismissed it with a smile as something totally unthinkable; but God is God of the unthinkable and impossible, and He was holding in store many more exciting things for the new-lywed couple.

🕎

PART II

Chapter 4

GOD HAS SPOKEN

*L*eon was still in the grip of agnosticism. He was not only dismissing earlier Christian views he had accepted, but he was doubting the very existence of God and the entire Jewish religion! Propagating his theories to his friends, he succeeded in shaking their faith in God. He remained in this condition for more than a year, but as long as he was raging, like a volcano, spitting ashes of unbelief, God kept silent. By the end of that year Leon had no desire for the Bible, using it only now and then to pick out a verse here or there, as unbelievers typically do, to argue with his religious colleagues to enforce or prove his point of view. However, there finally came a time, when for some mysterious reason, he gradually began to lose interest in religious arguments, except occasionally, when challenged by a close friend.

Once, as Leon was using a verse from memory, desiring to prove the vanity of religion — that there is no use in believing and serving God, and that there is no profit in praying to Him — he was urged by his friend to substantiate this notion by showing an actual entire quotation from the Bible. Arguing that one cannot prove anything by separating single verses from the context, this friend provoked and challenged Leon.

As Leon went home that night, he took his long-neglected Bible, the *"Tanach,"* from its bookcase, and began to search. His first glance fell upon Ezek.

18:4: "Behold, all souls are Mine..." Paying no special attention to it, he went on until he found the verse he was looking for in Job 21:15: "What is the Almighty, that we should serve Him? And what profit should we have if we pray unto Him?" Suddenly, he remembered the challenge of his friend and began to read the preceding verses, and when he did that, he realized that his friend was right about separating verses from the context. In this passage Job meant the *UNGODLY!* At this point Leon's theories began to shake...

Once again Leon looked at the previous passage, the one he saw first and dismissed as insignificant, namely: "All souls are Mine..." These words kept buzzing and ringing in his ears. He tried to get rid of this "noise," but soon became aware that it was the voice of God — the searching love for the lost sheep which had strayed so far away from Him. Soon Leon learned the meaning of the words: "Thine arrows are sharp in the heart of the king's enemies..." Ps. 45:5.

God met Leon by touching the sore spot in his life which was the cause of his backsliding, namely, the death of his mother. It is God's way to deal with people according to the statement of Ps. 18:25-26: "With the merciful Thou wilt shew Thyself merciful; with an upright man Thou wilt shew Thyself upright. With the pure Thou wilt shew Thyself pure; and with the froward Thou wilt shew Thyself froward." These words began gradually, more and more, to hammer in his mind, until he stopped to think: "What is the meaning of this?" Of course he understood the words at once, but it was an empty phrase to him until the inner voice of the Holy Spirit interpreted the phrase to him in the way of an argument which sounded something like this:

"As high as you think of yourself, you acted very foolishly in wasting so much time and energy in fighting against God, Who according to your new philosophy, does not exist. If so, you were merely beating the air. Your argument is: there is no God and no soul. If there is no soul, what happened to your mother? Nature took its course, your mother ceased living and no one is to be blamed. You became vexed because God took your mother, acting unjustly as you thought, and this was the particular reason why you could not believe in God being love, and eventually began to deny His very existence altogether. If your mother had no soul, explain what happened to her. God definitely did not take the body of your mother. You and your relatives buried her. Think hard and search your heart."

These thoughts went on for a while in a very simple way: "What happened to your mother is the mystery of life. You will never solve it unless you admit that there is a God, an Omnipotent Creator, and the life of mankind is the living soul. It is about you and your mother that God says "All souls are Mine." The soul of your mother belonged to Him, and whatever He took of your mother was His. Who art thou to rebel against your God? Has not the potter the right to make of the clay anything He wants and to dispose of things which belong to Him any way He chooses?"

Suddenly, Leon remembered the solemn vow he had made in connection with his earlier Christian convictions, that as long as his mother lived, he would not make any public confession of his faith in Christ. Brokenhearted and full of shame, he said to himself: "Yes, I wanted to spare my mother. I denied the truth, giving preference to superstition and prejudice." Then he was reminded of the words of the Lord, "Whosoever shall save his life shall lose it..." (Mat. 16:25).

Leon applied this verse to his mother, whom he put so decisively between himself and the Lord. It became necessary for him to be humbled by the mighty hand of God, to experience the faithfulness of 1st Peter 5:6-9, "Humble yourself, therefore, under the mighty hand of God, that He may exalt you in due time, casting all your anxiety upon Him... be sober and watchful; your adversary, the devil, as a roaring lion walketh about, seeking whom he may devour. Withstand him, be steadfast in faith."

Now another verse from the book of Job became very precious to Leon: "I have heard of Thee by the hearing of my ear; but now mine eye seeth Thee; Therefore I abhor myself and repent in dust and ashes" (Job 42:5).

There was another reason why Leon had to go through such an experience, not only in regard to the loss of his mother, whom he worshipped as an idol, but also to make him come to a better knowledge of himself. Self-righteous as he was, brought up in the atmosphere of a religion of self-righteousness, he needed such correction. Although his rabbinical makeup and environment protected him against many an evil thing, yet it prevented him from coming to a real knowledge of the wickedness of his own heart and of his need of the Savior. God had to lead him in this peculiar way.

ψ

Chapter 5

THE NEW BIRTH
AND A NEW LIFE

Shadows disappeared and a new light came over Leon after God met him that memorable evening, which led him to a deep conviction and real repentance. Truly, the Lord does not leave the work of His hand unfinished. He had a great purpose in all this and was removing all obstacles in the way of a new and wonderful walk.

Crushed under his new conviction, Leon went to see missionary Silberstein, who was pleasantly surprised to see him again after such a long time. Together they went to see missionary, L., who, in turn, also expressed joy over the unexpected reunion. Both friends manifested their sympathy and understanding for all Leon had gone through.

The Bible reading, neglected during the period of spiritual darkness, was resumed with an unparalleled desire and eagerness. There was a real spiritual hunger for the Word of God. Leon came more and more under the deep conviction of his sin against God and his denial and rebellion, even blasphemy. He felt brokenhearted, realizing how much he had harmed the souls of his colleagues and friends by injecting into them the poison of agnosticism. The solemn words of the psalmist resounded in his heart: "Out of the depth I cry unto Thee, my Lord. Hear my voice; let Thine ears be attentive to the voice of my supplications. If Thou, Lord, should mark iniquities, O Lord, who shall stand?" Psalm 130:1-3

Leon began to see the Bible in a new light. The Word of God began to come alive. When again the enemy tried to interfere, whispering in his ear all of his merits, and that his resentment should be considered and justified, being, after all, only the result of his love for his mother, and he should not feel so miserable and crushed, two particular passages of Scripture helped him out of his new dilemma. One of them was: "The fool hath said in his heart, 'There is no God.' They are corrupt, they have done abominable works, there is none that doeth good. The Lord looked down from Heaven upon the children of men, to see if there were any that understand and seek God." (Ps. 14:1-2). And the other, concerning his merits, that he was always zealous and did not commit any wrong things, was the word of Isaiah 64:6: "But we are all as an unclean thing and all our righteousnesses are as filthy rags."

In this new light of the Word of God, Leon realized that the religion of his people was deprived of the most essential thing. While a Jew can cry from the depth of his convictions as a sinner, this does not bring him nearer to God, because this is no longer the avenue of approach. The means for reconciliation and forgiveness of sins, and for fellowship with Himself which God had provided for His people in the past, have now been fully abolished by Him. The Sanctuary was destroyed; the sacrifices ceased, the Shechinah Glory was no longer over the Mercy Seat. Remorse and repentance alone, without the substitutional *"Korban"* (Sacrifice) of the One Who gave His innocent life, would not suffice. "Without the shedding of blood there is no remission of sin" (Lev. 17:11 and Heb. 9:22). Leon felt, as never before, that all the substitutes which the rabbis provided, demanding slavery of obedience in fulfilling them, were empty means, not having any face value before God, Who is against lip worship: "When you spread forth your hands I will hide Mine eyes from you" (Is. 1:15 and 29:13).

If the sacrifices of old, which were brought by the people out of impure motives, were considered an abomination (Is. 1:14), how much more so their own means of substitutional sacrifice, their own temples, their own ways of observing the Sabbath as practiced today, are abominable in the eyes of God.

By plowing deep furrows for the new seed, the Lord had prepared Leon's heart for the necessity of the Savior for reconciliation and forgiveness of sin. Before that, Leon's admiration and reverence for Jesus was at best due to the head knowledge of Him. He acknowledged His teachings as a high standard of philosophy, but this did not withstand the storms in time of testing. It was necessary to experience what the Lord Jesus said to the very moral, well educated rabbi Nicodemus: "Ye must be born again." Without this new birth, nobody can see or comprehend the Kingdom of God and no one can enter it unless he is born of the Spirit — born from above.

In this new light Leon saw the meaning of the Messianic predictions in the book of Daniel Chapter 9, of Messianic Psalms, and Isaiah Chapter 53 as overwhelmingly convincing. Furthermore, he could better understand the Messianic intimations in the Talmudic literature, Midrashim and Yalcoutim, especially in the mystical writings of the Zohar and other Cabbalistic books, which were suggesting that many of those rabbis were searchers after the truth.

After this experience there was no difficulty whatever for Leon to see the necessity of the vicarious death of the Messiah, since the rabbis too, taught that *Muthath Tzadikim Mekapreth,* the death of the just, provides forgiveness of sins for the people. This teaching is based upon Num. 35:25, namely that the sin of a man who killed someone by accident, not willingly, and escaped to the place of refuge, would be released without any penalty after the death of the high priest. In other words, such a man was set free by the death of the high priest. How important and significant to Leon became Isaiah 53 after its truth was revealed to him in the New Testament! The testimony of the Apostle Peter concerning Jesus and His resurrection, in Acts (KJV), Chapters 2 and 5, made an indelible impression upon him, particularly the words: "The God of our fathers raised up Jesus... Him did God exalt with His right hand, to be a Prince and a Savior, to give repentance to Israel and remission of sins, and we are witnesses of these things and so is the Holy Spirit, Whom God hath given to them that obey Him."

Overwhelmed with joy, Leon experienced in a real sense the blessing of his new birth, the spiritual one. The praise to God in the words of 1 Peter 1:5, resounded very clearly in his heart: "Blessed be God, the Father of our Lord Jesus Christ, which according to His abundant mercy hath begotten us again unto a lively hope by the resurrection of Jesus Christ from the dead." (KJV) Leon could wholeheartedly join the poet who wrote the beautiful words of a popular hymn "It Is Well With My Soul," the last stanza of which goes as follows:

My sin, O the bliss of this glorious thought,
My sin — not in part, but the whole —
Is nailed to the Cross, and I bare it no more.
Praise the Lord, praise the Lord, O my soul!

℧

Fanny's Disappointment

℧

To the greatest dismay of Mrs. Rosenberg, she discovered that the convictions of her husband were more deeply rooted than she thought. They were not only revived after a long spell of religious lethargy, but became more intensified, bringing about a real conversion. Although she was glad that the sorrow of the last several weeks, which robbed him of appetite and sleep, had given way to happiness and joy, she could not understand the reasons for it.

Leon explained to her how the first change in his attitude towards Christ came about, and how he became a backslider. He revealed to her the vow he had made, and that it was God Who had dealt with him in His most peculiar way. He tried to make it clear that he now understood God's dealings, and that he had come to a deeper knowledge of himself and of God as the righteous and merciful One — but his words fell on deaf ears.

Tearfully, his beloved wife tried to persuade him that if this new faith was his determination, he would utterly ruin his career and make their lives miserable. Leon asked how a man as happy as he was could make anybody's life miserable? The misery would come if he were to disobey God and be ashamed of the "Name which is above every name," the Name of his Messiah and Savior. He would indeed be miserable, if he were to yield fearfully to the opinions of those fanatical, zealous, self-righteous men who think more of themselves than of God.

Leon was caught betwixt and between those two sides. He loved his wife very dearly. Embracing her, he said, "Darling, do you remember what I told you the other day, why I lost my beloved mother? She was your aunt and I know you loved her very much, but God had to intervene. We should love Him with all our heart, with all our soul and with all our might and ability. You know how much I love you, but please do not cause me to interfere with God's plans once again."

It was not easy for Leon to rebuild that which he himself had torn down during many months of uncertainty. His wife used his former arguments in discussions on this matter. She was absolutely sincere and would not allow anything to stand between her and her beloved Leon. Her answer was, "I shall never share such beliefs with you." Leon solemnly decided not to compromise his beliefs any further but make a public profession of his faith in Christ before his colleagues and friends. He was no longer afraid to visit the Bible store in his free time, and if there was an argument between visitors and missionaries, Leon would not hesitate to make his opinion known to those present, defending the truth which had become so precious to him, As was only to be expected, Leon's testimony brought upon him a wave of severe persecution. His father, whom Leon from early childhood learned to know as a zealous priest of a high rabbinical caste, after trying in vain to persuade his son to give up and publicly renounce his faith in the *"Toli,"* made it impossible for Leon to remain any longer in the country. He was compelled to flee across the border. His wife was taken by her parents to another province as they could not endure the "reproach" brought upon them by Leon's actions.

☙

Love Undiminished

☙

Nevertheless, the couple's love for each other remained undiminished. Both suffered from this forced and sudden separation. Leon could not understand why his letters to Fanny remained unanswered, but later he learned that her father intercepted Leon's mail in an effort to make her forget her husband and to give up any hope for a reunion. Thus his wife, not knowing where Leon was, could not write to him. Her father went as far as to forge a statement to the effect that her husband had joined the British Forces fighting against the Boers, and had been killed in action in South Africa. She did not believe this for one moment, but was confident that some day she would hear from her beloved.

☙

New And Useful Contacts

☙

Continuing his flight, Leon purposed to go to England, but on reaching Hamburg, Germany, he had to wait for a boat. Being a stranger in the city, he felt safe in attending a church on Sunday. This was the very first time in his life that he entered a church. Not knowing the difference between the various denominations, except that there were Catholics and Protestants, he asked a policeman to direct him to a Protestant church in the neighborhood. The policeman said to him: "Young man, every spire you see in this vicinity represents a Protestant church." Leon attended the nearest one, and after the service introduced himself to Dr. W., the minister. This pastor, being a friend of the Jews, became interested in Leon, and after a short conversation invited him for a get-acquainted chat in his office on the following morning.

The story of Leon's conversion made a deep impression upon the minister, all the more so when Leon presented to him his credentials and a letter of recommendation from missionary L. to his friends in London. Dr. W. encouraged Leon to stay in Hamburg to see first of all the superintendent of Jewish Missions, Dr. A., and also Pastor F. Leon followed this advice and met with both men. They too became quite interested in him and invited him to stay at the Mission, at least temporarily, which Leon agreed to do. They advised him also to watch for the Lord's guidance. It became obvious that it was God's will for him to stay in Germany, to be near his homeland, where the possibilities of contacting his wife, and perhaps getting her over the border, were much greater than they would be in England. Furthermore, under the leading of the Lord, he felt encouraged to prepare himself for the Christian ministry while still in Hamburg, being more fluent in the German language, than in English.

ψ

The Hour Of Deliverance

ψ

Meanwhile, Mrs. Rosenberg, though not having heard from her husband for a considerable period of time, continued to nurture the hope that he would find ways and means for their reunion. Leon, on his part, regularly mailed letters to her. Months elapsed, but there was no reply from his beloved wife. Leon prayed and waited patiently.

One day, while visiting a church not far from the Russian border, where he was sharing his conversion experience, Leon was introduced to a smiling man who was eager to know the address of Mrs. Rosenberg's parents. Being a Christian man, he offered to assist in establishing communication between the forcibly separated young couple. He knew the district well, and became a messenger for both parties.

It was a great surprise to dear Fanny when a Gentile stranger, who came on business to her father, cautiously handed her an envelope as from her husband. If the messenger had been a Jew, Mrs. Rosenberg would probably have had some hesitancy in accepting anything from the hands of a stranger. A shadow of suspicion might have interfered, since the rabbis provide an easy way for a woman not to be left as *"Aguna"* (forever separated from her husband), in that she could be divorced through the medium of a witness by handing her, in a sealed envelope, the *"Get,"* (actual bill of divorce recorded in Deut. 24:1). The messenger had only to say, "I am the witness that with this you are divorced," this being sufficient for legal separation from her husband, and she would be permitted to marry someone else.

Of course there was no danger in the case of Leon and his beloved Fanny, yet as a matter of precaution, religious Jewish women are strictly admonished in the absence of their husbands not to accept any sealed messages, supposedly from a husband, handed to them by a Jewish messenger. A Gentile could never be a witness in such a case.

Unspeakable joy filled Fanny's heart when she saw the handwriting of her husband, and especially the loving message, briefly explaining the situation and giving his proper address, as well as means of reaching him. She had time for only a very brief reply. The messenger whose business transaction was only an excuse, had to leave in a hurry.

ψ

Good Tidings

ψ

Mrs. Rosenberg's message was very brief. It spoke of hardship, of her great longing, but it also contained really joyful tidings. She congratulated her Leon on being the father of a lovely, healthy girl, called after his mother, Gali Eugenia.

Since this happy contact was established, Leon planned to get his wife to Hamburg as soon as possible, but this was not an easy undertaking. Many things had to be considered, because her crossing the borders had to be kept secret. Her papers were strictly guarded by her father, and he would never give his consent for her departure.

ψ

Means Of Support

ψ

Leon had to make provisions for a home for his family and for their support. He had never learned a trade, and being in a foreign country it was not easy for him to find something to do without being interrupted in his studies. A deacon of the church Leon attended suggested to him that he try working in his stained-glass factory. The work was not hard but required intelligence. Leon soon acquired the skill and made steady progress, which enabled him to earn sufficient money for the support of his family.

Family's Exodus

By secret appointment and cautious procedure, mother and child left the parental roof and, with the help of the kind messenger and other friends, both safely crossed the borders and came to Hamburg. What a joyful reunion it was! Traces of deep anxiety and suffering were visible on Fanny's beautiful face. How happy she immediately became in her own little home! The new environment, however, was strictly Christian and it made a strange impression upon her. In spite of her intelligence and tolerance she could not easily adjust herself to this atmosphere. She found her husband's visitors friendly folk, but their thoughts and words were strange to her. She did not relish their conversation, which revolved around one topic: Christ and the Gospel. Leon's Hebrew-Christian colleagues tactfully endeavored to testify to her of their own conversion. They tried to share with her the story of how they became believers in Jesus, the Messiah, and to portray their joy in Him, but all their efforts caused her much inner pain, which she tried valiantly to conceal. She did, however, tolerate the Bible readings which her husband gave in their home and was not at all averse to listening, as long as they were taken from the Old Testament. She did not dare to read the forbidden book which she called "The Christians' New Testament." She adhered strictly to the rabbinical traditions and no one hindered her in this preference.

Chapter 6

THE DAWN OF A NEW DAY

Shortly before Easter of that year, Fanny, as she was known in her Christian surroundings (her Hebrew name as we mentioned earlier was Frymet), began to experience a deep concern and fear which she couldn't understand. As a daughter of Israel, she could not be indifferent to the false stories of Easter which had always brought real horrors to her people in some so-called "Christian" countries. Many were the weird tales spread abroad in those days, one of them being that "Jews use Christian blood in their unleavened Passover cakes." Because of these fantastic stories, told year after year by the enemies of the Jews, inspired by hostile fanatical priests, ignorant mobs attacked Jewish homes, plundering contents and killing people. Under the sting of these memories (it had not been long since a ritualistic accusation trial had brought tragedy to the Jews of Nakel in northern Prussia) Fanny felt uneasy being in the same land at Easter time, and worst of all, that her husband confessed faith in the crucified Christ, in whose name these atrocities were committed. Yet at this very time she felt more than ever an inner desire and an earnest longing to know the truth about Christ.

In her distress she cried to God. Once her husband found her weeping and asked about the cause of her grief. She sobbed, "I wish I could agree with you! I have tried my best; I have followed your advice. I cried to the

God of Abraham, Isaac and Jacob, asking Him to reveal to me the truth as to Jesus being the promised Messiah, but without avail. God does not answer me. Indeed, I am tormented by an inner conflict and more and more the distance widens between Christ and me. Watching you closely I must admit, I envy you because of the influence of this faith in your life. It makes you entirely different from all other Jewish young men I have known. Your joy and your happiness impress me; yet there is a deep fear in my heart that something must be wrong with your mind, that you can confess faith in the crucified babe, Yeshua."

Leon urged her to tell him frankly what she had against the Messiah, Whom he had shown her to be the fulfillment of all of the Old Testament prophecies. She cried, "I cannot see any similarity or comparison between the promised Messiah and the little babe Jesus of whom you speak."

The emphasis she placed on the words "little babe," in connection with Jesus, raised a question in her husband's mind and he asked her to explain more clearly her concept of Jesus. She was provoked, but after some hesitation exclaimed, "How in the world can it be that a helpless child in his mother's arms, when killed, is to be accepted as our promised King Messiah?"

Leon could instantly see that childhood impressions, carried through the years and repeatedly strengthened by icons and images of the Virgin Mary with the Babe in her arms, had veiled her eyes from seeing the true Man of Sorrows, the Lamb of God, the Promised Redeemer. When this became evident, he began to depict to her the earthly life of Jesus in its entirety — from the time of His incarnation — born of the Virgin, according to Isaiah 7:14, etc., to His full-grown manhood, when

He walked among His own people, the Jews, and wrought great miracles. Then on to His death on the cross where, according to prophecy, by Divine determination, He laid down His life as the final, everlasting and effectual sacrifice for sin, becoming the Savior of the world. The veil was lifted from Fanny's eyes. Isaiah 53 was carefully read and its wonderful details explained to her. She drank in the reading and meaning of this marvelous passage and all the other predictions in the Old Testament. She listened with rapt attention to the comments made by her husband, regarding their fulfillment in the New Testament. This made an indelible impression upon her mind, and the Word of God, that "two-edged sword," cut her heart to the quick.

The Lord opened her blind eyes and Mrs. Rosenberg, in a wonderful way, experienced a new birth. This spiritual experience also affected her physical condition in a very tangible way. Until then, her health was impaired because of her deep inner concern and the trials in her parental home.

ψ

The Lord's Call For His Service

ψ

All the preparations Leon had made since he was three years old, and later through the rabbinical training together with secular education, created indeed a good outfit as far as the human side was concerned. There was, so to speak, much fuel gathered, but without the Heavenly Spark, so most of it was dead material. While there was one thing in Leon's life which he had to give up, which could pave for him the way to social glory among his own people, there were other things which he had to consider before answering the call of the Lord.

Just to repeat the words used by young Christians who look with great aspirations to the field of labor, saying "Here I am, send me," was not sufficient for Leon. When confronted with the possibility of lifetime service, he argued that these words belonged to the unique experience of the prophet Isaiah and were never repeated by others. His spirit was closer to the spirit of the prophet Jeremiah, who received his call in a different way, and resented it with excusing himself because of his youth and, as he thought, his unfitness. Arguments with the missionaries before his conversion showed Leon how difficult it can be to deal with Jewish fanatics or sophists. He did not want to be a missionary. Again it was the enemy who interfered. The experience of persecution because of the New Testament, the scene on the street in Warsaw, when Scriptures and tracts were torn by the zealots, was still vivid in his mind, but conviction of being chosen by God for the mission field among his own people came loud and clear through a passage from the Book of Jeremiah 1:8-9 and 15:19-21 (KJV): "Be not afraid... for I am with thee... I have put My words in thy mouth... and thou shalt stand before Me: and if thou take forth the precious from the vile, thou shall be as My mouth: let them turn unto thee, but return not thou unto them. And I will make thee unto this people a fenced brazen wall: and they shall fight against thee, but they shall not prevail against thee: for I am with thee to save thee and to deliver thee, saith the Lord. And I will deliver thee out of the hand of the wicked, and I will redeem thee out of the hand of the terrible."

Being thus convicted and convinced, Leon and Fanny dedicated themselves earnestly to the Lord's service. After a period of seminary preparation and an ordination in Hamburg, Germany, Leon passed his final test and examination before two famous theological professors, J. Dalman and Kittel Sr. of Leipzig. His rabbinical training was also taken into account, because it included fluency in Hebrew and added much to his knowledge of the Old Testament.

Their first missionary exposure was in Krakow, then a part of Austria in the Empire of Franz Joseph, who was known to be a friend of the Jews. Realizing fully what a task it would be to serve among the vary strict religious Jews, Fanny and Leon (by then an ordained minister) cast themselves entirely upon the Lord.

This field served as a hard test with many trials. It was a pioneering ministry, and Leon had to lay a foundation for it by contacting individual Jews. He was literally a front-line missionary, serving where no one had served before.

It was not difficult at all to recognize a Jew, even from a distance, because of the long garments, the black felt hats and beards even on the youngest of faces. Religious Jews in those days never shaved, while today, no matter how religious a Jew may be, he may remain beardless without ever using razor by simply applying to his face some hair removing chemicals. This is the means by which they evade the rabbinical interpretation of the words in Lev. 21, where it reads in verse 5: "They shall not make baldness upon their head, neither shall they shave off the corner of their beard, nor make any cutting in their flesh." Although this behest was originally given to the priests, the rabbis extended it to every Jew.

The first Jew whom Leon contacted on the street, turned out to be a sympathetic listener. He became very interested in the message presented to him, concerning

Israel's problem and God's peculiar dealing with her. Proceeding on the Scriptures speaking on Messianic hopes of the nation, Leon purposely stopped and invited his new acquaintance to his home. He cordially accepted Leon's invitation not knowing who he was. The man came one day and their first talk was not entirely missionary, but more of an introductory in nature. Another appointment was made at the convenience of the Jewish friend, and he came on the following Saturday when Jews are usually free from all their business and other obligations.

While Leon's home, as neatly and invitingly as it was arranged by Mrs. Rosenberg, had no offensive symbols, yet one thing still attracted the visitor. On the wall he was facing, hung a nicely-framed text that seemed highly strange to him. It read *"Yeshua HaMashiach, Hallelujah,"* which means "Jesus the Savior, Hallelujah." Surprised by the presence of this strange text, the visitor asked: "Who is this Yeshua? Who is this Savior?" This question only hastened the presentation of the Gospel message. The "spring board" of the previous conversation was used to jump directly into the depth of prophecy concerning the Messiah, found in Isaiah 53. With the visitor's permission they read this chapter together, at first without any comments. Leon only asked if the man knew of whom the prophet spoke; who was this individual to whom the prophet referred as a person? The man knew, of course, the rabbinical interpretation, applying this chapter to Israel as a nation, but he admitted that he had never noticed it before and did not know whom the prophet had in mind, when he spoke of someone despised and rejected and sentenced to die, but who though buried, was exalted, and who had the authority to justify man, and so on.

Leon pointed to the wall and said before going any further: "Let me tell you, friend, that the answer is given in the very name *"Yeshua."* The man began to argue about the meaning, about the simple translation of the word by which the Jew usually expresses any kind of help. Translation of *"Yeshua"* generally bears the meaning of "help": financial help, all kinds of temporal help, help in times of sickness, and help in all things is expressed in the word *"Yeshua."*

"Yeshua" is also a name," said Leon, "and in this case it is the name which is above every name, and because of His greatness, He is the only Helper. In other words, the Helper for the greatest need, namely, the need of sin. He is the Savior from sin, the Victor over sin!" Now they had reached the point where Jesus, the Yeshua, became the center of their conversation.

However, as long as the conversation was in the Hebrew tongue, there were many questions the visitor was asking, wanting to receive clearer explanations, but when he realized that Leon meant Jesus of Nazareth, he immediately excused himself and said that he would continue the conversation at another time.

Leon waited one day, and the man did not come. A whole week elapsed, and another Saturday began, but he did not return. On Sunday, between 9 and 10, the man appeared at the door of Leon's home just when the family was ready to leave for the Sunday church service. The man urged Leon to take a little walk with him. Seeing an opportunity for further discussion, Leon decided to go with the man while his family went on to church.

When the two men stepped out into the street, the new friend gently took Leon's arm and led him into a public square. It was full of Jewish people who liked to spend the two idle days of the week there. On Saturdays they observed their day of rest, attended their synagogues and spent time with their families. On Sundays, when the Gentiles attended their churches, the Jewish businesses had to be closed, so all of their business transactions took place in the city square and were conducted much like in a stock exchange.

As the two men approached the square, Leon still naively believed that this friend was leading him to his orthodox friends for more discussions, but the gentle "guide" suddenly loosened his grip on Leon's arm and waved his hand towards a group of people. Responding to this signal, two men began to run towards them and one, red-bearded, came close very hastily...

Leon's new friend turned out to be a traitor. Pointing to Leon, he shouted towards the crowd: "This is the man!" The one with the red beard was his brother with whom he, evidently, had shared everything he had heard from Leon recently at his home. Raging with fury, shouting and swearing, the man attacked Leon, saying: "You came here a stranger to deceive and convert our people? You will have no success in our midst!"

His loud shouting attracted other Jews, and when he explained to them who this man was, a real turmoil started. The Jews, who enjoyed all the freedom under the rule of the emperor Franz Joseph, felt themselves very free indeed. They were not afraid to express their protest against Christ and Christianity in a very unkind and rude manner. Leon was surrounded by a great number of fierce people, real fanatics, whose treatment of him was very rough. One man pushed himself to the forefront of the crowd, grabbed Leon's face between the palms of his hands, and began to pat it very softly, while others were roaring with laughter. The reason for the laughter was that the man was smearing Leon's face with soot. In a peculiar way this protected Leon from greater trouble at the hand of these very excited fanatics. They were distracted by this treatment of Leon, who not knowing what turned rage into laughter, continued to answer questions, asked by one or another of the men in the crowd.

Suddenly, an elderly man with a gray beard pushed his way out of the circle and approached Leon. In one hand he held a large umbrella. "I will teach him a lesson!" he shouted, but listen first to a story I will tell you." He began to tell a little fable about a fox and a crow, a hunter and a dog. It went like this: a fox was trying to persuade a crow to come and share with him a piece of meat which he supposedly had in his den. When the crow expressed fear that the fox might consume her, the fox told her not to fear "for the Messiah is here and we should not harm one another." When a hunter approached with his dog, the fox ran away. The crow shouted to him: "Why did you tell me the Messiah is here?" To which the fox responded: "The dogs do not believe in the Messiah!" (Jews called Gentiles dogs.)

Evidently, this man did not grasp the nature of the whole argument. He thought that Leon was an infidel who denied the Messianic promise. After listening to the story, Leon replied: "Truly, you cannot call me a dog, because not only do I believe in the Messianic promise, but my argument with the people here is to show them that God has already fulfilled His promise by sending the Messiah." The man became even more enraged and shouted: "What? What did you say?!" Others told him that Leon was a missionary who wanted Jewish people to believe in the *"Toli"* as their Messiah. Being a typical fanatic and zealot, the old man was beside himself with anger and began to beat Leon on the face with the big umbrella. Leon was trying to turn his face away in self-defense and, if possible, avoid being permanently disfigured. However, the man did not give up until with one more heavy blow he dislocated Leon's jaw. This did not escape the sharp eye of the people and caused some commotion. In severe pain, and not being able to speak, Leon pushed his way through the crowd which was showering him with clumps of mud.

When Leon arrived at home, his wife did not recognize him at all. His face was black-and-blue, completely covered with mud, soot and blood. He could not explain to Fanny who he was because of his dislocated jaw, but she soon came to conclusion that this bloody black mass was indeed her husband Leon.

After a successful operation on the jaw, Leon remained in bed for quite some time. Fanny comforted him by saying that she was more pleased with such a beginning than she would be with an immediate and easy success. "This will be a safeguard," she said, "against our pride, and we will always remember that the wise one should never boast of his wisdom, neither the strong of his strength, but that nothing can be done without the Lord." This was indeed a lesson with a lifetime impact.

ॐ

Chapter 7

A CHANGED ATTITUDE

When Leon showed himself on the street after his painful experience, he was astonished that many Jewish people greeted him in a very friendly way and all of them expressed regret for the attack which so unwisely and unfairly was wrought upon him. Some blamed the fanaticism, others blamed the crude behavior on the lack of culture, and all pleaded with Leon not to make an issue out of the sad incident and to try to forget it. Later Leon discovered that they were afraid, that if the Christian public would find out that the attack was not against a Jew, but against a man who represented Christianity, the consequences might be deplorable for them.

This circumstance presented an unprecedented opportunity for Leon to show further the praises of Him Who brought him out of the darkness into His marvelous light: from darkness of superstition, vengeance and hatred into the bright light of the loving, gracious Messiah and Savior. People began to listen to him and many became really interested in his message. Hearts and doors began to open and the house of the missionary became an open home for many.

ॐ

First Fruit

ॐ

Among those visitors who often came to the missionary's home but did not like to be seen by others, was a young man of a well-known Orthodox family who was a student at the Rabbinical High School. His last name was Stern. He was not only keen in his arguments, but also truly sincere. It was a pleasure for Leon to deal with this young man, although he had to spend many an hour in arguments. When Mr. Stern saw that he could not prevail, he decided to invite one of his intimate colleagues to assist him in this fight which he at the time considered a fight against heresy. By and by, a few others from his class were invited to these special meetings with Leon, and heated discussions became a regular thing at the Rosenberg home. Shortly before Christmas, Rosenbergs had a great surprise. It happened not long after Fanny had sent a letter to her parents telling them of her whereabouts. She never stopped writing to them, although her father had strictly forbidden her to do so. His last message to her was very unpleasant. It was a reply to her first confession of faith in Jesus in a letter from Hamburg, telling them of her joy in finding in Him her Messiah. She really poured out her soul in that letter, telling her parents of her inner conflicts and her final victory over prejudice and superstition. Her father's reply at that time was very condemning, enough so to break her heart. He quoted several passages from Deut. 29, cursing his beloved daughter. A portion of his letter, which was written by her mother, was stained with tears. Mother was telling Fanny that now she must consider her beloved Frymet as dead, that she would forever deny her as her child. She made it quite clear that from then on there would remain between them an impassable gulf. She closed her letter with "Do not ever dare to write to us again."

However, under God's obvious leading, some changes did occur. Fanny's parents agreed to the suggestion by their other daughter, Helen, to allow her to go to Krakow to visit Fanny and Leon. They were confident that she would succeed in winning them back to Judaism. Helen was warmly welcomed by Leon and Fanny. At first she was careful not to reveal her parent's real reason for letting her come. The Rosenbergs proceeded with their lives in the usual manner, conducting their customary daily home worship as, they believed, every Christian family should. They determined not to compromise nor to hide the "light" for one moment. Christ was the Head of their house from the very beginning of their Christian walk with him.

Helen was free to prepare her food as she pleased, and she was cautious in her conversation not to impose, neither to offend. She listened carefully to Leon's discussions with Jews, who came to his house, and she showed keen interest in their opposing arguments. Being very clever and fairly well equipped educationally, she made excellent use of her ingenuity. She did not come to argue with Leon, but mostly with her sister Fanny. These arguments. however, developed into real discussions. Fanny talked with her wisely, patiently, aiming her message directly at her sister's heart. When Helen saw that her arguments failed, she talked about their mother's deep sorrow and touched Fanny's heart with her tears. The two sisters loved each other deeply and both were devoted to their parents. The only thing dividing them was blind religious fanaticism on one side and a living experience of faith on the other. Helen was especially pleased when stubborn hotheaded rabbinical students came to argue with Leon. She surely hoped for defeat of the one who in her mind entangled her sister and made her as crazy as he himself undoubtedly was. She particularly loved to listen to arguments by the classmates of Mr. Stern, and how pleased she was when one evening the discussion broke up at his suggestion, "No use to argue with you and no use for us to waste any more of our time." In Helen's mind this constituted a crushing defeat for Leon.

As time went on, and Helen's expectations of winning back her sister failed, she began to make preparations to leave for home. Her father, too, became uneasy and urged her to return. But for some unknown reason she lingered on. Then something happened...after being absent for several days, Mr. Stern appeared at the Rosenberg's house one evening and began to apologize for breaking up the last meeting with his rude remarks. "I had no rest," he said, "your arguments, based not only on Scripture, but on historical facts, entered deeply into my heart. Ever since that evening I was under conviction. How I wish I could have shared this openly with my friends! I am ashamed for acting so cowardly, but I am sure you will understand. You know how it is among our people. One loses everything — one's best friends will become enemies; but you must know what I think and feel. A fierce struggle is raging inside my soul and I need to talk to you. I wanted to give up, and I will frankly admit that I wanted to do it for my own sake and for the sake of my people; but I cannot resist the truth any longer. I am convinced that Jesus is the promised Messiah and Savior, and I cannot resist this truth any longer. I was purposely harsh and unkind, hoping that this would close your door to me, but your patience, your friendliness overwhelmed me again and again and I said in my heart: 'I will try to restore our friendship.' So here I am. You greeted me as if nothing happened. I saw how your face beamed when you saw me."

Hearing what Mr. Stern had to say, Helen was more than amazed. His confession was more than any other proof to her. She stood up and went to her room.

Mr. Stern changed the time of his visits not to be suspected by his colleagues, who might have watched him, though none of them had shown up at the meetings for a considerable length of time prior to his confession. He began to attend the family worship times at the Rosenberg's residence and one hymn made an especially deep impression on his heart: *'In den stillen Nachtzeit Stunden, horch was klopft in dir...*" — "In the stillness of the night hours, hark, what beats in you."

♆

A Testimony Of A Child

♆

One morning, beaming with joy, little Eugenia, who shared the same bedroom with her aunt, came to mother and whispered, "Last night Auntie Helen was reading the Bible. She did not go to bed at all. I saw her reading before I fell asleep, and again when I awakened. Today she asked me whether you and Daddy taught me religion. I did not understand what she meant, but I told her that I too love the Lord Jesus. Than she asked if you and Father read the Bible and sang and prayed together before she came. I said: 'Of course, Father does not only read the Bible, but he preaches it too! Why does she ask me these questions?"

"Never mind, dear child," Mother said, "you answered her nicely and I am glad. We should pray more for your aunt, that the Lord Jesus might open her heart and her mind."

Helen did not come to breakfast that morning. When she came down for lunch, about noon, one could notice that she was deeply troubled by something. Nobody at the table mentioned the fact that they could see that she had been crying. As soon as the meal was finished, she returned to her room and closed the door. She showed up again only for the evening family devotions. When the whole family knelt for prayer, Helen slightly bent her neck but did not join them on her knees.

Little Eugenia was on her knees next to her aunt and was pulling her down by her skirt to a kneeling position. Not wanting to offend the child, Helen knelt down and folded her hands in prayer.

Some hours later Helen went to Fanny and opened her heart before her. There were many earnest questions in her mind, but mainly, it was the Messiahship of Jesus, in which she could not believe. Suddenly she made an odd admission: "In our religion we only have much chanting, reading of prayers, many ceremonies and fasting, but not one satisfactory answer concerning salvation."

It became evident to Fanny that her sister was an earnest seeker after the truth, and that it was God's obvious leading that her father gave his consent to Helen's coming to visit her sister. Thus the ice was broken.

In spite of the urging of her parents to return home, Helen decided to prolong her stay in some way. However, after she had become convinced that all the predictions concerning the Messiah pointed to Jesus, she did not know what to do. She still loved her father and mother more than the Lord. Again and again she said, "1 cannot yield. It will be a deadly blow to my father and my beloved mother." But the Lord Jesus, Who came to seek and save the lost, overruled all obstacles. He granted victory over Helen's prejudice and delivered her from all fear. One morning she came out of her room triumphantly, embraced her sister and brother-in-law, and shouted through tears of joy: "I am saved! Now I know that my Redeemer liveth!" Helen was saved. What a victory! What joy! That was the first family "trophy" of Dr. and Mrs. Rosenberg. Others followed soon. Altogether, not counting their children, seven more family members eventually became saved.

Soon another urgent letter came from the father. Leon and Fanny agreed that now the time had come for Helen to return to her parents. "I know," she said, "what awaits me there, but I also know that the Lord is with me." When the father met Helen at the railroad station, his first question was, "What did you accomplish through your long visit with your apostate sister?" Helen kept silent. The father noticed that something was wrong and insisted: "Tell me!"

Helen said, "Father, I realize how you feel about Fanny, but I wish you could know her and Leon as I have learned to know them. I did my best to persuade them that they were wrong. I tried it again and again. They did not impose their idea upon me. It was God's Word through our prophets which persuaded me! My eyes have been opened through reading the Word of God, and I believe with all my heart that they really have found Him of Whom Moses and the prophets spoke. Their Messiah has become my Savior too."

Helen did not talk much with her parents as her return was shortly before the solemn days of Israel's national repentance, the New Year, and the Day of Atonement; but her life had undergone a real change in many respects. The change was so obvious that the parents began to notice it. On the Day of Atonement Helen accompanied her mother to the Synagogue, but said to her: "I am just going to accompany you, because I already have my atonement, which is not dependent on my doings, but rather on God's mercy revealed through the Messiah."

After 24 hours of fasting and praying, the parents returned home. Helen's father solemnly said to her: "My child, I hope that God will mercifully accept our prayers. I have pleaded with God on your behalf, that you might be soon freed from this evil spirit which possessed you." Helen calmly answered him, saying: "Father, first of all, do you have the assurance that you are right with God? Can you really say that He answered your prayers concerning the greatest thing, namely, the real atonement?" He said: "I hope so." Helen said: "If our Yom Kippur of today, our fasting and praying, were sufficient, why do we cry to God to restore our temple, our priesthood, our sacrifices? Why do we so solemnly chant the whole procedure of the past, recalling the act of the high priest when he entered the Holy of Holies with the Korban (offering) to sprinkle the blood of the sacrifice upon the Ark? Our nation truly lives in recollecting the things of the past, not having a single thing of our biblical religion, described in the Torah, in the Books of Exodus and Leviticus."

Her father, astonished to hear from his daughter quotations from the Bible, became enraged and shouted: "We pray and fast for the coming of the Messiah, our 'Goel,' and when He will come He will restore everything!" His anger really reached its peak when she said, "But father, why does not the merciful God answer our nation's prayers, offered with such fervor and lamentation for nearly two thousand years? Why does not our 'Goel,' our Messiah, come?" His answer was (as it is by many orthodox Jews today): "We are not worthy." Then Helen said: "Is not the main reason for the Messiah's coming to redeem Israel from her sins? He is the Messiah for sinners and for the so-called 'just.' Don't we read in Psalm 130:8, 'He shall redeem Israel from all his iniquities'? And in the book of the prophet Isaiah 59:20, 'The Redeemer shall come to Zion, and unto them that turn from their transgressions in Jacob.' I thank God that my eyes were opened to see myself as God sees me, an unworthy sinner, and that He, in his mercy, fulfilled His promise and sent the Messiah."

In his anger the father added one more "curse" to the many he already pronounced on his wayward daughter: "Thou shall be there where thy Jesus is!" to which Helen said simply "Amen." This was too much for her rabbinical but benighted father, and he slapped her face.

From that time on Helen was ostracized by all members of her family and thrown out of her home. In her goodness the mother allowed her to take her belongings, so Helen quickly packed her things and left, not really knowing where she would settle down.

While Helen was led into the "desert" for testing of her faith, and came into "deep waters" and into "a furnace of affliction," the promise of Isaiah 43:2 was literally fulfilled in her life. When most of the testing was behind her, Helen used to say, "It was the prayers of my sister Fanny and her husband Leon that carried me through."

What happened to Helen should be told in a separate special sketch on her life. It is a story of God's dramatic dealing with another lost sheep of the House of Israel. Here we can only say that she dedicated her entire life to her Redeemer and Savior Jesus. She became a missionary, and the Lord used her mightily for many years in Russia, Yugoslavia, England, and Israel. She never married but chose to serve the Lord as a deaconess-missionary well into her old age. Her last years on this earth Helen spent as a missionary in Jerusalem, where she passed into glory in the early nineteen sixties.

🕎

Chapter 8

MOVING CLOSER TO A FULL-TIME MINISTRY

ψ

An Answer To Prayer

ψ

Just before the birth of the second child, Elizabeth, the Rosenberg family was completely without funds for the necessary hospital care for the mother and child. Both parents, naturally, spoke to the Lord about it, mentioning in their prayer a specific sum of money they so desperately needed. The next day the mailman brought a registered letter from a friend in Germany who was not aware of their circumstances. The envelope contained the exact amount for which they prayed. The donor, in relating how he was led to send this gift, asked not to mention it in their reply letter, but instead to mark one corner of the envelope with a tiny cross, which they did. This was but one of such instances wrought by the Lord in the lives of the Rosenbergs. They were greatly encouraged by this nearness of God's divine hand and its gentle, caring touch, and were emboldened for further and broader missionary ministry for which they did not have to wait long.

A Macedonian Call
From The Homeland

✡

After receiving yet another call to do ministry work in
Warsaw, Leon was not sure it came from the Lord, and
answered with a definite *"NO!"* Warsaw was the place
of many unpleasant memories. It was there that Leon
was rejected by the well-educated and cultured friends
who used to esteem him so highly when he was still in
the grip of agnosticism and even atheism. But as soon
as he shared with them his new belief in the Messiah
and told them who the Messiah was, they were quick to
humiliate and despise him.

However, the call kept coming repeatedly and per-
sistently, and Leon learned the profound lesson that God
has His way in storm and the wild wind; that our thoughts
are not His thoughts, and that the way of obedience is
the way He expects us to go.

✡

Vain Excuses

✡

To each letter which came regarding the Macedonian
call, the answer was polite but in the negative. Then a
short message came suggesting to Leon to consider what
the Lord said to the Gadarine in Mark 5:19, "Go home
to thy friends and tell them how great things the Lord
hath done for thee, and hath had compassion on thee."

This settled the inner conflict for Leon. Encouraged
by his dear companion, co-laborer and wife, Fanny, he
decided to respond to the call in a positive way, trusting

132

the Lord that He would overrule all difficulties and that He had a definite purpose in all of this.

☙

Unrecognized

☙

During the prolonged absence of Leon from Warsaw, rumors had spread about him and his wife not being together. When he left the city for the last time, no one really expected him ever again to appear in the city, let alone with his wife.

Being aware of many speculations about them, the first thing Leon and Fanny did, as soon as they had settled in their new home, was to take a long walk through the streets of the Jewish quarters to let people know that they were there. On one corner of the thickly populated streets they met a friend who used to be very close to them in the past. They stopped and looked at each other. But soon the former friend shook his head and turned away, not able to believe his eyes and thinking to himself, "No, they are only doubles." Leon went after him but to no avail. Suddenly, this friend's face changed color and anger flashed from his eyes as he said: "So you *ARE* here! I have nothing to do with you and I would advise you, if you do not want more of the same kind of trouble you had here before, to leave our city at once!" But he was so curious as to who the lady was with whom Leon walked arm-in-arm that he asked: "Who is the lady at your side?" "It is Frymet," Leon said. "So she *IS* with you after all!" exclaimed the man and ran away. He was in a hurry to spread the news as if he was hired and well-paid to do so.

Profitable Curiosity

By and by some former friends and acquaintances began to appear to see for themselves those who dared to come back to their city as apostates, those who accepted the religion of the gentiles and now returned here as soul hunters, "*Meshamudim*," abhorred, despised, exposed to open criticism and seemingly not afraid of constant threats. At first, when Leon left alone, the comforting thought for many was that Fanny did not leave with him because she held on to the religion of her ancestors. But now *BOTH* of the Rosenbergs were here and this was a puzzling thing to all who knew them.

Especially dramatic was the reaction of some relatives, who pleaded to be spared such a shameful reproach and humiliation, as that which was brought upon them when Leon and Fanny showed up once again in their city. They even promised to assist Leon with means if he would consider leaving to go abroad. Some relatives manifested sincere love, and it was painful for Leon and Fanny to see tears in the eyes of people whom they loved and for whom they had deep concern.

However, it became more and more obvious that it was the Lord's will for them to sow His good seed, and to experience that those who sow with tears, shall reap with joy.

Two of Leon's younger brothers ventured to come to see him. They had little to say, but conveyed a familiar message from their father and repeated his pleadings and his generous promises. The appearance of Leon's modest home made it evident that it was not of the kind which Jewish people usually think of when a Jew becomes a neophyte to the Christian religion, assuming that he was well paid and changed his religion for material gain. Many thought that it must be a good business, because the Gentiles are so interested in getting a few into their ranks. Another motive, namely, that some Jews who wanted to marry a Gentile girl would for her sake change religion, did not fit Leon's and Fanny's situation, because Leon married an Orthodox Jewish girl out of the ranks of his own relatives.

They knew that Fanny did not become a Christian for material gain, because Fanny was well-off, managing a large business prior to her marriage to Leon and conversion to Christianity. They knew that Leon also gave up an honorable career among his own people.

The only explanation of this puzzle was expressed by one of Leon's brothers: "We do not know what has happened to you. We do not see any advantage in your choice. You have not gained any profit through it. You did not even marry a Gentile girl. There is only one explanation...we are afraid that you must have become a *'meshuge'* (crazy)." In his ignorance this brother applied the common Talmudic view, that a man does not commit a sin unless he becomes possessed by the evil one.

When Leon's brothers went back to their father and told him about the failure of their mission, the father was deeply grieved, but decided to try a personal contact, without allowing Leon to enter his house, and without entering the house of his, now "pagan," son. He sent a message suggesting a meeting in a neutral place. Since he had to come directly to Warsaw from the nearby province, he proposed to meet in a hotel. Being afraid that their conversation might become rather loud, because he knew his own temper as that of an excitable Cohen, he advised taking a quiet room on the outskirts of the city so nobody would meet him on the way to his rendezvous with his apostate son. Leon gladly agreed to have a man-to-man talk with his father.

When the appointed time arrived, Leon and Fanny went together, but she to serve only as a guard to be nearby, fearing some unpleasant occurrences. They prepared themselves for this important event by much prayer, which in the end proved to be very necessary, for this encounter left a truly indelible mark on their lives.

Father's arguments were incisive and heart-searching, but they alone could not address the serious issue at hand. Before long, the weapons of rabbinical scholasticism were exhausted between father and son. The son, however, had one advantage, for besides his rabbinical training, based mostly on the Talmud, he was well-versed in the Word of God, expressed in both Testaments, and against this double-edged sword Rabbi Eleazar, the priest, could not prevail.

To Leon's deep sorrow, the gap between father and son widened even more, and their long and heated conversation ended with a curse upon him from his father's lips and a closing statement: "I once more tried my best to bring you back to God and back to your people, but you are lost and 'I will go down into my grave unto my son mourning.'" (This later part of Leon's father's statement was a quotation from the words of Jacob regarding his son Joseph when he believed him dead. (Gen. 37:35) These final words of his father pierced Leon's heart and the two unbendable men parted silently with lumps in their throats, fighting tears in their eyes.

Waiting in the lobby, Fanny was glad to see her husband returning to her unharmed, but she was deeply distressed when she heard about the results of this solemn exchange between father and son.

All of Leon's siblings were forbidden to contact their apostate brother personally or by letter. Leon, however, had a deep longing to see his youngest sister, Frieda, whom he had not seen since she was a baby, and whose birth caused the death of their beloved mother. In order to do so, he had to go secretly into town and ask a friend to take a snapshot of his sister as she played with her friends in the backyard of their house while father was not home.

♆

Encouragement

♆

Not everything was unpleasant in the city of Warsaw during the Rosenberg's ministry there under such adverse conditions. Some happenings were indeed quite pleasant. The Lord had tangibly blessed their efforts by giving them souls to win for Him. But on the other hand, this brought upon them various attacks by those relatives who became convinced of the truthfulness of Christianity and had accepted Jesus as their Messiah. The reason for this negative reaction was, that they too had to pay a heavy price for their faith and were not ready for it.

At times, the pressure from these relatives seemed unbearable and caused much earnest pleading with the Lord to show them another open door and means of reassurance and strength. Some indeed triumphed over the circumstances and developed resistance to persecution through deeper knowledge of the Word of God. Some fell by the wayside for the time-being only to recover later with sadness and regret in their hearts for their failure to stand firm from the beginning.

Though things were moving along at a satisfactory speed, and some fruits were reaped from among the local Jewish population, Leon and Fanny felt a subtle "tug" on their hearts, a call to something bigger and more significant. Thus a new page in their story was opened, introducing a new period in their stormy and eventful ministry, a period which was destined to last for about twenty years.

🕎

PART

III

Chapter 9

ODESSA

At the turn of the twentieth century, the relatively new, but rapidly growing city of Odessa on the Black Sea in South Russia, became widely known as the largest port and the main gateway to the Orient. Commerce flourished there, and because it was an unrestricted zone for Jewish settlements, the sons of Abraham flocked from the surrounding areas and settled in Odessa.

The Jewish community consisted of about two hundred thousand, or 30% of the entire population of the city, thus becoming the majority among the many non-Jewish ethnic groups. Besides the rival parties of natives, the so-called great Russians (*vyelikorossy*) and little Russians (known as *malorossy* or the Ukrainians), Odessa sheltered a number of Tartars, Turks, Greeks, Bulgarians, Romanians, Chinese, Japanese, Serbs, Persians and Armenians. There was also a considerable number of Germans and a few Americans and British. There was a tremendous diversity of religions, cults and denominations, beginning with the most prominent State Greek Orthodox Church, followed by less numerous Roman Catholics and various Protestant groupings, and finally, Muslims with their mosques and temples.

Odessa impressed some as a Babylon of sorts, not only due to the variety of tongues spoken there, but also because of the prevailing low moral standards.

The Jewish community there was divided into three religious groups. The Orthodox were in the majority, with 53 synagogues, large and small, and with considerable staffs of rabbis and their assistants. The Reformed Jews constituted the next group in size, with their modern synagogues which were called temples. The minority were the so-called *"Karaites"* (in Hebrew *"Karaim,"* or followers of Scripture), who kept themselves separate from the rest. Their rabbis were called *"Chachamim,"* meaning the "wise men." Their assistants were called *"Chazzanim,"* and their synagogues were called *"Bet Ha-Knesset,"* which means "House of Assembly" (today's Israeli parliament, the Knesset, is such a house of assembly). These people, though Jewish, enjoyed many privileges of the non-Jewish peoples. These were granted to them because of their rejection of the Talmud, although actually they had their own traditions and did not differ from the other Jews in their attitude towards other religions.

There were other distinctions in the Jewish community among the Orthodox as well as among the progressive groups. The influence of the so-called spiritual leaders *(Tzaddikim)* was strongly competitive and each of them had a considerable following, which openly defied one another. Yet there was a great difference between the Orthodox Jews of Odessa and those of Warsaw, or the district, known as Russian Poland. Those in Odessa were more open-minded towards the *Haskala,* the Jewish renaissance, and thus Odessa became the center of this movement.

From this city came the real "Macedonian call": "Come over and help us." Though the previous call to come to Warsaw sounded also as a call from God, and no doubt constituted such a call for that time, it was a call for a preparatory assignment, designed for training before the final location would be indicated and all the proper provisions could be completed. That location proved to be not Warsaw but Odessa, Russia (today's Ukraine). The Mission, under the leadership of which the Rosenbergs went to Odessa, was the British Mildmay Mission for the Jews. No one ministered to the Jews of that area at that time.

Some work among Jews was tried in Kishinev (Moldavia), a city also with a very large Jewish population. The Rosenberg's call came in the days of Joseph Rabinovitz, a Jewish lawyer from Kishinev, who shortly after his return from Palestine, boldly appeared among the Jewish people of his city with his testimony that Jesus Christ indeed is the long awaited Jewish Messiah and King.

Prior to his conversion, Rabinovitz was sent by the *"Chovevei Tziyon"* (Lovers of Zion) to find out about the possibilities of colonization on Eretz Israel, or the land of Palestine. While there, he came across Christian places and monuments, such as the Church of the Nativity, Gethsemane and Calvary, which so captured his attention that he read the New Testament in order to learn more about them. This resulted in his conversion and he returned to his home and to his friends with the message, saying that the key to Palestine, to their historic homeland, was in the hands of their brother, Jesus, and he founded the so-called "Christian Synagogues"; but severe persecution soon put an end to his efforts.

In Odessa there lived in those days a retired minister from the North, the famous pastor Gurland, a Hebrew Christian, who because of his ill health was ordered by the doctors to live on the shores of the Black Sea. Being greatly handicapped by his ailment and mostly confined to his home, he did a splendid work for the cause of Jewish Missions with his ever ready pen. Soon he passed away to be with the Lord. Leon cherished the memory of this dear servant of God and counted it a privilege to have been with him if only for a short time.

The way to Odessa was not as smoothly paved for Leon as he expected. As soon as he arrived he had a very sad experience. Leon had left his family in a German settlement near Warsaw for a summer vacation and traveled alone to Odessa to acquaint himself with the living conditions there. While attending his first Sunday worship service in a German Baptist Chapel, he was handed a telegram with very sad news: his little son Philip, his only boy (and his third child), suddenly passed away. This necessitated his immediate return to the family, and he left Odessa.

ש

Buried In A Cradle

ש

When little boy Philip died, the minister of the Protestant congregation of the area where Fanny lived, refused to permit the burial in their church cemetery only because Leon's family was not on the membership rolls of his church and did not belong to his denomination. While waiting for Leon to arrive Fanny was desperate and really did not know what to do. In the heat of the summer she could hardly keep the little corpse in the house. The only thing left to do was to bury her dead son in his cradle filled with wet sand.

Traveling in those days in Europe was not very fast and it took several days before Leon arrived at home. After the local Police intervened on Rosenbergs' behalf, the minister allowed them to bury their little son in a far corner of the cemetery with one condition that the father of the little one would officiate himself at the funeral service. For this denomination this was quite a unique event that a Jewish Christian minister was going to bury his child in their church cemetery, and curiosity caused many to attend the peculiar service. Father and mother who had to dig their son's grave themselves, did so bravely because they knew Him, Who is the Resurrection and the Life, to Whose hand they entrusted their darling. Taking advantage of this occasion, when so many people had gathered at the cemetery, Leon gave a real Gospel message which touched the hearts of many leaving an indelible impression on them.

After the funeral, an elderly man introduced himself as a retired teacher who once taught at the school run by this Protestant denomination. With tears in his eyes said that he was deeply ashamed of the narrow-mindedness of his minister, who because of some very minor difference between the two denominations refused to officiate at the funeral of a tiny innocent boy. The old teacher added that he was glad that things turned out this way and he was able to hear Leon's message, which was a great blessing to him and he hoped also to others. This man suggested to Leon to arrange some private meetings. "I am certain," he said, "that many who listened to your message today would gladly come." It was truly from the Lord Who sweetened the sorrow of the sad experience with the blessed results of the gatherings which were regularly held for several weeks in a garden. People came in great numbers and many souls were saved. The death of a child was used of the Lord in this community to His glory.

While Leon was tempted to remain in the city where his little boy died, and was about ready to give up the idea of returning to Odessa, it "just so happened" that Fanny, whose health had suffered a downturn from the births of the first three children and now the loss of one of them, her only son, was advised to go to a warm southern climate, and in the Fall of 1905 the family moved to Odessa where God had already prepared a great ministry for them.

♈

Chapter 10

OBSTACLES

*U*nknown and unforeseen difficulties were awaiting the humble beginnings of a new public Gospel ministry among the Jewish population of Odessa. At that time, Russia, with its Orthodox State Church, tolerated the presence and activities of some foreign denominations, giving religious freedom to some German and English-speaking groups to hold services in their own languages. Russia also allowed the Orthodox Jews and other non-Christians to practice their religions. However, the actual mission work and open preaching of the Gospel in the native Russian language was strictly forbidden. This right was reserved exclusively for the State Greek Orthodox Church with its services in the Byzantine tradition and style. As a result of all this, many obstacles had to be overcome before Leon was given permission by the Government to open a book store with Christian literature for Jews.

ψ

The Sign In The Window

ψ

Considering the conditions in Russia in those days this was indeed a great achievement, and so, after much prayer and strife, a sign was placed above the door of a rented building with an inscription, *"Sklad Bibleiskikh Kneeg"* (Bible Book Store). An open Bible with underlined passages in the Old and New Testaments was placed in the shop window, together with other Christian literature, and a placard in Yiddish telling of the nature of this exhibit. These underlined places were changed every now and then and Jewish passersby stopped to read them. This was new for Odessa and attracted the attention of many.

One day a Jew stopped at the window and began to read the story of Zacchaeus, a Jew in the New Testament who wanted to see Jesus. The passing-by Jew became interested in this story but could not read the continuation of it in the window. He came into the store and asked for the story about the little man. He was handed a New Testament, paid for it and left. Whether this man knew what he had purchased or not, remained a big question. But a few days later, another man came to the store and said that a certain book was recommended to him by a friend and that he would like to have one. By-and-by more Jews became interested in the new store and its books. Some began to ask questions which in turn gave ample opportunity to proclaim the Gospel.

ॐ

Warnings In The Synagogues

ॐ

The rabbis, who had heard about this unusual bookstore, gave warnings to their congregations not to have anything to do with the *"Meshamudim,"* but these warnings aroused greater curiosity among the people and an urgent desire to go and see for themselves what it was that alarmed their rabbis so much. The bookstore became, so to speak, a battlefield of opinions, not only between the missionary and his opposition, but also because of difference of opinion among its visitors. Though Leon was spiritually and intellectually well equipped and prepared for such events, physically they became too hard to handle. The need of a helper became evident, but in the Jewish mission field of that time it was a matter of much prayer and consideration. Jewish missionaries were sparse, uncommon and hard to locate. Total trustworthiness and adequate knowledge of the Scriptures would be the two main qualifications, so Leon and Fanny turned to earnest prayer.

ψ

Police

ψ

One Saturday, when the Bible Book Store was packed with Jewish people so that some were even crowding outside, lively debating some subject, a Russian higher police officer came over, attracted by the commotion, and began to shout, "What is here? It this a synagogue or a meeting?" (The word "meeting" then was a very suspicious thing. It was always linked with conspiracy against the Government and such meetings were strictly forbidden.) The people became frightened, but Leon approached the officer and said, "No, it is neither a synagogue nor a meeting. It is a place authorized by the Government to sell literature."

"Did I not hear you talking to them?"

"Yes," Leon answered, "you have."

"What were you talking about? What kind of speech were you giving?"

"I was just praising the literature we sell," replied Leon.

"Is this then an auction?"

"No," replied Leon, "but I wouldn't mind selling all of my literature at once and supply another stock."

"I have never seen such a thing," said the officer, "Jews never buy goods on Saturday."

"Yes, but they want to know the nature of the books to pay for them the next day."

"What kind of literature do you have anyhow?"

Quietly Leon took one of the books out and said: "This is the New Testament of our Lord Jesus Christ, in Hebrew."

The amazement of the policeman was so great that he could not catch his breath or believe his ears. He shouted, "The New Testament and the Jews?!" In his mind this Book was associated only with Christians and could not also be in the Hebrew language for all Jews to read. After the officer calmed down sufficiently, he was offered a seat, and he was obviously becoming more and more interested in the goings-on at this unusual bookstore. Leon used this opportunity to explain to this "Christian" the essence of Christianity and how it originated in the Old Testament of which the New Testament is but a fulfillment, and how it pertains to the Jews. Jews watched how the officer examined the store's license, and then listened with rapt attention, when he, being himself a religious man, said to Leon: "I am pleased to have such a place in my locality."

The officer filed a report with his headquarters and for a while nothing threatened Leon at least from this side, and he enjoyed relative peace and even a sense of protection.

Chapter 11

BUILDING OF A FIRM FOUNDATION

♅

First Bible Class And An Undesired Visitor

♅

*I*n one-on-one conversations with individual Jews, Leon explained how the the Old Testament Messianic predictions were fulfilled in the New Testament and verified by history. This indeed became a tremendous eye-opener to many. The simplicity of the Gospel proved to be the power of God unto salvation to those who believed.

Faith became naturally evidenced in private secret testimonies of those whom missionaries rightly called then and still do today, "the secret believers." One by one these secret seekers of truth expressed their desire for further studies and a wish to be admitted to Christian fellowship for the purpose of setting aside some quiet hour for regular Bible study.

The first such class started with only three Jews, whose names were, Kudashevitz (who was the eldest), Pidtz and Ebin. But even for such a small gathering great precautions had to be taken. "Meetings" were not only strictly forbidden by law, but were watched by vigilant eyes of the secret agents of Pobedonostzev, the General Procurator of the Holy Synod of the State Russian Orthodox Church. These agents were constantly looking out for possible signs of secret group meetings for the purpose of propagating and promulgating the Gospel. The reason for such alarm and vigilance were the pioneering activities of the so-called *"stundists,"* or evangelicals who dared to study the Bible on their own in small home groups. With fear and trembling, humanly speaking, Leon decided to follow the command of his Lord and the group began to grow. Because of precautions, one had to be sure of the trustworthiness of those who were allowed to attend these "meetings" which in reality were merely Bible classes.

As a means of precaution, Fanny Rosenberg set a Russian *"samovar"* (a self-boiler of hot water for tea) on the table and served tea. Before each of the visitors was set a cup of tea and little snacks were placed beside each open Bible. Should the police come, it would look like a private group of friends, gathered for conversation around the samovar, the ever present feature of every Russian home. These gatherings were held mostly in the evenings behind locked doors.

One evening Leon's sharp ear caught a repeated faint knock on the door. As the man of the house, he was the one who answered the door during such meetings. To his amazement, a very humble looking bearded Russian man, whose appearance seemed typical of those who were known as *"stundists,"* stood outside the door and greeted Leon with a Christian greeting, *"Mir vam, bratetz"* (peace unto you, dear brother).

"I was told," he said, "that you are a Christian Hebrew, a missionary, who has the book store on 25 K Street."

"Yes," Leon said, "it is true. How can I help you?"

"I am a *stundist,* a brother, and I know you would be able to answer a few questions from the Word of God."

Leon said "maybe," and told the man that he was at present busy and "would he please come at another time." The man said he was sorry but he would not be able to do that, because he lived in another city. The determination and persistence of the visitor were suspicious. They did not display the usual meek spirit of a stundist. But Leon had to yield and let him in. Meanwhile the Jewish brethren casually sipped their tea. When the man was admitted to the table, he continued to play his game, repeating his greeting to the others and expressing his delight in being privileged to meet with Hebrew Christian brothers. He was offered a cup of tea which he gratefully accepted, but left soon after finishing his tea, seemingly uninterested in anything else. Leon was convinced that the man was not sincere, but did not reveal his suspicions to his guests.

Two days later, the secret police came to investigate and accused Leon of holding religious meetings in his home, insisting that among the visitors were some members of the Russian Orthodox Church. This, of course, was not true, but from that time on Leon's activities became even more guarded. The gatherings continued at different homes and at different times and the Lord set His seal upon these little meetings. They became a foundation of much greater work in Odessa.

♆

Chapter 12

LIGHT IN THE DARKNESS

Such conditions could not last long. The powers of darkness caused much sorrow and suffering to those faithful pioneers, the stundists, and their cry went up to Heaven. Their persecution was unbearable, but nothing could stop them, in spite of the fact that the aforementioned Pobedonostzev had ordered this movement to be crushed by its enemies in an attempt to keep the Russian people in religious darkness, represented by the firm grip of superstitions taught by the poorly educated *"bateushkas"* (endearing term for *"batia,"* or father, as the Russian priests were called).

Evangelicals, who dared to study the Word and to gather in the precious name of their Lord, were the ones who realized the impotence of the ceremonies of the official church. These simple believers in Christ were deliberately given a foreign name, *"stundists,"* so that the strong nationalistic Russians would despise them for their supposedly foreign origin. In the original German, the word *"Stunde,"* from which the name *"stundist"* is derived, means either an "hour" or a "lesson." These evangelical believers met for an "hour" of prayer and study, or for a time of learning, to take a lesson from the Holy Scriptures. They were also called "sectarians" for creating a "sect" or a break-off group from the main body of Orthodox believers. But these early Russian evangelical believers, including the Rosenbergs, spent countless hours in prayer and learned profound lessons from the Scriptures. God answered their pleas and deliverance did eventually come, but not before much more severe testing of everyone's patience and faith.

As for the Jews of South Russia, the period between 1904 until October 1905 was indeed a very trying one. The Russian-Japanese war so inflamed the nationalistic feelings of the vast Russian Empire and the Holy Synod with the entire Orthodox hierarchy, that they expected to overcome the enemy simply with thousands of icons, which were presented to the Army chief, Kuropatkin. Instead, they were deeply humiliated by the defeat of the Russian Army and Navy. The underground socialist movement was looking for a chance to obtain some freedom from the government for their people, who were persecuted under the Czars, and incited a mini-revolution which was quickly put down for the time-being. The young Emperor, Nicholas II, yielded to the demand and advice of his more liberal government advisors and granted his people constitutional freedoms to avoid future problems.

This was celebrated by millions of oppressed and underprivileged people. Needless to say, the Jews, although being a small minority (only about 7,000,000 in the whole Russian Empire) rejoiced that day, too, anticipating some new privileges and freedoms from the desperate conditions to which they had been subjected for so many centuries, being restricted to certain settlements and not allowed to live in the old Russian cities like St. Petersburg, Moscow, Kiev, Kharkov, etc. They were the only taxpayers (very heavily taxed by arbitrary methods) who were deprived of many social rights and excluded from the political process. Though their sons had to serve in the army, they could never advance to the rank of even a corporal. The religious anti-semitism was nurtured and supported by the official State Church by means of persecution. The Jews were driven and tempted to accept the Greek Orthodoxy, which they staunchly resisted.

The reactionists, who were the Russian vast majority and the most privileged in the country, disapproved of the new constitution and organized a counter-action, spreading wild rumors of an overthrow not only of the government, but of everything in "Holy Russia." For a scapegoat they chose, as was historically quite often the case, the despised and defenseless Jews. The Jews were kept under constant suspicion in the minds of the people because of their separateness and different religious style aimed at fulfilling God's commandments according to their concept and knowledge of them.

This counter-action of the reactionists was organized to threaten the Czar and to warn him that his liberal action caused the rage of his loyal subjects, and that there would be great tribulation in the country, which might destroy the prestige of his monarchy in the whole civilized world. They explained that in order to avoid all this, they had organized a counteraction to serve as a lightning rod and to be aimed mainly against the Jews.

The gendarmes (police officials and priests) began to agitate people against the Jews, promising full freedom of action, protection, and liberty to take the spoils during attacks on Jewish businesses and homes. Thus the massacre of the Jews began to rage all over the country. Mad mobs, intoxicated by hate and alcohol which was given to them free of charge, were agitated by political and fanatical propagandists. They began to attack Jewish shops and settlements, robbing, pillaging, wounding and killing. In Odessa such inhumane attacks raged for three days. Hundreds of Jews were killed, several thousands were wounded and great masses left without a roof over their heads. The aftermath of this three-day unbridled slaughter was horrible.

ψ

Ministry During The Jewish Pogrom

ψ

In those hazardous days of political turmoil, the Jewish population of Odessa was subjected to cruel attacks by well organized mobs. On the first day of the Russian Orthodox Easter the police were secretly withdrawn from the streets and the Jews were declared outside the law. Thus the "green light" was given for blind hatred and unbridled pillage which has been known in Jewish and world history under the Russian name *"pogrom,"* meaning massacre.

The so called "Christians" identified themselves by putting icons in their windows or crosses over their doors. Seeing this, a number of Jews, in an attempt to save themselves, came to the Rosenbergs' house expecting that they, as followers of Christ, would also mark their home with Christian emblems of some kind. But when they saw that no sign was placed in the windows or on doors, they urged pastor Rosenberg to do so for his own protection, to which he replied that he did not believe in any of these emblems as sources of protection, and said that his trust was only in the Lord Himself, and his home was under the sign of the blood of Christ which reminded his family of the miracle on the first Passover night in Egypt. Hearing this, some of the Jews remained in the house, while others did not feel sufficiently sheltered and returned to their homes exposing themselves to the fury of the mad mobs.

Rosenbergs' house was facing 'K' street in the immediate Jewish section. Looking out of the windows, it was indeed horrible to see these organized mobs which, with crosses in one hand and a hammer or an ax in the other, were breaking in the doors of Jewish homes and stores, robbing them and carrying away their goods. It was heartrending to hear the voices of the innocent victims, of the many tortured men, women and children.

Humanly speaking, there was no hope of survival for the Rosenberg family either, but the protecting hand and watchful eye of the Almighty was over His own. Nevertheless, all faithful believers were ready, if necessary, to give up there lives. Pastor Rosenberg's assistant, brother D., for instance, came with a large Bible under his arm and declared, "If something happens to me, I would like to die with my Bible in my arms."

As never before, the words of the 91st Psalm became most reassuring: "He that dwelleth in the secret place of the Most High shall abide under the shadow of the Almighty." To the Jews in Pastor Rosenberg's home the reading of this Psalm sounded as if he was preparing them to die, because the first words of this Psalm are usually placed as an inscription over the gates of Jewish cemeteries. Women began to sob and even some of the men cried. They too preferred to escape, but there was no time to do so because the murderous attacks were in full swing under the windows of their shelter and in every section of their Jewish neighborhood.

Pastor Rosenberg explained the meaning of the 91st Psalm as being a psalm of consolation for living believers and not for the dead. This calmed the whole group and they spent much time in prayer. The noise of the hammers and axes, breaking and demolishing Jewish property, added acutely to the solemnity of this unusual prayer hour. Many times the enraged killers passed the praying home of the Rosenbergs, but nothing happened to them during three days of the great havoc of pillage and massacre. This experience made a deep impression on those Jews who spent the time of the pogroms with the Hebrew Christian missionaries. They were drawn closer to accepting the Lord Jesus as their Messiah and Savior.

On the fourth day the organized pogrom suddenly stopped. Police, who had laid down their uniforms to lead the mobs as civilians, appeared again at their posts. Mounted Cossacks were sent into the streets to prevent any further outrage. The threat to the Emperor that his constitution would incite anarchy and lead to his dethronement did not materialize, and the order came from the government to stop the pogrom at once.

However, the result of this anti-Jewish action, which carried the name of a "counter-revolution," was shocking. Broken Jewish furniture was strewn everywhere and the demolished Jewish stores were a stark evidence of pillage and robbery. The many corpses of dead Jewish men and women in the streets and in the homes mutely spoke of the real nature of human cruelty and violence.

When the streets were cleared for traffic, Pastor Rosenberg took the first opportunity to visit the homes of those Jewish friends whom he knew personally, especially the Hebrew Christians.

On the first streetcar he took, there were only a few Jewish passengers. The discussion among the rest of the passengers was focused on the events of the previous three days. Some approved the action, others considered any action against the Jews both unchristian and inhuman and were openly outraged. This gave Pastor Rosenberg an opportunity to read out loud from his

Russian New Testament and to speak of the true nature of genuine Christianity.

☖

Miraculous Escape

☖

Pastor Rosenberg's trade as a "tent-making" minister was that of a cabinetmaker. On the day of the outbreak of the pogrom, he hurried home from his shop to be with his family. On the way he was encircled by a group of malicious foes. "Stop, you dirty Jew!" they shouted, "open your mouth!" The leader pointed a revolver at Leon, intending to shoot a bullet into his mouth. Leon asked permission to read a passage from the New Testament before he died. The man with the revolver in his hand was astonished to hear a request from a Jew to read a word from the Holy Gospel and said: "You, a Jew, will read something from the Holy Gospel?" "Yes," Leon answered, "I am a Jew, but I believe in the Lord and Savior Jesus Christ." Having said this, Leon took out his New Testament and read the words of the Lord Jesus which He uttered while hanging on the cross and praying for His enemies, "Father, forgive them; for they know not what they do."

The leader of the group patted Leon on the shoulder and said: "Go in peace, brother."

This experience left an indelible impression on Pastor Rosenberg's heart. He repeated the story many times with tears in his eyes, emphasizing not so much the miraculous deliverance itself, as the faithfulness of the Lord Who protected him and his family during those three evil days.

Pastor Rosenberg's assistant also experienced something short of a miracle. He lived with his family right in the middle of the Jewish settlement, the so-called *Moldovanka.* There the sight of the aftermath of the pogrom was truly shocking. The whole area looked as if struck by a hurricane. When Pastor Rosenberg approached the corner house with smashed windows where his assistant lived, the whole family was delighted to see him. All still bore traces of agitation over the recent experiences, but were joyfully praising God. Mr. K. showed a bullet, pointed to the ceiling and then the floor and said: "This bullet was fired into the house, struck the ceiling and came down half an inch from me. How easily I could have been killed or mortally wounded, and yet here I am with my family and all six of us are alive. Several times the raging mob was about to break in and kill us, but ironically, the Lord used the owner of this house, a Russian Orthodox Christian who, unlike many others, is a very fine man. He stood the entire time in the doorway of his house, and when danger approached, bravely defended us by asking the mob if "they were now also killing the Christians?"

In one instance, the leader of such an atrocious group noticed brother K. with his typically Jewish features, and said to the defending landlord: "Why do you say he is a Christian? How can he be a Christian while looking so typically Jewish?"

Brother K.'s landlord replied: *"Nye smotry na yevo zhydovskooyoo mordoo, on khristianin v dooshe"* (Do not look at his Jewish muzzle. In his heart he is a Christian).

On his way back home Leon was told that in the courtyard of the Jewish hospital were thousands of refugees — men, women and children, — who barely escaped the hands of the murderous, vicious mob. He rushed into that courtyard and found there a horrible scene of misery: starving, pale, frightened, shivering fathers, mothers, boys and girls were filling the yard. The crying and lamentation over the loss of their loved ones ascended to heaven. Some, being in a state of shock, were silent in their desperation. There were also signs of mental disorder. For instance, one woman with disheveled hair and insanity in her eyes, was shouting and dancing, while her two little children pulled on her skirt, crying, "Mother! Mother!" She was oblivious to their crying and continued her frenzied dance, twirling and jumping. Leon learned later that this dear woman witnessed the brutal murder of her husband and rape and murder of her two daughters. The two smaller children watched from their hiding place somewhere in the house the horrible scene which made their mother lose her mind.

Seeing so much misery, Pastor Rosenberg could hardly enjoy the benefits of his own miraculous rescue; even the fact of the accepted constitution, granting new liberty and freedom, was overshadowed by the harsh reality played out before his eyes. The question was how to approach a Jew in the name of Jesus, when such cruel things where done to them in the name of Christianity, and yes, even in the name of the Cross. The words of the prophet Jeremiah echoed in Leon's heart "For the hurt of the daughter of my people am I hurt; I am black; astonishment has taken hold on me. Is there no balm in Gilead, is there no physician there? Why then is not the health of the daughter of my people recovered?" (Jer. 8:21,22 KJV).

Leon thought of the divine injunction of the Lord given in the story of the good Samaritan. Arriving at his home, he shared his experiences with his wife, stressing those in the courtyard of the Jewish hospital. Fanny suggested starting at once a relief effort; no matter how modest, it would be a beginning. Encouraged by the words in Isaiah 58:7-8 about the meaning of a true fast, they knew how to go about helping the needy, namely "...deal thy bread to the hungry and bring the poor who are cast out to thy house. When thou seest the naked, that thou cover him, and hide not thyself from thy own flesh. Then shall thy light break out as the morning, and thy health shall spring forth speedily; and thy righteousness shall go before thee; the glory of the Lord shall be thy reward." (KJV)

They understood that the Lord wanted *THEM* to deal *THEIR* bread to the hungry and share *THEIR* house with the destitute — at least with as much or as little as they could afford. They put the emphasis on the right words, "thy" and "thine," "thy bread" and "thy house." Fanny said: "God does not want us to wait until we have our own bakery or a large institution. We must begin in a small way and go one step at a time with the Lord leading us. When we have shown faithfulness in small things, God will entrust us with greater."

ψ

Step Of Faith

ψ

The beginning of this badly-needed Samaritan work was indeed small. The first group brought into their home to be fed and sheltered numbered only a few. The first meals were frugal. Bread and tea was all they could afford. This served as appetizer as well as dessert. However, sanctified by prayer and under the blessing of God, such meals brought tears of gratitude and thanksgiving from the heart. The first company of beneficiaries consisted of two of the most miserable and exhausted among the thousands of homeless who had escaped into the courtyard of the Jewish hospital.

This simple act of practical Christian charity exercised among the destitute Jews in the name of the greatest Lover, their Messiah, our Savior, soon became known not only among Christian friends in the city of Odessa, but also in the whole country and abroad. Relief on a much larger scale was soon organized. Appropriate, roomy quarters were provided for the many homeless, with food for the hungry. Group after group, numbering from sixty to one hundred, were not only sheltered and fed, but re-established in their businesses or other previous activities. Homes were repaired and furniture replaced. This relief was administered wisely and carefully under a special committee, and was carried on until life returned to normal.

ψ

An Effective Testimony

ψ

The Rosenbergs were grateful to the Lord Who had enabled them to display such generosity at this particular time of need. The preaching of the written Word and the practice of loving deeds blended into most effective testimony to the glory of the Messiah, Who Himself went about doing good and preaching the Word. This language was understood by the afflicted Jews, but caused some opposition on the part of the most fanatical ones. However, this was gradually overcome and a regular, widespread Gospel activity was established. A blessed work among orphans and destitute children was founded and continued through most of the rest of the Rosenbergs' lives.

Organizations were established and large-scale relief, particularly Jewish relief, was organized in the USA, England and other countries with substantial Jewish communities. The nature of this Christian and truly Messianic testimony had its unique place and received approbation as well as opposition. Appreciation came from those who were helped in a quiet way, not merely by charity but in a personal friendly manner, which comforted and rehabilitated broken hearts without any obligation. Opposition came from the organized rabbinical circles of those fanatics who looked upon missionary activities as a means of soul hunting. The motives of missionaries were misinterpreted and deeds were considered as a means to bribe or buy the Jews into Christianity.

Under the new Constitution people made use of their liberty, and open discussions about the current events became commonplace. Opposition was strong but divided, and soon it became evident that there were more defenders of missionary activities of the nature conducted by the Rosenbergs, than opponents to them. Large crowds began to gather around the benefactors; people came to listen to the Gospel message and it became necessary for the Rosenbergs to call in other missionaries to assist them in proclaiming the Gospel of Jesus Christ. The few workers they already had were not sufficient because the meetings continued all day from early morning until late evening. One group would replace the other and so it went on all day long. Two brothers were summoned from Warsaw, well known missionaries, L. and Z.

This provoked the rabbis of the city and they ordered a delegation to enter into an open discussion with the missionaries. One day, while a huge crowd was gathering for an open meeting, this delegation arrived and everybody could see that they were charged with hostility. Without asking for permission, a leading rabbi jumped on a chair and lifted his voice addressing the gathering, but instead of giving a message to disprove the teaching and preaching of the missionaries, he accused Pastor Rosenberg of selling himself out to the enemy of Israel by deserting the God of Abraham, Isaac and Jacob, and believing in the "*Toli.*" He further accused Pastor of being a brother to those murderers of the Jewish fathers and mothers, sisters and brothers, and partaking in wrecking and pillaging their property. Then he attacked the audience, telling them that they were bribed and had sold themselves to those apostate enemies of their nation.

People listened but could not understand a word of what was said, and began to whistle, hiss and stomp their feet. They urged Pastor Rosenberg to call the police, but instead of doing that, Fanny Rosenberg stood with her arms crossed, silently looking at the venerable leader who, in his spiritual blindness, could not do any better. Not knowing her personally, the speaker decided at first that he had found in her an attentive listener, but soon Fanny opened her mouth and began to respond. She told the rabbi that he had nothing to say in self-defense and quoted a phrase from the Talmud that "he who slaughtered his fellow man publicly had no part in the world to come." This was too much for the self-righteous rabbi and he answered, "I do not consider you as a fellow man."

"Do you not consider those present, or even some of them whom you do not know, as your fellow men?" The speaker went silent, but only for a moment, and then said: "Yes." Then Leon said: "Your 'slaughter' was addressed not only against me, but against those innocent ones present. You called them renegades, people who sold themselves to the missionaries, and this is not true. Our motives are peculiar. We preach the Word of God. We prove from the Scriptures that the prophecies concerning the Messiah were fulfilled, and it is only because of Him, the great Lover of our people, the good Shepherd, Who laid down His life, Who prayed for those who were against Him and Who commanded His followers to love not only their friends but also their enemies, that we undertook this action of helping those who needed to be helped and who appreciated our help."

The rabbi realized that he had lost his case but still called the people to follow him. No one budged and only those who came with him left with him.

This attack in itself was a good testimony against all "slaughter" and evil speaking because the people knew well that what the rabbi said was a lie. The majority of those present did not need help but came just to listen to what was said, still others were simply curious to see the missionaries of whom they have heard so many diverse reports. After the relief work came to an end, and after life gradually returned to normal, the scattering of the good seed and the time of the harvest began in earnest.

ψ

Chapter 13

SOME UNUSUAL ENCOUNTERS
AND HAPPENINGS

☙

Meeting With Nilus

☙

*T*he name of a Russian man, Sergeus Nilus, became widely known in connection with a certain pamphlet entitled, "Protocols of the Learned Elders of Zion," which he had published. These protocols were destined to become a menace to the Jewish nation through the hands of the Jew-haters and anti-Semites all over the world for decades to come.

It was in 1906 in Odessa, right after the horrible Jewish pogroms, that this man introduced himself to Pastor Rosenberg as a missionary to the Jews, commissioned by the Russian (Greek) Orthodox Church. He came to Leon on the pretense of being interested in his missionary activities, and though he presented himself as a friend, he turned out to be a wolf in sheep's clothing. He hoped to secure from Leon the religious secrets, the Jewish mysteries of the strict pious sects. He was well informed about Leon's background — that he came from such a religious sect and was familiar with all the rabbinical teachings and customs.

Nilus told Pastor Rosenberg of his acquaintances among the outstanding Jewish leaders, but added that he could not expect them to reveal to him that which he was so anxious to know, as they were strict Jews and he was a Christian. "But you," he said, "are a learned Jew and a good Christian."

Based on this fact, Nilus wanted to obtain information that would be damaging to the Jews. It was compulsory in the Orthodox Church that, before being baptized by immersion, the Jewish convert (*Neophyte*) would renounce his people, his parents, relatives and the devil. Hence, it was expected that such a "convert" would be naturally opposed to his own people, the Jews. Ignorant on the subject of spiritual birth, which is generally not taught in the Orthodox Church, Nilus assumed that Leon was just that kind of nominal "convert."

Leon asked Nilus why he was so very interested in the Jewish mysteries, to which he replied that he was publishing an interesting booklet and wished that Leon would listen to the content of the yet unpublished manuscript. Leon was curious enough and expressed willingness to go through it with his guest, who told him that it was a translation from the French original. The booklet was the infamous "Protocols of the Learned Elders of Zion."

As Nilus read, Leon listened without a comment, but when asked of his opinion, he realized the full danger of this booklet, and yet knew that he had to be careful in the presence of this man. He asked Nilus if he was familiar with the writings of Luto Stanski, Roling and others who dealt with similar subjects. Nilus did not admit anything, but Leon saw his embarrassment, which he attempted to conceal. Leon asked if Nilus would oblige him by showing to him the original of these "Protocols." His grasp of the French language was sufficient to understand the original text. Nilus promised, but Leon never got to see them. He told this strange visitor that he wondered how it was that the strictest Jewish religious society would write the minutes of their secret session in modern French, the language of the *"goim,"* against whom they were plotting, rather than in ancient Hebrew or some kind of a secret code. Again it was difficult for Nilus to conceal his embarrassment when Leon questioned the original text of this, his discovery.

Attempting to be polite and calm, Leon pointed to the highly incredible way in which the original protocols were revealed. He drew the attention of his guest to the introduction to the translation of the original document in which the translator stated that "a Christian servant girl in the house of a very influential Jew in Paris noticed that from time to time, a group of Orthodox, well-to-do Jews met secretly at the house of her employer. She, as a Christian, suspected that there must be some plotting against the Christian Church and against the government and noticed also, that following each meeting, her employer placed a book in his safe. At a given opportunity she secured this book and disappeared."

The introduction ended with the following conclusion: "This book proved to be the original of the "Protocols" and the men who met at that home, were the "Learned Elders of Zion."

After Leon focused the attention of his guest on the total incredibility of the story about the origins of the booklet's manuscript, and the highly unlikely behavior of the "Elders," Nilus excused himself and left.

Leon shared his odd experience with his wife and co-workers. One of his associates, Mr. K., said that he did not believe this book would cause harm, as any fair-minded person would see, at once, that this was a forgery conceived in the minds of enemies of the Jews. But the meeting with Nilus soon proved harmful to Leon himself and to his work. A few weeks later he was visited by agents of the Secret Police who thoroughly searched his home and the Mission property. Leon was ordered to appear before the Chief of the Gendarmes. After long and thorough questioning he was permitted to return home but was repeatedly harassed by the civil and secret police.

Years went by, and the story of the "Protocols" was forgotten. First World War, the Bolshevik Revolution and Second World War changed the face of the world and consequently the direction of the Rosenbergs' Mission, but when in God's providence, Leon and Fanny reached the free world, Leon discovered that the "Protocols of Zion" had found wide circulation, even among Christians. Brother K., who in the early days of Fanny's and Leon's ministry in Odessa, was prophesying that fair-minded people would easily discover the forgery and foolishness of it, was dead wrong. Anything and everything against the Jew is readily believed. This booklet surfaced again and again all over the world, and is currently resurrected in Russia, after the fall of communism in the nineties, as we are writing this biography.

But let us not run too far ahead in our story. For now, let us return to the presentation of events which took place immediately or shortly after the pogrom. The above mentioned encounter with Mr. Sergeus Nilus, translator and publisher of the infamous die-hard "Protocols," was only one of many remarkable events of that time in the life of Leon and Fanny Rosenberg.

♆

Misused Liberty

♆

Alongside many blessed encouragements there were many discouraging events which appeared in the form of obstacles, laid in the path of the missionaries by the ever-present adversaries.

For quite a while there were watchmen located before the entrance of the Mission to keep Jews away from Gospel meetings. Placards were placed at the entrance of each synagogue, warning the Jews about the missionaries. But these warnings indirectly served another purpose: they were drawing the attention of those Jews who did not know much about this place, and aroused a desire to come and see for themselves. Another favorable result was that only the brave and sincere "seekers of the truth" came.

However, these activities of the opposition did not last long. The adversaries soon grew tired and gave up. More serious were the fervent attacks of the radical groups. Windows were broken and only by God's mercy no one was hurt by those heavy stones that were thrown. Once Leon was attacked by a man who threw a flask of acid at him which could have easily deformed his face or blinded him. Instead it only ruined his new suit and fell to the ground in pieces. On another occasion a severe attack endangered his very life, but he escaped unharmed.

Failing to succeed by these means, the enemy turned to other methods. In those days in Russia there were many dangerous groups, some called themselves anarchists, others "Black Ravens," or such terms. In western countries they would have been called gangsters and racketeers. Many citizens lost their lives in bomb attacks on stores or missions. Virtually the entire population was indeed terrified.

One day, two men came into the Mission Book Store introducing themselves as members of the "Black Raven" group. In the name of their organization they demanded that the Mission cease its activities because it was a hindrance to the progressive march of time, and because it kept people in religious darkness. Knowing their methods of terror, talking to them was by no means an easy task.

Pastor Rosenberg and his assistant K. tried their best to appeal to their consciences, but those malicious people showed no conscience at all. Finally, Pastor Rosenberg told them that they came too late, that he was already warned by a "Supreme Authority" to continue with the work and not fear any threats. They wanted to know what organization it was, and was it not, perchance, a group of reactionaries.

"No," Pastor Rosenberg replied, "This warning was given by the "Most High, the Almighty One." Mocking Pastor Rosenberg and threatening to blow up the whole Mission, they left. Things became very serious; the conditions demanded special care and protection. But what could be done? If they were to follow their feeling of fear, there was only one thing to do — to liquidate everything and close the doors forever. On the other hand, this matter was not personal in nature, because the lives of others — of the visitors and regular attendees — were in danger. Pastor Rosenberg and Mr. K were earnestly concerned about the whole situation, and they committed themselves and the threatening of the enemy to the Lord in prayer. Claiming the promise of Psalm 27, they decided to keep this decision to themselves and not tell their wives and children.

ψ

Testing Of Faith

ψ

When the day of the next meeting approached, the two brothers were in earnest prayer before the Lord. The enemy again and again put the responsibility for those innocent lives upon their hearts, saying, "Even if you are ready to die and some others with you, there will be people who are not prepared at all."

The temptation was great just to give up the meetings at least for a certain period of time. But on the other hand the words of Psalm 27:1-3 gave comfort and confidence:

"The Lord is my light and my salvation; whom shall I fear? the Lord is the strength of my life; of whom shall I be afraid? When the wicked, even mine enemies and my foes, came upon me to eat up my flesh, they stumbled and fell. Though an host should encamp against me, my heart shall not fear: though war should rise against me, in this will I be confident."

Brother K., however, suggested that he would stand at the outside of the door, and when he would recognize one of those malicious men, he would take it up with him in some way to prevent him from carrying out his threats. K. was very serious in suggesting that, and could not be denied this privilege. He was really willing to give his life for the cause of Christ.

♆

A Moment Of Groundless Fear

♆

The meeting-hall was packed to capacity. On Saturday afternoons the attendance was usually the largest. Pastor Rosenberg conducted the service, taking his place behind the pulpit. Nobody understood why he did not read the Sabbath portion from the Pentateuch as he usually did, but instead began to read the 27th Psalm. His prayer was also very solemn, and when he finished praying, he just started to speak, depicting the Savior as the shining light in the darkness, the only helper in every need, particularly the Savior from sin.

He was suddenly interrupted in mid-sentence by some kind of disturbance at the back of the center aisle. A strange man pushed his way through the blocked entrance and walked into the big hall. Behind him with outstretched arms followed brother 'K,' watching his every move. The man seemed also very agitated. Looking from one side of the aisle to the other, he finally spotted an empty seat by one of the windows and sat down.

Pastor Rosenberg, himself expecting something unusual, stopped preaching. Nobody understood the reason for his silence. Finally the man turned to brother 'K,' who was still waving his outstretched arms in front of him, while he searched his pockets for "something mysterious" — or so it seemed to brother 'K' — but it turned out to be nothing more than a handkerchief. Poor man! He was for the first time at such a meeting and was himself scared; he could not understand why he was met at the door by that odd-acting man who continued to follow him wherever he turned. He was looking from side to side of the hall, searching for an empty seat. Pastor Rosenberg and brother 'K' exchanged sheepish glances and both smiled. The Lord put both of them to shame. They feared a handkerchief! What a relief it was when the Lord once again proved Himself victorious.

Pastor Rosenberg resumed his sermon by reading Exodus 14:13: "Fear ye not, stand still and see the salvation of the Lord, which He will shew to you today; for the Egyptians whom you have seen today, ye shall see them no more forever." There was great rejoicing in the hearts of those who just minutes before feared their own shadow.

After that encouraging experience the work of the Gospel went on with renewed strength and joy. Many Jewish men and women yielded their lives to the Lord accepting Him as their personal Savior. Some could really say with the Apostle Peter, "Lord, we left everything behind and followed Thee."

However, these decisions for Christ caused much persecution to many. Not only were the young men who had accepted the Lord ostracized by their families after they confessed faith in Christ as their Messiah, but fathers and mothers were also often rejected by their sons and daughters and many husbands divorced their wives who believed in Jesus, and wives left their husbands because of their confessed faith in Him. Nevertheless, all this was in harmony with the promise in Romans 8:28: "All things work together for good to them that love God," and the final result was always a tremendous blessing to the hearts of those who took a firm stand for Christ in the face of persecution. There were many heartrending events and many moving individual stories which, if retold, would fill a separate book.

One story was especially touching. Brother P. was driven out of his home by his wife and grown children because of his faith. They quickly discovered his "soft spot": being a Christian he would probably not demonstrate any resistance or vexation to their chicanery. Brother P. bore everything with quiet resignation considering it a special privilege to suffer for his faith in his Savior. His face was always beaming and if anyone deserved the name "walking prayer," it was he. One could hear his voice raised joyfully in prayer at every meeting. He gained the growing trust of his Jewish boss through his faithful service. His co-workers mocked and ridiculed him, but he kept quiet amid persecution and constant scoffing. His courageous testimony about his Messiah not only conquered the roughness of his opponents but also won his boss to such a high degree that he too started attending meetings frequently and became increasingly interested in the Gospel of Christ.

It was indeed a victory for the Gospel when this intelligent and highly educated industrialist was so seized by the power of the Holy Spirit that in one of the meetings he suddenly cried out with tears in his eyes and asked if there was any forgiveness for him. When the "Sun of Righteousness" rose in his heart and he found peace for his soul through the blood of the Lamb, he became a joyful child of God and a faithful witness for the Lord.

Soon his wife too became a Christian and this happy brother realized that he could no longer continue in his business as before. This, in turn, led to much ridicule and mockery from his business colleagues and a boycott by Jewish businessmen, and he was forced to close his business altogether. He and his family had to migrate, trying to find another place in which to "pitch a tent," unable to go out as did their father Abraham "with great herds."

When his boss left, brother P. lost his only source of income and a period of hard suffering began. Deprived of even the basic commodities and regular meals, he developed a stomach ailment from which he never recovered. There was no place for a Hebrew-Christian in any well-equipped hospital, and he checked into a Russian hospital for destitute people. Even during his grave illness he remained patient, as his custom was, in all tribulation, and his fellow-sufferers could see how quietly and submissively a Jew, who had become a sincere believer in Jesus, was able to endure his sufferings.

The Russian Orthodox nurses could not understand how this sick Jew with cancer in his stomach managed not to cause any disturbances while other patients forced them to run around and serve them all the time. This Jewish Christian often asked them to attend the other patients first, and when they asked him "why?" he answered that they had to endure more while he was strengthened by his Messiah Who suffered on the cross for him. All nurses soon began to call him a "holy Jew."

He diligently read his Bible and, as long as he could, spoke about his Lord to those around him who were willing to listen. His journey heavenward proceeded with ever greater speed, but it just so happened, that shortly before his going to heaven Pastor Rosenberg had to leave on one of his missionary trips. Brother P.'s desire was to see his beloved pastor once more, and the Lord granted him that joy.

His greeting of Pastor Rosenberg was unforgettable. With his last remaining strength he raised himself up and stretched out both hands towards his beloved pastor. His eyes filled with tears but his face beamed as he whispered: "Brother Rosenberg, I wanted so much to see you once more to thank you before I depart into eternity and to ask you to pray with me."

With Pastor Rosenberg came his wife Fanny and several brothers and sisters from the fellowship. They all knelt down by the bedside of the dying brother and thanked the Lord together with him for a life well-lived. When they arose from their knees, they saw that brother P.'s family stood also at his side. The hospital administration had called them in. No one from the group of believers said a word to them, but the Russian Orthodox nurse said to brother P.'s wife: "Your husband is dying as a saint." The sorrowing woman did not respond but the words made a deep impression on her. Her eyes filled with tears as she stared at her husband, whose face became even more radiant as he recognized his wife and children. He tried to whisper something but could not and quietly gave up his spirit. His death glorified the Lord Whom he loved and served in humility of his heart.

ψ

Satisfied Longing

ψ

Before his death, brother P. expressed a desire that his two youngest children should be reared in some Christian family. This seemed impossible because his wife in her unbelief did not want to give up her children. After the death of this dear brother, the fellowship which he had attended lost touch with his family, but his wife had no rest after the passing away of her husband. Suddenly she started to attend the Christian meetings which had had such a transforming influence on her husband. Months passed and she came and went with her heart untouched by the sermons. The Lord, Whose ways are often past finding out, chose to speak to this woman through privation and want. He does not always use suffering as a "staff" to lead people to Himself, for He has another "staff," called "grace," but in this case it was necessary to use suffering.

One day, a Mennonite brother, who had no children, came to church expressing a desire to adopt one or two children of Jewish Christians. At once all thought of brother P. When approached, the widow said an adamant "no" and all convincing was in vain. Her fanatical mother intervened and the whole affair seemed hopeless. The Mennonite brother prayed with the congregation about it for the sake of the departed brother and his poor children. Suddenly, out of nowhere appeared the widow and declared that she was ready to give her little girl to the friend of the church, but it was obvious to all involved that something needed to be done with both of her younger children. However, the poor woman was not ready to part with her little son, and the Mennonite brother left for the train station, giving up all hope.

Fortunately, it is the Lord Who directs human hearts like streams of water. He spoke to the heart of brother P.'s widow, and only a few minutes after the kind man left, she came with her two children, ready to let them both go. A carriage was called (no automobiles were at the church's disposal), and it rushed to the railroad station with the mother and her two children.

Pastor Rosenberg also came along. At the very last moment he was able to board the train (there was no time left to buy tickets) and began to search for the Mennonite brother. To his surprise, he did not have to look long, as he was in the same section, preparing his berth for the night. In Russian trains at that time there were three berths, one above the other, for sleeping passengers. The departing brother did not notice brother Rosenberg and the children at once, but when he finally did, his joy was great because he recognized the leading hand of God in the fact that despite the great haste of departure, Pastor Rosenberg and the children were in the same section of the train where he was, with just a few seconds left to turn the children over to him and hastily leave the train.

Thus the Lord answered prayer and satisfied the longing of a dear brother by providing a Christian home for his small children. They eventually received a good education and found their Lord and Savior in the Person of the Lord Jesus. As for the mother, she frequently visited the Mission fellowship, earnestly seeking the truth. One day she too accepted Jesus as her Savior and Redeemer and found peace for her soul in Him.

ψ

Chapter 14

ONE STEP FURTHER

☰

The Founding
Of The First Hebrew-Christian Church

☰

*T*his chapter begins with a barely readable scribbling on the margin of one yellowed by time page in the handwriting of Pastor Rosenberg. We were able to decipher the following: "It seems to be necessary at this time to tell about the First Hebrew-Christian Church in Odessa because of its peculiar origin and nature, testing and triumphs."

The above mentioned statement is an excerpt from the Hebrew-Christian Alliance quarterly of October 1931, which contained a report given by Rev. Leon Rosenberg at a Conference at High Leigh, England, in July of 1931. Below we quote parts of that report, followed by additional information derived by us from other sources:

"It was in 1903, after the savage pogrom at Kishinev, that I first went to Odessa, that beautiful harbor on the Black Sea, with its Jewish community of about quarter of a million. Odessa was subject to much hatred and many restrictions that form a well-known and pathetic chapter in the history of our people in Russia.

"The conditions I found there were very depressing. Anti-Semitism was exceedingly bitter although at that time the Jews could not be accused of taking the lead either in finance or politics. Nevertheless, they were violently hated. A religious element predominated in this. In churches and schools the priests and teachers endeavored to implant in young and old a spirit of revenge for the crucifixion of Christ. *'The Jews have killed our God'* was a well-known expression in Russia, and the Jews were made not only object of revenge in this way, but they were made the scapegoats for all the mischief and calamities that from time to time were taking place in the country.

"No wonder the Jews were strongly opposed to Christianity and were hostile even towards Christ Himself, in Whose name they had been so profoundly ill-treated. We found difficulties in spreading the Gospel because the Russian Government, strongly supported by the Orthodox State Church, strictly forbade the propagation of the Gospel..."

In 1905, after the Russians had lost the war with Japan and the country was engulfed in revolutionary calamities, the conservative party did its utmost to place the blame upon the Jews who as the result of this attitude suffered severely.

However, an unexpected blessing came through these cruel happenings and upheavals in the country. Forced by circumstances, the despotic Russian regime issued a Constitution containing a provision for "Religious Freedom and Liberty of Conscience." It was a happy change not only for the despised, rejected and persecuted Jews, but also for so called *"stundists"* or evangelicals, and much praise ascended to God for many answered prayers. A door was opened for the blessed Gospel. Room was provided for missionary activities, and Pastor Rosenberg and his helpers could now safely testify to the love of God, revealed in Christ Jesus.

As we began to tell in the previous chapter, when the pogrom was over, the missionary work of the Rosenbergs began with expression of practical Christian love, a necessary and legitimate means of service to the Master in those days. This testimony in words and deeds in the name of the Lord resulted in large crowds of Jews gathering, eager to hear the living witness, and this continued for weeks, despite the severity of the Russian winter, before the alarmed rabbis tried unsuccessfully to do something about it, going as far as accusing Pastor Rosenberg of being the originator of the *pogrom!*

Nothing worked, and the missionaries rejoiced to see the Gospel of Christ proved to be the power of God unto salvation to Jewish men and women, young and old. A large number of those who were deeply interested requested continuation of regular Gospel meetings, but there was no proper place and no means to provide it. All that the Rosenbergs had was a spacious living room in their home, and by the grace of God, they were able to provide seats for about ninety people. Thus began in Odessa a regular congregation of Jewish believers in Christ.

Yet, in spite of the complete legality of these meetings, a storm of opposition broke out. All groups and parties, from strict conservatives to extreme radicals, turned against this legitimate outreach. Those who attended the meetings were watched and persecuted. The Orthodox Church was exceedingly bitter because Jews were brought to the knowledge of Christ and the acceptance of Him as Savior. One would naturally assume that as Christians they could only rejoice at such a prospect, but alas, much like the elder brother in the Gospel story of the prodigal son, they were jealous and raving mad at the return of the wayward prodigal brother into the loving arms of the Father.

The socialists, in turn, were against all missionary activities and hindered them wherever they could. But under all this pressure from the enemy the Rosenbergs were greatly comforted and encouraged by the real presence of the Lord in His mighty Spirit, and continued fearlessly in their work with His obvious seal of approval upon their activities, manifested in the widening and deepening of their efforts.

Before long the living room space proved too small and Fanny Rosenberg decided to empty one of the adjacent rooms (a bedroom) and to fill it also with rows of chairs. Through an open door one could clearly hear the speaker and everyone was happy.

A year later even more Jews came to believe in the Lord Jesus as their Messiah, the true Lamb of God. They all received pardon and redemption and were growing stronger in faith, despite the storms of trial and difficulty. This unique group did not know whom to join for Christian fellowship. They were simply Jews who had found in Jesus their promised Messiah and recognized in Him the fulfillment of all that God had predicted through Moses and the Prophets and in the Psalms. They wished to remain in one group and be called Hebrew-Christians.

These, born of God, simple Abrahams, Isaacs and Jacobs, Sarahs, Rebekahs and Leahs would never have found a satisfactory understanding in the churches around them. All this pressed a burden upon the hearts of the Rosenbergs. It was essential for the believers to obey the Lord in baptism, and to continue steadfastly in the breaking of bread and prayer. On the other hand, the country in which they lived had no civil office for the registration of births, marriages, and deaths. Each clergyman of each denomination was responsible for all of this in his congregation, and the Jewish believers were quite isolated.

Pastor Rosenberg talked the matter over with leading Christians in other areas and the most considerate and understanding among them recognized and appreciated his problem. As a result, much prayer was offered on his behalf.

Of course, various attempts were made by the Lutherans, reformed Baptists and other groups to take the Jewish congregation under their wing, but their conditions were unacceptable. The Rosenbergs much regretted the many splits and divisions and various names by which the denominations were called. All of this was not in accordance with their Messianic ideas, or hope of one Shepherd and one flock. Their desire was to have all possible fellowship with all true believers in every denomination.

After having reached at last a sufficient number of members to qualify for legalization by the Government, they organized into an independent Evangelical Community of Hebrew-Christian Believers. In this they were advised by a dearly beloved and trustworthy brother from Sevastopol, and received the good wishes of most of the Evangelical believers in South Russia (today's independent Ukraine). A capable brother was ordained as pastor of the Hebrew Christian Church to assist Pastor Rosenberg; the converts were examined as to their faith and knowledge of the Scriptures, and a large number of new Jewish believers was soon baptized and joined the new congregation. They were all happy that the Lord had saved them and was adding more and more to their number.

But still, it was not easy for them to obtain government recognition. Although new religious liberty was granted by the Constitution, the disposition of the local government, supported by the State Church (Russian Orthodox) and its clergy, was against the registration of this unique congregation. They followed the Russian proverb: "God is high and the Czar is far away," so the new church met with all sorts of trickery. Pastor Rosenberg had to travel repeatedly to St. Petersburg to argue his cause before the officials there. After much prayer, the group was at last successful in carrying through the registration. Pastor Rosenberg could not forget the reaction of the Minister of the Department of Religion when he told him that the new church was based on Evangelical fundamentals. The minister was quite disgusted and exclaimed: "When Christ gets into Jewish hands our Orthodox Russian Church is doomed!"

Having said this, he refused to call the Jewish believers "Christians" but rather *"Evangelicals,"* as most non-Orthodox Christians were called, and included a clause in the registration document to the effect that although these Jews confessed Christianity, they remained under the same deprivations and limitations as all other Jews in the country. This only proved to be a safeguard to the young church against political and economic opportunists, who were encouraged to accept Christianity as a form for personal advantage. Many of these people came to the new church and begged to be received into the membership, but there was no place in this congregation for unregenerated souls.

In writing about this part of his ministry, Pastor Rosenberg stated: "I am sorry to say that our stand as Hebrew Christians was not understood by all, not even by pastors and clergy who were often confusing their religious and national viewpoints, saying that a Jew can never be a Christian, and a Christian can never be a Jew, forgetting that a Jew is first of all a member of his nation or race.

"Realizing from the Holy Scriptures that the New Testament is the fulfillment in the Lord Jesus of the longing and hope of the Jewish people, we found it quite right to emphasize with the Apostle Paul our position as Jews by race, Christians by faith, saved by God's grace through the atoning death of His Son Jesus Christ."

Finally, a written statement put an end to these queries. It was based entirely on Scripture and made clear the fact that the great Apostle Paul himself, after his conversion from Judaism, called himself a Jew. References were given from the New Testament: Romans 11:1, Acts 21:39 and 22:25-28. Paul also made a distinction in his position as a believer in Christ, calling himself a Christian minister of the Gospel, a servant of Jesus Christ and, because of his nationality, an Israelite. In reference to his citizenship, he called himself a Roman. Becoming a Christian, he gave up Judaism, accepting the teaching of Christ, according to the Gospel, but he never ceased to be a son of his nation and remained a Jew.

Although this was a Hebrew-Christian Church, it was strictly evangelical, following the apostolic line, as recorded in Acts 2:42: "And they continued steadfastly in the apostles' doctrine and fellowship, and in breaking of bread and in prayer." Strong emphasis was laid on the unity in Christ of all believers as members of the one body (Eph. 2:3 and 1 Cor. 12:12-27). Emphasis was laid on the words *"Hebrew-Christian."*

Some attempts were made to gather Jews who acknowledged the Messiahship of Jesus into special groups, but these attempts in the course of time proved failures. One group wanted to remain in the synagogue, to live and act as Jews, like the others, causing trouble with the unbelieving Jews. This was also a handicap to the spiritual growth of the believers.

One group called itself "Israelites of the New Covenant" and kept in their place of worship two symbols, the old and the new, but they too were "putting new wine into old wine skins."

The Hebrew-Christians did not compromise, but followed the apostolic line they had adopted and the name which was given to the first believers in Antioch. As a testimony, they never denied their national origin as Hebrews, but their faith was purely Messianic. Believing that "the middle wall of partition was broken down," they made no distinction in the realm of spiritual fellowship between themselves and Christians of other nationalities.

This church became in a very real sense, a missionary church. Each member, whether young or old, rejoiced in his salvation and enjoyed the blessings and privileges of Christian fellowship, knowing also his place of responsibility in the church.

ψ

The Inner Life Of The Church

ψ

Christian friends from all over the country and from abroad began to show interest in a Hebrew-Christian Church. This was an entirely new thing because of its purely evangelical nature, and there was much suspicion and fear that this might be just another new sect. However, this fear was soon overcome and the church benefited spiritually by the visits of many renowned Bible teachers from Britain, America and other countries, and their sound and benevolent advice was always appreciated.

Various branches of Christian activities, promulgating the Gospel and doing good, enjoyed the blessings and favor of God. Soon similar churches were established in other places where precious souls were won for Christ through the faithful ministry of the spiritual children who went out from the First Hebrew-Christian Church in Odessa.

The whole Bible was their standard; they believed in the divine authority of the Old and the New Testaments. This was the foundation for the church and for life and practice of each member. However, the emphasis was always laid upon salvation by grace. A little booklet with rules and regulations was published to give outsiders and the government an idea of the beliefs and teachings of this unique church.

The Lord provided from within the body a good number of elders and deacons, as well as other volunteer workers, who shared in all of their joys and difficulties. The inner life of the church was built up by preaching and ministering the Word of God, Bible study and prayer.

While Gospel (evangelistic) services were held for visiting Jews on the Jewish Sabbaths for the sake of those who were free on those days, baptized believers assembled regularly on the first day of the week, the day of resurrection of the blessed Lord and Savior. These services were also open to all. In the evenings, the Gospel was preached and hymns were sung in several languages. Nobody could complain or accuse the group of being like a Jewish synagogue.

Knowing that our God is the God of order, and that His Spirit is the Spirit of harmony, the Rosenbergs sought earnestly to adopt the best means of carrying out the work, relying a great deal on the advice of friends who came from abroad: Britain, Germany and America.

Ψ

Establishment Of A Christian School

Ψ

The leadership of this new church sought to care for their children and young people and, in answer to prayer, our Lord gave them a nice day school for Jewish children. A generous Gentile noblewoman who had been converted in this new Hebrew-Christian Church, being blessed with financial means, felt the burden of this need and, as a rightful stewardess of the Lord's provision laid the foundation for a school. Soon the difficulties with the Board of Education were overcome and Rev. Rosenberg was licensed to establish a school with grade classes for juniors and seniors. A fine staff of teachers under the supervision of Mr. Goering, a devoted non-Jewish Christian and true friend of Israel, made the school a worthy institution to the honor and glory of the Lord.

The establishment of a special school was necessary because of the attitude of the Jews toward converts and the unwillingness and even inability of new believers in Christ to send their children to public schools where religious instruction was conducted by the priests of the State Russian Orthodox Church. The parents desired to bring up their children "in the nurture and admonition of the Lord" and had no place to turn to for such training. For obvious reasons, children of believers could not be sent to Jewish schools which would have no place for them. This Christian school was especially important for Jewish girls, who were generally neglected both educationally and religiously by their families, where all attention was directed towards the proper upbringing of the boys. A vivid example of this may illustrate this point: in a Bible class for older children, the teacher, speaking of Abraham, asked who of the boys and girls knew about this great hero of faith. A twelve-year-old girl raised her hand and said: "I knew him. He was our neighbor, (referring to a very religious shoemaker). He was very poor and died a fortnight ago of consumption."

At the School, lovely Bible stories, hymns and choruses were eagerly absorbed by the children like dew or rain by dry soil, and many of the boys and girls opened their hearts to the Lord Jesus, receiving Him as their Savior and Friend. Through the influence of their children many parents were exposed to the Gospel of Christ.

Believers were trained in the spirit of the Scriptures and knew that "it is more blessed to give than to receive." On the first day of the week each gave his contribution for the work of the Lord as God enabled. All, even the poorest, learned about their duty in this matter, and their generosity was a real encouragement. The funds were controlled by a trustee appointed by the Church, and acts of benevolence became a regular practice for all. Care was taken that funds were used, not stored, and the Lord honored this practice, for funds were never exhausted! Those who benefited from the Church treasury usually returned the amount of assistance as soon as they were back on their feet financially. The Old Testament practice of tithing was never introduced, the reasons for which were explained by Pastor Rosenberg in a series of sermons which became a very popular brochure.

By this stage in the life of the new Church the term "missionary" entirely lost its sinister connotation among the Jewish neighbors, and completely disappeared together with the derogatory term *"Meshamud."* Members of Pastor Rosenberg's Church were called *"Jewish Evangelists"* (evangelicals) or *"Stundists,"* and were regarded with great respect by the people around them. Believers had the confidence of the Jews and persecution was rare. The services had an entirely Jewish-Christian flavor in all their expressions: from singing to prayer to sermons; so the Jews, who came to them, were not caused to stumble. The one "offense" was "Christ crucified" and this was presented in a quite wholesome way. Very soon the power of God in the Gospel of Christ broke through the "offense" and many were saved and added to the Church.

The development and growth of this church was further proof that the movement was sound and blessed by God. The brethren who were born again in Odessa and felt called by the Lord into His ministry, were sure that aggressive methods in spreading of the Gospel and the definite purpose of gathering and linking up of the saved Israelites into communities, were the only right ways, and they endeavored to carry this into practice in their own mission stations.

Despite great difficulties, two other churches arose, one in Yekaterinoslav (today's Dnyepropetrovsk), founded by brother Smoljar, and another in Kiev through the efforts of brother P. Gorodishz.

ψ

The Jewish Hymn Book

ψ

It is a well known fact that songs are used much in Jewish synagogues and Jewish homes. The Hebrew nation is a singing and dancing people in spite of their tragic history. Even the reading of the Torah, the Scroll of Law, is done by chanting it using an ancient oriental melody. The songs of the Jews changed after their Babylonian captivity, the destruction of the Temple, and the loss of their homeland. They became quite different from the songs sung in the old sanctuary. The harps, which accompanied the joyful singers in the Temple, were now "hanging upon the willows," and the song of Zion turned mute. It could not be sung in a strange language. Israel's songs in the *"galuth"* (the dispersion) sounded monotonous and heartrendingly sad.

After becoming a believer in Christ the Redeemer, the Jew received a new song, a song of praise and of victory which resounded in the assemblies of the righteous.

Like other believers, the Hebrew-Christian longs for Gospel songs of faith and thanksgiving. It is not easy to translate songs in general, but in the case of the Rosenbergs' fellowship of Hebrew-Christian believers there arose other difficulties, and among them the need to adapt to Jewish thinking and Jewish ideas.

When the task of creating a Hebrew-Christian song book was assigned to pastor Rosenberg, he realized how dependent one is upon the Lord if the songs were to become real Gospel songs. The first edition of 151 Jewish songs was produced with great effort and the congregation was finally able to sing their own songs during the gospel and prayer services, as well as on all other occasions.

One of Pastor Rosenberg's co-workers showed musical talent and became an excellent choir leader, and the choir drew many listeners to the meetings, exposing them to the Gospel through this means.

Chapter 15

FATHER'S VISIT

One day, quite unexpectedly, a word was received at the home of the Rosenbergs that Leon's father, who expelled Leon from his home and declared him "dead" at the time of his conversion to Christianity, intended to pay a visit to the now missionary family in Odessa.

The children did not know their grandfather, but from what they heard about him from their parents, they could feel nothing but a joyful anticipation, for they held him in high esteem.

Each of the children held a small bouquet of flowers as they lined up in the hall to meet the honored guest. The warm reception deeply touched the heart of the old man. For his greeting he used the words once spoken by the patriarch Jacob when after a long time he again saw his son Joseph: "I had not thought to see thy face: and lo, God shewed me also thy seed."

Leon and Fanny thought that grandfather's outward appearance, in the typical Jewish orthodox apparel, would seem strange to their children who grew up in a different environment and were brought up in a different way, but they did not act as if they saw anything unusual. In their sincere childish way they admired everything about him. They loved to gather around their grandfather, patting him tenderly on the face and hands, not understanding why tears rolled down his bearded cheeks. They watched him with great respect, especially when he would put on his prayer shawl and the phylacteries. They found everything quite attractive and interesting, and their only question was why their father did not have or use such things.

The Rosenberg children felt hurt when grandfather refused to participate in the family meals. He took only tea and did not touch any other food. According to the rabbinical ritual ordinances, food prepared in regular cooking utensils, even in the prescribed way, would not be fit for him to use. Not only would new vessels be required, but a Jewish Orthodox person would have to do the cooking, and the food would have to be purchased in a special place supervised by an Orthodox Jew.

This was impossible for the Rosenbergs, for they no longer lived "under the Law," but "under grace," and from the very beginning of their Christian experience did not mix the two. However, Leon did go with his father to a Jewish restaurant and their relationship was not affected by the meal they ate together. It turned out that father's visit was business related in nature (or at least he pretended it to be so). The economic conditions in the world had affected his financial affairs.

And yet, all that Leon's father saw in the home of his son during his visit, as well as their open discussions, did soften his attitude toward this once rejected son and his family. He made Leon promise that whenever he should happen to be close to where his father lived, he would be sure to drop in for a visit. This was a far cry from the initial "curse" and Leon gladly fulfilled his father's desire and took full advantage of his visits to plant the divine "seed" in the heart of the old man. On a later visit he noticed a great change in his father, but it was not in the position towards Christ. Father remained very reluctant to reveal his attitude in this matter.

However, shortly before his death, Leon's father told those around him, that Leon was his best son. No one knows what he meant. Leon was not present at his father's bedside at the time of the old man's passing. He was not notified in time of the impending death of his father, because some relatives did not want him, a believer in Christ, to take any part in the funeral. To the very end of his life Leon carried a conviction that his father secretly accepted his Messiah.

🕎

Chapter 16

A GANGSTER
AND HIS CONFESSION

One day, just before the lunch hour, brother K. who was in charge of the Bible-Depot, was getting ready to go home, when a young man entered the store. He said he had something important to say to the manager. Brother K. reported the visit to Pastor Rosenberg and left for his lunch.

Pastor Rosenberg came into the store to greet the visitor, but the young man did not want to be disturbed while talking with him, and did not want anyone to see him through the glass door, so he asked permission to go with pastor Rosenberg into another room. Once there, he took out of his pocket a revolver and very politely asked his host to sit down at the table, while he would lock the door. He locked the door with the key that was in it and kept the key. Then he took a seat by his host's side and produced another revolver, and so he sat there with two murderous weapons in his hands. Looking Pastor Rosenberg straight in the eye, he calmly said: "I have come to you on a very serious business in which only you can be of help." Pastor Rosenberg pointed to the guns in the hands of the visitor and asked him what they meant. The young man allayed his host's fears, saying that the guns were not dangerous for him, although they were loaded, and began to tell his story:

"I am the son of honest, hard-working Jewish parents from a small town, and was brought up in a strict orthodox way. Two years ago I came to Odessa because a Socialistic agitator promised to help me learn a trade in some work-shop. Soon my modest means were exhausted and I never reached the promised place of employment. My parents were killed during the pogrom and all their belongings were plundered. As I could not pay for my night-quarters, I was evicted. In the summer I was able to sleep in parks and gardens, or wherever I could find a place to lay down my head, but I soon came in conflict with the police. I was ashamed to beg, and when I finally stretched out my hand for help to one or another passerby, I was brushed aside with a remark: 'You are too young to beg, go and find work.' I tried, but couldn't find any work. Meanwhile, my clothes wore out, which even further lowered my chances to find decent employment. My rich uncle to whom I went to seek help, responded with anger and contempt and threw me out into the street.

"One morning, feeling severe hunger after several weeks without a square meal, I stole a couple of rolls from a passing peddler, but she raised such a racket, that I barely escaped trouble by running away.

"Soon I found a companion who invited me to join him in order to find a way out of our troubles together. 'We have to help ourselves,' he said, 'society has no money for such sufferers as we are. They help when they have to and not when they should.' Then he asked me if I had any rich relatives. I told him how my wealthy uncle had thrown me out, to which he replied: 'I can give you good advice as to how to get help out of your uncle, but you will have to swear that you will be my partner in everything' Being on the verge of despair, I didn't give it much thought. What, after all, did I have to lose? Meanwhile, my new companion whispered into my ear: 'I have a gun, and if you go to your uncle and he refuses to help you, point it at his head and he will be more than willing to oblige.'"

At this point in the story this strange "visitor" became excited and tightened his grip on the revolvers. Sighing deeply, he continued:

"Anyway, I was desperate, and became a tool in the hands of this stranger, not having any will of my own any more. He took me with him and gave me a loaded gun, accompanied me to the gate of my uncle's house, but kept himself at a distance. When I entered the house and found my uncle alone, I again pleaded with him for help, but he showed me the door, slandering and abusing me verbally. Then I took out my weapon and said, 'You *WILL* help me, or it will cost you your life!' My uncle's face became pale as death and in a meek voice he said: 'I only have 250 roubles here.' He took some money out of a desk drawer. I could hardly believe my ears, as I had not expected such a large sum. Hastily I grabbed the money out of his hands, and according to all the rules of a perfect hold-up, told him not to move and to keep quiet until I had left the house, or else...!

"My companion took a lion's share of that loot and I was again in his hands and had to do his will. We bought new weapons so we could continue our 'business'."

While this man was telling his story, Mrs. Rosenberg came in to call her husband to eat. As she heard some one talking with him, she pushed the curtain aside to see who it was. When she saw the strange visitor with a gun in each hand, she almost fainted, but that became known only later. Meanwhile, the strange visitor continued his story:

"Two more men had joined us and we all were under the leadership of my first accomplice. After the first holdup we had several successful robberies." Among the victims he mentioned was one of Rosenbergs' friends, so Pastor Rosenberg knew that this man was telling the truth, and asked him why he was so frank with him. He replied: "I know what I am doing... I am very well informed. I have been to your meetings and I know your views."

Pastor Rosenberg asked him what he had in mind and received an interesting answer: "I am tired of this kind of life, and cannot stand my companions any longer. Only you can help me to start a new life. I want to learn a trade to be able to earn a living peacefully and honestly, as did my parents. I promise you that if you help me to do this, I will never participate in any holdups again. I haven't participated in any for several weeks, although I suffered loss. I learned that there is no gain or joy in stolen goods and my conscience is bothering me. I hold these weapons only to show you what kind of man I am. They are not meant to harm you, and I do not mean to blackmail you. These are only my witnesses that I am telling the truth. Please, help me!"

These, his final words, sounded like a plea. Pastor Rosenberg possessed nothing of any value, but he took out his wallet and said: "This is all I have; it is not much, but it will get you through the next several days. I am not rich, because ministers of the Gospel and missionaries seldom are, but I promise to do my best for you in the name of my Lord and Savior Jesus Christ."

The strange visitor took the few roubles, thanked Pastor Rosenberg, and said: "I do not demand any money from you. All I want you to do is to buy me some cobbler's tools and pay my rent for a few months. A friend, who is going to teach me this trade, will give me board."

This experience made a deep expression on Pastor Rosenberg. He found that the intentions of the "robber" were honest and was glad to help him. He began to attend the Rosenbergs' meeting regularly, received the Lord Jesus as his Savior, and learned the cobbler's trade. He married a nice woman and never reverted to his old ways.

In Pastor Rosenberg's long experience as a minister of the Gospel and a missionary, this was the only time when a man sought help from him with a gun in each hand, and no one ever was as adamant and resolute as this strange Jewish visitor who came to him seemingly out of the blue — but not without God's marvelous intervention.

♁

Chapter 17

AN EBEN-EZER

*I*n the year 1913, the first Hebrew-Christian Church decided to celebrate its 10th anniversary, counting from the day of the formation of a small fellowship in the home of the Rosenbergs, prior to the pogrom and the official registration as a Hebrew Christian Evangelical Church. The desire was to express thanks to God for honoring the first "covenant" among the initial few faithful brothers to begin missionary work among the Jews of Odessa. In their minds and hearts this initial group was in the sight of God "a church."

In addition to giving thanks to God for the blessing of the initial group, this much larger official assembly of Jewish believers wanted to thank God particularly, for blessing the ministry of Pastor Leon Rosenberg.

Taking advantage of their pastor's absence (he was on a prolonged missionary itinerary), the church made preparations to surprise him when he returned. Ministers and friends from other cities gladly accepted the invitation, and everything was arranged in the most pleasant way. It turned out to be indeed a great surprise and a real *"Eben-Ezer"* to the glory of God.

The festivities were opened by the assistant pastor who, after a prayer, gave a brief sketch of the blessed years of missionary and ministerial activities of the senior pastor. Bishop Albert, a personal friend from a nearby town, gave an inspiring message in which the importance of missions to the Jews was stressed. Bishop Albert praised God for the tangible evidence of His blessing in this unique Hebrew-Christian congregation and, among other remarks, said:

"I am an old minister of the Gospel and have traveled far and wide and visited many churches, but nowhere have I seen a congregation like this one. Not only is this a Hebrew-Christian Church, but all her members are the fruits of the Gospel faithfully preached here by the senior pastor and his assistants."

The opening statements by several other prominent friends of the church were followed by an interesting and uplifting program of testimonies by young and old and singing by the Hebrew-Christian choir in Hebrew, Yiddish and other languages. Special numbers were given by the students of the school. All of this was greatly enjoyed and appreciated by the local members and visiting friends. In the closing address, Rev. Rosenberg related some of his experiences, giving glory and honor to God.

On the nicely decorated and lavishly set tables, there were many contributions by Christian farmers from the surrounding Mennonite villages, and a real shower of gifts was presented to those whose anniversary in God's work was being celebrated.

Among the gifts was a sealed envelope and in it Pastor Rosenberg found a check for ten thousand Russian roubles (an equivalent of $5,000 in gold) The enclosed message revealed that this gift was from a friend of the Rosenberg family and was designated for the purchase of a home for them in recompense for their private home which they had given up to make room for the extension of the church.

Overwhelmed with joy, Rev. and Mrs. Rosenberg, seeing the hand of the Lord in this development, were convinced that this gift, although designated for them personally, should be considered as an earnest from the Lord in answer to their prayers regarding various needs of the Mission, the Church and the School. With the approval of the donor who was present, the amount was dedicated as a foundation fund for an orphanage for Hebrew-Christian children, for whom there was no room either in the Jewish or non-Jewish institutions, a home for aged women, a hostel for the many new believers, who were ostracized by their families for Christ's sake, and a technical school with industrial workshops and other trade-teaching facilities for young graduates of the middle school.

The Lord blessed this enterprise, and the same year a property was purchased for fifty thousand roubles ($25,000 in gold) without a penny of debt. Donations towards the extension of the work on this occasion amounted to more than 50,000 roubles.

Thus the groundwork was laid for a greater and broader outreach into the community; but clouds were already gathering on the horizon with new hindrances in store.

Ψ

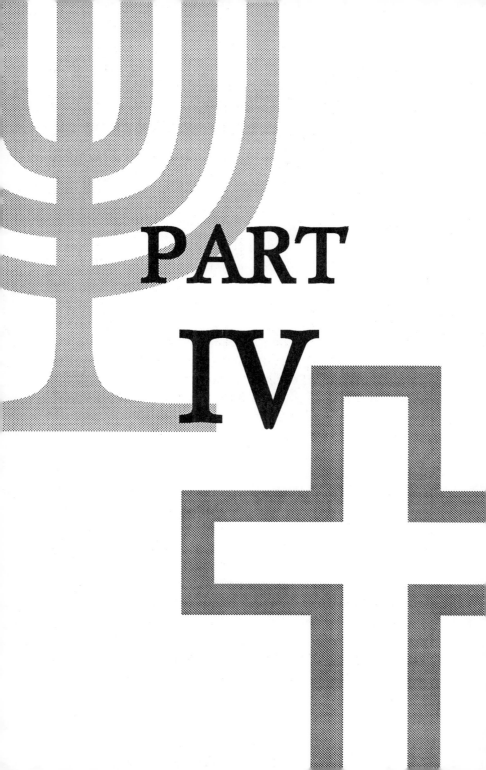

PART
IV

Chapter 18

THE FIRST WORLD WAR
AND ALL THAT CAME
WITH IT

*I*n the year 1914 the first great World War broke out. While in itself this calamity was a severe test, the adversary of God and His work on earth took full advantage to cause harm and damage to the young Evangelical movement which had spread so mightily throughout Russia. As his tool, Satan used ecclesiastical authorities of the Russian State Church, to whom this movement was "a thorn in the flesh," and they found this an opportune time to hinder as much as possible all genuine Gospel-related activities. Every native Protestant institution and all activities of native Protestant ministers were branded "unpatriotic," based on the following assumption: "The German Emperor with whom we are at war, is a Protestant, and all Protestants are controlled by him and therefore all are dangerous to our country's security. We must immediately stop all their activities and exile their leaders and ministers."

This kind of propaganda in the clerical and the so-called, "patriotic" press, appealed to the military governors under whose authority the country was placed in the time of war. South Russia was governed by Mr. Ebeloff, a former Muslim, now converted to the Russian Orthodox religion. He knew nothing about Protestants, so when the agents of the Holy Synod brought before him their accusations, he immediately ordered all Protestant ministers and missionaries whose names were submitted to him by the priests, to be exiled to Siberia.

The name of Rev. Leon Rosenberg was well-known because of his various Gospel related activities, both as a pastor and a missionary, as well as director of the Mission School, so it was placed at the top of the list. There were special accusations against him, for the accusers knew that some of his converts, men and women, had been regularly sent abroad (including to Germany) to study at some quite prominent Protestant schools.

ψ

Exile To Siberia

ψ

The Governor General's order was carried out immediately and with the aid of the local police, innocent men were roused from their sleep in the dead of night, arrested and transported to the far north region of Siberia. On the way there they were moved from prison to prison, enduring unspeakable hardships, privations, scorn, ill-treatment, and filthy sleeping conditions on the long march to the region where ice and snow never thaw.

Siberia was the most dreadful word for those who heard it applied to them personally. A thorny path into an icy desert was usually traveled not by train, but by foot from one prison to another, until all prisoners were gathered together. Only then were they put on one of the many prisoner-transportation freight trains.

Regardless of the crime committed, the exiles were forced to travel with the most dangerous criminals and were treated as one of them. There was no difference in the food rations which were almost unbearable. So long as one had some money of his own, succeeding in miraculously hiding it from thieves, one could buy some food along the way, but the time of real suffering began when the train would finally reach its destination.

When an order was issued to exile all preachers from Odessa, all meeting-halls were closed and converted into hospitals because of the still raging war. Many of Pastor Rosenberg's co-workers were untouched and could continue their work in secret. The Lord had His own purpose in permitting this time of trial. A lesson from Romans 8:28 was learned in a practical way by all involved, that "All things work together for good for those who love God..." Brothers, who in the past were separated by denominational and other man-made barriers, learned to know each other better in prison cells, to love one another as children of the same Heavenly Father, members of the same Body of which Christ is the Head, and they began to voice their needs in common prayer.

At this testing time the Hebrew-Christian Church was not only deprived of its minister, but also of its church property, which was confiscated by the military authorities and used as a hospital. And though many of Pastor Rosenberg's co-workers were not arrested or harassed in any way, all missionary activities were strictly forbidden. One thing, however, could not be taken away from them, nor from the believers in general, namely, their private prayer and fellowship with their Lord. They fervently prayed to their Heavenly Father, interceding for their pastor and the scattered students of the Mission School, and their prayers were answered.

While Pastor Rosenberg was still away traveling from place to place, exiled from home and family, his Christian friends in higher circles in St. Petersburg became greatly concerned for him. Among them was Count Palin, a Senator and a true Christian. He befriended Pastor Rosenberg while serving as Governor of W. By divine providence the Governor General of Odessa was Count Palin's former adjutant and, as such, provided an important link. Senator Palin wrote a letter of recommendation for Pastor Rosenberg and asked the Governor General of Odessa to order him returned from exile as soon as possible. This was also done by other friends in high office, guaranteeing Pastor Rosenberg's loyalty and stating that he was known and trusted by many friends in Britain and America.

Letters from these high-placed friends impressed the Governor General of Odessa, and in his next official publication it was announced that Rev. Rosenberg was permitted to return from Siberia. An order was dispatched by wire to the Governor of Tomsk in Siberia for his immediate release. When Mrs. Rosenberg was advised by Senator Palin to go to the Governor General with a copy of the letter he himself had written, the Governor's answer was: "It is all done. Your husband will soon be home." The order to return Pastor Rosenberg was published the next day in the local news release, and the officials in Tomsk, Siberia, where he was held and supposed to remain until the end of the war, were advised by a special dispatch to release him immediately.

ψ

Happy Return

ψ

After a few months on the road to Siberia, Pastor Rosenberg was permitted to return to Odessa without reaching the place of exile appointed for him by authorities. The weighty influence of Count Palin, Countess Perovskaya, Princess Lieven and many other prominent persons and high-ranking officials, forced the same Governor General who had ordered the exile of pastor Rosenberg and all other Protestant ministers, to change his mind and cancel his order concerning Rev. Leon Rosenberg, reversing his decision and allowing the persecuted pastor to return to Odessa.

The very first step undertaken by Pastor Rosenberg upon his return, was to visit the Governor General and thank him for his intervention in this matter and to ask him for permission to resume missionary activities. Under the prevailing conditions this request was granted only in part.

Since the church had been taken by the Red Cross, Pastor Rosenberg was allowed to hold church meetings in his home and keep them exclusively Hebrew-Christian. However, as soon as the Hebrew-Christian gatherings were allowed, other Christian friends also started attending them. One elderly Russian brother said: "I specifically prayed to the Lord to return at least one of our Russian ministers, and He returned you to us. God answered my prayer and did above all that I asked or hoped. Your preaching in several languages can better serve our Russian and German speaking brothers."

This was a challenge to Pastor Rosenberg which involved new difficulties, because of the vigilance of the spies of the hostile Russian Orthodox clergy. Pastor Rosenberg was warned more than once to keep within the limits of the permit given to him, but the Governor General did not exercise any pressure against him. The preaching of the Word was blessed and the spiritual life of believers was invigorated.

The enemy evidently disliked this kind of cooperation among believers for a new wave of persecution started. Secret police came and took the names of all who attended the church meetings at the Rosenbergs' home to find out how many other nationalities were among the Hebrew-Christians. Any fellowship with people who had German names and spoke German was strictly prohibited during the entire time of the war.

It just so happened that a friend of the Rosenbergs, a military doctor, died suddenly of a heart attack. His family and relatives, who were German and Dutch-speaking Mennonites, wanted Pastor Rosenberg to see that the body of the deceased brother would be delivered to his home town, Orlov, and that he himself would conduct the funeral service. He did as they had requested, but strangely, the authorities in Odessa in a very short time knew not only what was said, but even what was *NOT* said at that funeral! The fact that Pastor Rosenberg spoke and preached in German among the German-speaking Mennonites, was considered a great crime. Police repeatedly inquired about him at home and searched his house. He received word that police were looking for him and it would be wise for him not to return home.

Pastor Rosenberg decided to call on the City Governor who favored him and in whose home the Bible he had presented to him at an earlier time was held in great esteem. Pastor Rosenberg explained to him the whole situation and it paved the way for him to call on the Governor General as well. This time he was only rebuked in a benevolent sort of way which caused much vexation to the "black" foes of all Evangelicals, the Russian Orthodox priests, who were once again behind this attack on Pastor Rosenberg. The Lord had prevailed over the powers of darkness and the ministry in Odessa continued unhindered at least for a while.

☰

Chapter 19

MISERY AND BLESSINGS IN REFUGEE LIFE

The First World War not only cost millions of lives on the battlefields, but also caused much damage to the country, as many cities were destroyed by the enemy. Especially hard hit were the border regions stretching from the Carpathian mountains in the south to Eastern Prussia in the north. Thickly populated by Jews, these areas suffered tremendous damage. And what the foreign enemy didn't do, the Cossacks did. Ten thousand people were transported inland after losing their homes and belongings. An uninterrupted flow of cattle trains filled with refugees streamed daily to Siberia with many passengers perishing along the way from hunger and disease. many organizations were asked to provide for the filthy, hungry, homeless and sick, old and young people, children and women, but no one really cared for them. Time was ripe for caring, loving Christian service to take charge.

The Rosenbergs succeeded in obtaining from the Governor General permission to open "tea- houses" for refugees and other victims of the war. When the first such house was opened in Odessa, many hundreds of hungry and needy souls were able every day to take advantage of the free services rendered to them in the name of the Lord.

Pastor Rosenberg, his wife Fanny and their co-workers cared not only for weary, hungry bodies by giving them nourishment and clothing, but they also ministered to their sick souls. The Lord made it possible to spread this relief work over other places as well, and many benefited from this freely-provided assistance. Expressions of their gratitude were indeed touching, but the greatest reward from the Lord came in the form of wonderful encouragement through an answer to prayer.

ॐ

A Precious Find

ॐ

For many years pastor Rosenberg prayed for his own brothers and sisters, especially for the elder of his two sisters who, in many respects, reminded him of his beloved mother. It was virtually impossible to get in touch with them and they, in turn, knew nothing or little about Leon, other than that he had become a Christian. His 'other faith' deepened the gulf between the siblings.

During the terrible war with all its horrors, Pastor Rosenberg miraculously "ran into" his elder sister in one of the refugee camps in the city of Poltava. They had not seen each other for a very long time and would not have recognized one another were it not for the stark resemblance to their mother and the name which the woman gave when asked about it. Leon could hardly contain his joy when he introduced himself, but the sister was fearful and distant when he, with tears in his eyes, stretched out his arms to embrace her. He invited her to come with him to Odessa, but she felt embarrassed as she could not fellowship with a *"goy."* However, the Lord, Who was seeking this lost sheep and wanted to save her, saw to it that she agreed to come later.

One day, a marching band was passing through the town where Leon's sister lived, and she recognized the leader of the band as her former language teacher. She told him about the visit of her brother who "had invited her to come to Odessa." The teacher told her that he attended meetings there and a man by the name of Leon Rosenberg was the regular speaker. After she told him that this man was her brother, he earnestly urged her to accept his invitation, saying that it would be best for her.

Taking this advice to heart, she soon wrote Leon a letter, telling in it that she was ready to come if he would promise never to mention his faith to her. She intended to watch and listen and learn to know better the family of her long lost brother.

Pastor Rosenberg did not promise his sister that his wife would not talk to her. So she came, and it didn't take long before many earnest questions, which were in her mind, were asked and received an honest answer. Fanny was always very straightforward in her approach.

Soon the sister started coming to the meetings, and under the sound Gospel teaching, which proved to be "the power of God unto salvation," the Lord opened her heart and she became a happy, joyful follower of the Lord Jesus Christ. In obedience to His command she received water baptism from her brother. And thus, her refugee misery turned out to be a great blessing for her.

Among the victims of war who visited the "tea-house" in Odessa was a young man who also found faith in the Lord Jesus and was chosen by Him to be His servant. He found in Leon's sister his life's companion and for many years both were faithful helpers in many missionary activities of Pastor Rosenberg in Odessa and in other areas in later years. It was the Lord's will to allow both of these beautiful people, Alfred and Theophelia Malcman, together with three of their five children, to be martyred by the merciless hand of Hitler's henchmen in Poland.

But let us not run ahead of our story, let us allow it to take its course. Cataclysmic events followed World War I in rapid succession, each leaving irreversible impact on the Bethel Mission and its ministry.

ψ

A Modern-Day Lydia

ψ

In the years closely preceding the Bolshevik Revolution, there were many "free thinkers" and so called "progressive people." One such "modern society" lady, who cared little for God and her soul, suddenly lost her husband, a bank director, who was quite influential in the business world. At first she reacted to God's interference in her life with indignation and even anger, because her husband was her "all-in-all," but over time things began to change.

One of her lady friends, who had also lost her husband not long before, visited her and expressed sincere sympathy. The serenity and tranquillity of the visiting friend caused the bereaved woman to ask about the reason for such composure in her time of grief. She knew that this lady friend lived with her husband in great harmony and they were very happy together, and this forced her to puzzle even more over her friend's calm demeanor. The visiting lady was a devout Christian and took this opportunity to tell her grieving friend about her Savior, Jesus Christ. Having done this, she soon left.

At first the angry widow could not quite comprehend all that she had heard, but she started to think about it and seek a source of comfort and salvation. The Lord led her into one of the meetings where Pastor Rosenberg was preaching the Word with his usual fervor. Later they met again at the home of two sisters who were warm friends of Israel, and Pastor Rosenberg was able to hold a long conversation with her. It was a heart-to-heart exchange, but this time the Lord opened her heart and the sunlight of His salvation illumined her soul and the lost, erring "sheep" was brought into the fold of the "Good Shepherd."

She wanted to show her gratitude, and the Lord moved her to open her large spacious home for the preaching of the Gospel. Being the widow of a bank director, she had many friends among bankers. She invited a number of Jewish bankers and a few prominent lawyers to social gatherings in her home and called Pastor Rosenberg to tell them what he had found in Jesus. They were "all ears," this "modern society," and after the talk was finished, the subject of the evening refused to die down but continued in the form of an informal conversation. The "puffed up" modernism of this Jewish "society" fell apart when faced with the stern reality of the ever-living and ever-present Lord and Savior, Jesus Christ, the Messiah of Israel.

When a few days later Pastor Rosenberg met Dr. K. who had been present at the gathering and took part in the conversation there, the good doctor told him: "You do not know how deeply I was moved by all I heard from you and others who sat with us at the table. I would be very interested in hearing more." He offered his home for meetings and asked Pastor Rosenberg to deliver a discourse about Jesus. He gladly accepted the invitation, praying that the Lord would graciously grant that more souls would be won for Him out of this particular circle of people. And the Lord marvelously answered this prayer. In due time many souls responded to the inner call of the Holy Spirit, while Pastor Rosenberg humbly served as His willing instrument. Little did these people know, that very soon they would have to face the ultimate test of their young faith. Some crumbled under the pressure from the godless interrogators, but many showed remarkable strength of spirit, and even were instrumental in leading others to Christ during the most difficult times in Russia's history.

ψ

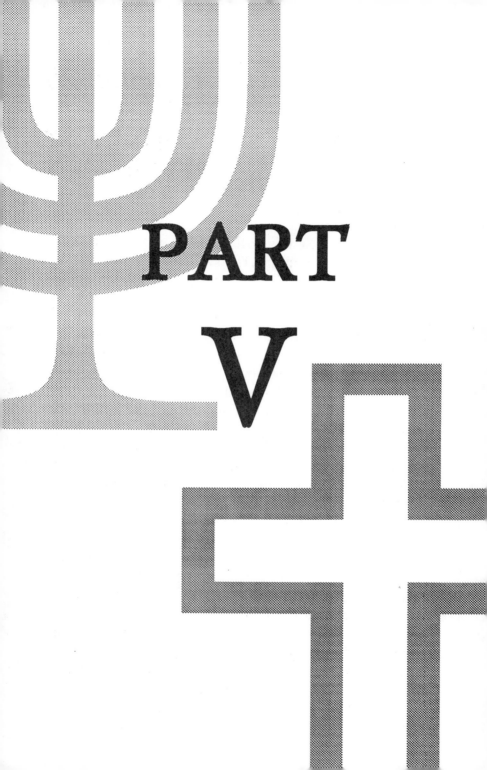

PART

V

Chapter 20

THE COMMUNIST REVOLUTION

*I*n 1917 the Red Revolution came in like a gigantic flood over the country. The seeds of injustice and discrimination, which had been sown for many years, yielded their harvest in due time. The oppressed masses, the impoverished peasants, the unsatisfied workers and soldiers embittered by the prolonged war, were ready for, and open to, propaganda of fiery orators and agitators, both domestic and foreign.

At first it seemed that the Civil War would never end. Organized and well armed groups, loyal to the Czar, valiantly fought against the rag-tag revolutionary bands and scattered armies. But eventually the revolutionaries prevailed and the whole country was flooded with red banners, marked in one corner by a new insignia — Hammer and Sickle implying, that workers and peasants were now holding the power. These red banners were hoisted in every city, village and hamlet. The long bloody years of the war and clashes between different political elements were accompanied by pillage, destruction, starvation and death.

This, the most horrible phase of the violent Communist Revolution, took millions of innocent lives. Terrible class hatred ensued and proceeded by different stages. In the very beginning the Communists were mainly against the highest-ranked people in society, starting with the royal family, high officials — military and civil — private domestic and foreign industrialists and other capitalists. Then their hatred spread to the middle class and the *"intelligentsia,"* Jew and Gentile alike, and in a few more years extended to the workers and farmers, whose hammer and sickle marked the new blood-soaked red banner. Not one single region was spared. Christian institutions of *ALL* denominations, including the former State Church, the Russian Orthodox, were uprooted and most ministers and priests exiled. No one could foresee such an outcome of the so-called "People's Revolution," but by then it was too late.

☮

A Holdup

☮

Dark times, laden with heavy trials, came over Russia and grew almost unbearable. Indescribable terror raged like a constant succession of storms. The number of acts of violence moved beyond anyone's ability to count. The Czar's family was brutally murdered and all who were directly or indirectly connected with the old regime were doomed to annihilation by the ruthless Soviets. Most human life counted for nothing. Bolshevism developed and spread quickly, changing its forms and gaining power through unbridled rampages of devastation and destruction. "The end justifies the means" was the directive given by their leader Vladimir I. Lenin, whose followers did everything and anything to reach a nebulous goal, masked by lofty slogans and empty promises of freedom and prosperity.

During the years 1919-1922 the terror in Russia reached its climax. For the Rosenbergs those years were worse than the pogroms, more terrible than the world war, and more dreadful than the revolutionary "over-throws" and bloody guerrilla (*partisan*) conflicts. What made it even worse, was the continuous famine with all its horrible consequences.

Suddenly, the Rosenbergs were entirely cut off from the rest of the world. The awesome responsibility for the vast missionary work fell heavily on the shoulders of the only surviving minister of the Gospel — Pastor Leon Rosenberg! Friends who had formerly actively supported the Mission could no longer do anything for it. Robbed of their estates, expelled from their homes, they were in a terrible state of deprivation. Many were shot to death or killed in more gruesome ways.

The Rosenberg family was helpless. Victuals could not be obtained even for currency. Those who had something to sell wanted only gold for their goods. The paper money had lost its value. Foodstuffs could be obtained only by way of trade or barter in exchange for clothing or commodities.

It was difficult to survive materially, but as if this wasn't enough, one Sunday morning the Rosenberg house was attacked by a band of armed robbers. Everything of any value was taken away but the attackers were still asking for "hidden treasures" of which there were none. The frightened parents were worried about their daughters as they did not know in what part of the house they were at the time of the attack. Only later did they discover them huddled together in the cold hallway and knew that all this time their children had been at the mercy of the bandits. Only after the bandits finally left with all that was worth taking were the frightened parents able to see that their children were safe.

After the robbery, the family could no longer barter things for food. One message of grief after another reached the house as in the case of Job. Many friends were suffering from hunger, cold and disease. Their ranks grew thinner and thinner as the typhoid epidemic took its toll. People were absolutely powerless against this uncontrollable onslaught of calamities. Many of the brothers and sisters walked about like shadows and it was painful to see these swaying forms in the meetings which for the time being were still allowed. Though the personal suffering was hard and distressing, it was more painful to watch the suffering of others, while being unable to help them in any way. Of course, the most piteous sight was presented by the willowy thin and sickly children.

ψ

The Refugees

ψ

At the time of the holdup, the Rosenbergs were sheltering in their home some friends, who had been robbed of their farm a short while before, and barely escaped with their lives. They fled to the big city of Odessa, where they believed they would be more secure, being unknown. This was a family of five. On their flight the grandfather lost his left hand from a bandit's gunshot and was in a lot of pain. These people were very happy to be able to stay with the Rosenberg family until suddenly the above mentioned holdup occurred. The bandits went through all the rooms and pillaged the room of the guests as well. Being arrested in another room and not allowed to move, the hosts knew nothing of what was happening to their guests in another part of the house. Though the robbers did not find much in the guest room, nevertheless something of value did fall into their hands. The farmer's wife had some pieces of jewelry and a few gold coins in a little sack hidden on her person. She was searched and the little sack was taken away. The refugee family took the loss of their last possession in quiet submission to the will of the Lord.

Not too long after this sad happening, the grandfather who lost his hand in a shoot-out, fell ill and died. The Rosenbergs wanted to do their best for their friends and their deceased loved one and give him at least a proper burial. The congregation tried to help, but it was very hard to find burial clothing for the deceased brother. It just so happened, that through oversight the bandits had left behind Pastor Rosenberg's black overcoat. It was decided to use it, but it turned out to be too small, so the back of the coat had to be ripped open to make it fit. No one would see the back anyway, and the bereaved family was comforted by seeing their loved one looking very dignified in his coffin.

At that time it was still possible to conduct Christian burials and Pastor Rosenberg officiated very meaningfully, making an already close relationship with this family even closer.

In God's providence he met these dear people years later in America, and they repeatedly showed their friendship in a tangible way, by filling many needs of a then fledgling Mission.

ψ

A Sympathetic Neighbor

ψ

After the brutal attack on the Rosenberg home, one of their neighbors, an elderly Jew, came to express his sympathy. Among other things he said: "What are you going to do now? You are entirely ruined! You are a poor man! They have taken from you everything you had."

When Pastor Rosenberg told the old man that the robbers were not satisfied with what they had found, and demanded that the "hidden treasures" would also be turned over to them, or they would hurt the children, the old man wanted to know if Pastor Rosenberg had complied with their demand. Not wanting to give a direct answer, in order to point out to him something more valuable than earthly treasures, Pastor Rosenberg looked at the man with an expression of inner peace, which the good neighbor could not miss, but not being able to understand it, he said: "For a long time you have been a puzzle to me. I have watched you on different occasions and always envied your inner calm. And now your face shows satisfaction, even in such hard times when you have been deprived of all your belongings and suddenly become very poor." In reply came the following words: "The loss of my possessions did not make me poor. The robbers could not take my greatest treasure."

Hearing this, the neighbor looked at Pastor Rosenberg with pleasure and said: "That is what I thought myself. You are a clever and courageous man, who knows how to hide his most precious valuables and how not to allow bandits to intimidate you." He naturally assumed that the words "greatest treasure" meant earthly goods. But when he heard about the threats to the children who were in such jeopardy, he thought that, perhaps, under such circumstances one should have given the bandits all, even if there were some hidden valuables, and asked: "What do you mean, your greatest treasure was *NOT* taken?'"

Pastor Rosenberg answered: "The greatest treasure of which I am speaking is my faith in the Lord Jesus, The Messiah, through Whom I have the assurance of salvation and eternal life." The old man bowed his head in silence and there were no more questions, but when he raised his head and looked in the eyes of his pastor neighbor, tears were rolling down his cheeks as this higher truth slowly filled his soul.

☙ ✡ ❧

A Stormy Sea Journey

☙ ✡ ❧

Once during those turbulent times Pastor Rosenberg had to travel to the Crimean Peninsula. He was concerned for the well-being of his daughter Elizabeth, who was there at the time, and he also wanted to visit some brothers in the Lord. Before his return home, his friends supplied him with all kinds of foodstuffs for his family. Thus on his journey back he had quite a load of valuable things to carry with him during a time when food was scarce. The boat from Sevastopol to Odessa was filled to capacity, but having no other choice, he boarded it. There was nothing left but to share the lot of many other passengers and to use his luggage for a seat on the upper deck.

The weather did not seem to be favorable from the beginning, but no one expected a real storm. However, as soon as the ship left the bay, the sea began to rage and the ship was tossed about like a cork. Large billows came over the deck and the officer on duty ordered all passengers to be tied to one another by a rope so that no one would be washed overboard.

It was a long, dangerous and very uncomfortable trip. Almost everybody suffered from seasickness, but no one was able to move. The sense of fear was dulled by the apathy caused by this unpleasant sickness. All passengers were soaked to the bone but no one complained. At least the waves were washing away human waste and freshened the air by removing the horrible smell. Gradually the ship approached the bay of Odessa where the storm became less noticeable.

As Pastor Rosenberg was leaving the ship, two "sympathetic" soldiers offered their services to carry his heavy packages. Seeing that only a few porters were available, he accepted their offer and even considered it very kind. But his disappointment was very great when after trying to follow the "helpers," he discovered that they seemed to want to lose him in the crowd, weaving through it as fast as they could with the valuable packages of food in their hands. Soon they disappeared all together and Pastor Rosenberg returned home empty-handed.

☙

The Poor Rich And The Rich Poor

☙

In addition to scarcity of food and hunger pangs there was a lack of clothing. The robbers took away, among other things, all of the shoes for grown-ups and children. Still, Pastor Rosenberg discovered that "all things work together for good to those who love God."

A leather sofa, ripped by one of the vandals, became of great profit to the family. Though Pastor Rosenberg never learned the shoemaker's trade, he knew that as a missionary he had to do many things, and having some deftness with his hands, made "elegant" shoes for the entire family from the ripped out pieces of leather from the now useless sofa. Because it was not really shoe leather, the shoes did not last long, yet many people envied the Rosenbergs, seeing them in the street wearing those nice-looking shoes, while other people had to wear rags on their feet and use sackcloth to make clothing.

People became quite ingenious. Some would wear a potato sack with three holes in it: one for the head and two for the arms with rope for a belt. A pair of trousers was often made from more than one color of material, loosely pieced together. It was painful to see some young men dressed like this, especially when remembering that in the past many of them used to be quite well-off, but now deprived of all their earthly possessions. With the loss of everything some of these people became poor also spiritually, but on the other hand, there were people who endured their losses with joy and dignity, becoming richer in the things of God than ever before.

One could hear people who used to have large estates and many other possessions, say: "In times of peace we often sang, 'Sever me from this earth, increase my faith,' but rarely was it meant in earnest, because not many were willing or ready to be severed from the earth, so the Lord permitted the earth to be severed from us. Now we have learned to treasure the heavenly realities more."

Chapter 21

DAUGHTER LYDIA

*F*anny and Leon Rosenberg were blessed with six children. Their only son Phillip, their third child, died at the age of one and a half years, but the five surviving daughters were being raised in the nurture of the Scriptures in a fine atmosphere of a solidly Christian home. The result was that all of the children accepted the Lord as Savior at an early age.

Eugenia and Elizabeth, who were born one year apart, gave their hearts to the Lord one day in Sunday School. They came home beaming and told their mother about it, but when she asked them if they had not believed in Jesus as their Savior before, loved Him and prayed to Him, the girls answered: "Oh yes, we believed and loved *YOUR* Savior, but now He is *OUR OWN* Savior."

Eugenia took an active part in the work of the Lord as a very young girl, and later, as a philology student at the Odessa University, became the secretary of the Christian Student Association. Elizabeth, who could not obtain her medical education in Russia after the Revolution, being the daughter of a minister, accomplished this in Germany and later went to India where she taught at the Women's Medical College and practiced as a medical missionary doctor. Helen, the fourth child, who also in her early youth gave her heart to the Lord, became a teacher and was in many other ways well prepared for service and faithfully assisted her father. In the thirties she led the children's work at the Bethel Mission in Poland.

Lydia was the fifth child in the family and was the pet of all. Not that other children were ignored or neglected, for there was never any envy between the siblings, but this little one was weak from childhood and always cheerful, like a bright ray of sunshine. Her disposition was so charming that she became the pet not only of her parents and sisters, but of all who ever met and knew her. She was always the first to arrive at day school or Sunday School. She loved her Savior and believed with her whole heart in the power of prayer.

All she ever heard from her mother, or in Sunday School, about the dear Lord Jesus, she told to the blind Captain W. M. who lived in the same house with her. During the time of the great trials, when the Revolution broke out and the family suffered at the hands of the Bolsheviks, she was a comfort and blessing to all around her. In the sovereign plan of God, divine purposes of which will be fully revealed and understood only in Heaven by all who loved and served Him here, it was appointed that in this hard time, when misery and want prevailed in the cities and villages of Russia, little Lydia's pilgrimage should come to an end. She became ill with the Spanish flu, but in her soul she was well prepared for her homegoing, though she was only twelve years old!

While she lay sick, no one dared to grieve in her presence, and even in the very last moments of her life one glimpse of her lovely face communicated deep comfort. Her favored hymn was, *"'Cause I the Shepherd's lambkin am, I rejoice in His good care."* The family stood around her bed and sang this hymn along with the dying child. As they began to sing the last stanza,

"Shouldn't I then happy be? I'm a lucky little sheep. When these evil days will pass, I will then forever rest. My Good Shepherd's firm embrace will receive me, yes, oh, yes!" After these words and a hearty *"amen,"* Lydia's face became more radiant, beaming with inner joy. Noticing tears in the eyes of her loved ones, because it was painful for them to part from her, she whispered the words of yet another favored hymn of hers, *"Let me go, let me go, that I soon may see my Lord."*

This was like a plea to her father and mother and her loving sisters to let her go without tears. They did not finish the last verse, "My soul is filled with longing to be received by Him for ever," when Lydia quietly went to be with the Lord. Father was holding her little hands in his right hand and covered her head with his left hand to close her eyes. He felt just a little quiver when her spirit slipped from her body into the loving arms of the Good Shepherd.

Many believers gathered at the funeral as this was still possible in Russia at that time. Children from the Sunday School were all present and hundreds of Jews came to hear what the missionary would say at the coffin of his beloved child. He read II Cor. 1:3,4 and it became a blessing to all in a very full measure:

"Blessed be God, even the Father of our Lord Jesus Christ, the Father of mercies, and the God of all comfort; Who comforteth us in all our tribulation, that we may be able to comfort them which are in any trouble, by the comfort wherewith we ourselves are comforted of God." (KJV) At the grave site several preachers addressed the large crowd.

Yes, the Lord did well in taking a little child before still greater tribulations came over the long-suffering family of a dedicated servant of His, and indeed the whole land. He took home His little lamb at the proper time, for He *NEVER* blunders.

Chapter 22

THE END OF AN ERA

Since the first year of the Communist Revolution, the Russian Government, as well as the entire nation, suffered the heaviest blows from Vladimir Ulianov, known by his party name "Lenin," commemorating his exile by the Czarist regime to a Siberian region on the river Lena.

With his fiery speeches, assisted by his fellow agitators, Lenin propagated his "new" ideas among the workers and peasants, promising the best for all the under-privileged. The slogans of the Communists sounded indeed lofty: "Land, freedom, bread" or "Land for the peasants and factories for the workers" etc. None were ever fulfilled and the new bondage proved worse than the previous one, but the propaganda swept like a brush fire through all cities, towns, villages and hamlets. It penetrated the army and the navy, whose personnel were tired of the cruel, prolonged war and eager to return home.

Soon the Communists were firmly entrenched in the seat of power. The Czar and his family were arrested and brutally murdered. Men of higher military rank, who did not escape in time, were also killed. *"Capitalists"* and the *"intelligentsia"* were nearly wiped out. A mere mention of belonging to those classes through ancestry or marriage was sufficient to land one in jail or be killed by a firing squad.

After dealing with political opponents, the godless hordes turned their wrath against all religious leaders regardless of creed or denomination. They virtually declared war against God.

Of course, Pastor Rosenberg was not spared. Having been a missionary and pastor of a church, the director of a Mission School, the president of all Evangelicals in South Russia, and an accredited agent of the American Relief Association under President Hoover for supervision of the relief campaign for the various Evangelical and Baptist churches in his district, he was "a thorn in the flesh" of the godless. He was arrested, and after a short trial by the revolutionary tribunal, sentenced to death and thrown into a dark, moldy dungeon. His experiences there were indeed unique.

Meanwhile, his faithful wife and fellow-missionary, as soon as her husband was arrested by the godless Communists for his Christian activities, bravely commended him to the faithful care of Jesus, Whose he was and Whom he served. "You are mine," she said through her tears at the time she was parting with Leon, "but first of all you belong to the Lord, and His will be done."

This woman knew her place before the Throne of Grace, and in the most severe of trials and testings she really understood how to talk to her Lord. Believing in prayer and trusting His leading, she taught the little ones, as well as the adults, who too were now under her care, how to approach God with their requests without anxiety. In answer to their prayers the Lord performed a needed miracle on behalf of Pastor Rosenberg. The promises of Psalm 91:14-16 were literally fulfilled: "Because he has set his love upon Me, therefore will I deliver him. I will set him on high, because he hath known My name...

He shall call upon me... I will be with him in troubles; I will deliver him and honor him." (KJV)

Pastor Rosenberg was delivered at the close of 1921 due to the intervention on his behalf by the International Red Cross. The Communists agreed to exchange him and some other prisoners for several persons who were important to them and were being held by the Germans. They ordered Pastor Rosenberg to leave the country.

As painful as his departure was for his family who at least had hope for an eventual reunion, it was almost devastating for his congregation. A "Letter of Thanks" from all of them partly reveals their pain:

LETTER OF THANKS
TO OUR SPIRITUAL FATHER
AND SHEPHERD OF OUR CONGREGATION
PASTOR LEON ROSENBERG:

"Circumstances are urging you to leave Odessa and go abroad, thus leaving us orphaned.

"For twenty-two years you were standing here in the service of our adored Lord and Savior as the Superintendent and leader of an Evangelical Mission. The Lord blessed you richly and gave you visible fruits of your faithful and diligent ministry to our beloved Evangelical Christian congregation of Hebrew believers, a congregation of which you, our spiritual father, can be rightfully called both the Elder and the Pastor.

"The years of our existence as a church are really a monument of God's grace and mercy (Psalm 73:1 and Romans 11:1).

"Yours was the duty to guide, with the Lord at your side, the little vessel of our church through many storms. When He opened a door, no one could close it. The witness of the Gospel was accompanied by God's strength from above, and the Lord added more and more to the number of believers in our church. A great number of brothers and sisters of our people, the scattered nation of Israel, who had to leave their father's house because of their faith in Jesus, are standing here today. Those who had to leave Odessa are living witnesses of the Gospel outside the borders of this country. Several branch-churches arose as proof of the blessing from on High, and many brothers and sisters in the course of time remained faithful unto death.

"You also served our little children. Your concern for them led to founding of a school, where they were brought up in the nurture and admonition of the Lord in a purely Evangelical way.

'How will it be now?' — we are asking ourselves. How will we get along without you? Yet, we are persuaded that it is the Lord's will for you to go, and we hope that someday He will bring you back to us. So we wish you Godspeed and call His blessings upon you and yours on all of your ways, and may He Himself be your blessing!

"Thanking you for your marvelous ministry from the depths of our hearts, we are saying sincerely: 'May the Lord reward you.'"

In His love,
Faithfully yours,
(*signed by the whole congregation*)
Odessa, May 1922"

The congregation was left in the hands of the Lord under the leadership of the assistant pastor, Philip Trostianetzky, and a year later he reported to the senior pastor in Germany that in spite of many hindrances, the church stood fast and firm in unity and love among its members, and that new souls had been added to their number. (Unfortunately, this time of relative freedom was not destined to last very long. By the early thirties all churches were closed and almost all ministers put behind bars.)

ॐ

Reunion And Attempts To Start Over

ॐ

In 1922, seven months after his expulsion from Russia, and once again by the intervention of the Red Cross, Pastor Rosenberg was reunited with his family in Germany. This was a miraculous and joyous event for the dedicated missionary couple. Fanny Rosenberg in her typical simplicity of faith said to her husband: "I never gave up hope, because I knew that God answers prayers."

Their missionary spirit was not quenched; and it was their longing and heart's desire to resume their activities as soon as possible. Under the name "The friends of Israel" (no relation to another mission under the same name which was formed much later in America), they started a mission in the city of Frankfurt am Main. A fine group of ministers became members of the Society, including as chairman the renowned *Prediger* (preacher) Waechter, vice-president of the Evangelical Alliance of Germany. Meetings and public lectures in the civic auditorium drew hundreds of Jews, among whom the Rosenbergs made many friends, and who in turn began regularly to attend local meetings in the newly formed mission. Two of Pastor Rosenberg's lectures before the student body of the University of Tuebingen, "Evangelical Christianity and the Jewish Question" and "Essence of Redemption," were published and reprinted in several editions. All of this looked promising, but was not meant to be.

Fate Of The Daughter Left Behind In Russia

When the Rosenberg family was leaving Russia in 1922, their elder daughter Eugenia did not join them. During her student years at the University of Odessa, while in the Christian Youth Circle of which she was the secretary, Eugenia met her future husband Sergei, an ethnic Russian of Eastern Orthodox background, who had recently experienced spiritual rebirth. They had known each other for four years and now, seeing that Eugenia might decide to leave Russia with her family, Sergei proposed, and they were married the same year that the Rosenberg family left for Germany. The second Rosenberg daughter, Elizabeth, and two other daughters, Helen and Maria, left with their parents.

Two years later, in 1924, Eugenia, together with her husband Sergei and one-year-old daughter Lydia, visited the Rosenbergs in Hartz, Germany. They stayed for two years, during which Sergei finished a Bible School and a bookkeeping course. He was eager to learn a trade, not sure if he would ever again be able to enroll in a University after the expulsion from Odessa University for his Christian beliefs. Another daughter, Irene, was born to them while still in Germany, and in 1926 they returned to Russia. By that time Eugenia was expecting her third child. She was not sure if she would be able to see her parents and sisters ever again, so their parting was painful and tearful.

During the same period of time that Eugenia and Sergei spent in Germany, an important event took place there, in the city of Wernigerode. The humble attempts by the Rosenbergs to start new work among the Jewish population there, were widely known among many believers, so it was not surprising that Pastor Rosenberg was invited to the dedication ceremonies of the now quite notable Mission "Light in the East."

Among well-known Evangelical leaders, besides Pastor Rosenberg, was the beloved Christian author and lecturer Vladimir Marcinkovsky. When a Bible School was added to this Mission, both of these brothers were able to lecture there for a short time.

Unfortunately, Nazism was already then raising its ugly head, in pre-Hitler Germany, and some so-called "Christian" groups were not immune to its philosophy. One of the local Protestant leaders, Mr. Ludendorf, "purged" the New Testament of "everything Jewish," insisting that Christian religion should have nothing to do with the Jews. Many German Jews, on the other hand, considered themselves German nationals first and believers in Moses second. After a while, this spiritual climate did not look inviting to Pastor Rosenberg, whose goal was to bring as many Jews as possible to a living faith in Jesus, and he began to pray for some other open doors and fresh guidance from the Lord.

ψ

PART
VI

Chapter 23

BUILDING A MISSION IN POLAND

*N*ew challenges were lying ahead for this tireless servant of God. Soon he was on the road on his first missionary itinerary to Poland.

Deprived of all their possessions in Russia and uprooted from their fruitful activities by the crushing blows of the godless, Pastor and Mrs. Rosenberg did not despair, but made plans for more service. The very first trip to Poland revealed that that country had emerged from World War I with a population of 34,000,000, of which nearly 4,000,000 were Jews. What a marvelous opportunity for spreading the Gospel!

In a special way the Lord had laid upon the hearts of His two faithful servants the desire to care for the dispersed Hebrew-Christians in that country, who were "scattered" in more than one sense, as Jews among Gentiles, and also as Hebrew-Christians among the various religious denominations. They had no contact with one another and also had no one with whom to share their inner needs and difficulties. It is true that at that time there was no distinction made as to race, as yet, and Hebrew-Christians were welcome to become members of any church of their choice; but the ministers and pastors of those churches had neither time nor training to occupy themselves with the particular requirements of the Hebrew-Christians. Quite frequently they lacked understanding of the needs of the Jewish souls, who before conversion lived in an entirely different and strange religious world and had had to sever their old family and community ties.

In 1927 the Rosenbergs, following a definite call of God, were contemplating a move to Poland. At that time there lived in Warsaw one Rev. Zimmermann-Carpenter, pastor of the Anglican Church, which was connected with the British Embassy. This man served as a representative of the London Jewish Missionary Society. Pastor Rosenberg expressed to him and his associates, Mr. Eisenmann and Mr. Bregman, his feelings of concern and found both men very responsive. After meeting these men, Pastor Rosenberg wrote a pamphlet entitled *"I Am Seeking My Brethren."* Not long after this, the first Hebrew-Christian Conference ever held in that country took place, and Pastor Rosenberg was not only invited to attend it, but was given an opportunity to speak and present his past work as well as his plans for the future. He was well received and one Austrian organization took him under its wing, forming a Mission under the title *"Peniel"* (meaning "the face of God" from Gen. 32:30). This organization was Lutheran and believed only in infant baptism.

It just so happened, that about that time, Pastor Rosenberg had led an interesting couple to Christ: the husband was a Jew and his wife, a Lutheran, had espoused Judaism at the time of their marriage. When both experienced spiritual rebirth through Pastor Rosenberg's teaching, they desired to be baptized by him, which he promptly did. The Lutheran organization was infuriated. Their belief in child baptism left no room for a second baptism upon the confession of faith in adulthood, and Pastor Rosenberg had to part ways with them. He could not deviate from the Bible teaching concerning baptism and compromise his belief. There was no bitterness in his heart. Seeing the hand of God in this matter, he soon founded the "Bethel Mission of Poland" in the industrial city of Lodz.

Poland had just emerged as a nation after the devastating World War I, and it was not easy to find a suitable place. Means were also lacking and raising funds in a postwar Europe would be almost impossible. But the Lord manifested His grace once again in two marvelous ways. First, a legacy from a friend in Britain had been awaiting Pastor Rosenberg for some time. Because of the dire circumstances which the Rosenberg family was in at that time, the money could not be delivered to them while they remained in Russia. This legacy of 100 English pounds, worth 500 American gold dollars, was a great amount of money in those days.

Secondly, the problem of a suitable location for a Jewish Mission in a Roman Catholic country was also wonderfully solved. A textile factory in the center of the city was damaged by fire. The municipal order was that no factories were to be erected or rebuilt in the business district. The owner, a Protestant Lutheran, was more than glad to let the Rosenbergs rebuild the place for missionary purposes. Interestingly enough, the name of the street on which this factory stood, was *"Navrot,"* or Conversion Street! Two huge halls were available for immediate use and a sign was erected with the name *"Beth-El,"* reminiscent of the renaming of Luz by the patriarch Jacob. After seeing the angels of God there and the heavenly ladder, he named the place *"Beth-El"* (the House of God), and then moved on to his next objective.

☰

Chapter 24

A MIX OF TESTING
AND BLESSING

As a faith Mission, "Beth-El" was often led through deep waters of severe testing of faith. There was a financial crisis in the country, accompanied by a joblessness of great proportions, so that many friends who supported the mission were forced to cut down on their support or even stop it all together. Amazingly enough, this was also a time of many answered prayers. The ministry was registered as an Evangelical non-profit outreach to the Jews with which the Catholic Church had no quarrel. The economic crisis affected thousands of children and soon it became obvious that it would be the next task of the Mission to serve these destitute little ones in whatever way possible. Children without parents or with parents of insufficient means for survival had to be cared for, and soon, because winter was approaching. For the summer plans were made to take them out into the country for a few weeks. This was a tremendously difficult task but in time miraculously brought much fruit for the glory of the Lord.

Many of the poor children attending the Mission Sunday School belonged to Hebrew-Christian families; but there were others as well who, along with the believing children, learned to be thankful to the "Giver of every good gift" and Friend and Savior of souls.

However, this branch of the ministry met with many obstacles. As children of the local Jews, these little ones were not welcomed to the countryside owned mostly by Roman Catholic farmers. It became an ever-present problem for the Mission to find a summer shelter for these Jewish children, many of whom were orphaned when one of their parents accepted Christ and decided to follow Him. The need remained acute and many prayers were offered by the staff to the kind and merciful God and Father of widows and orphans.

One day, a suitable parcel of land became available but the price was out of reach for the new Mission. Many local friends gave all they could and still it was not enough. Suddenly, from out of nowhere, came a letter from America in which a total stranger wrote the following:

"A friend of mine let me read one of your letters in which were described some of your blessings and needs. My heart goes out in a special way to the suffering Jewish little ones in your Mission who are won for Christ. I too have children and I feel it is my obligation to do something to help your little ones. I do it out of love for my Lord and my own children who currently are sheltered from any want.

"Please, receive this gift (she enclosed a check) as a gift to God for the purchase of a home for orphaned and otherwise needy Jewish children."

This was the Lord's direct answer to many prayers. The desired parcel of land was not yet sold, but the amount covered only two-thirds of the entire sum. The owner agreed to accept what was there right away and have the rest be paid in eight monthly payments. With some mishaps and difficulties the rest of the amount was eventually paid and "The swallow had found her nest" at last! The children's home in Helenoweck was soon enjoyed by boys and girls and was called by them a "Paradise." Officially, though, it was called "Loraine Johns Memorial Home" in memory of the generous giver's late father who was a great friend of children.

This home became not only a dwelling place for children but also a second mission station from which the Gospel went out in many directions.

Chapter 25

USING
THE NEW
CIRCUMSTANCES

*A*gainst all odds, the new Beth-El Mission began to expand its ministry in Poland. Although the Orthodox Jewry and the laws of the Roman Catholic government made it impossible to work with children without the consent of their parents or guardians, the Lord richly blessed Beth-El. Many Jews awoke to the fact that here was not a proselytizing institution, or Gentile agency of a certain church that would destroy Judaism, but a place with a sound Biblical message. Many came to listen to God's Word which was delivered to them in a loving sympathetic, yet firmly uncompromising manner, and a number of Jewish men and women were saved. An equally large number, afraid of an open confession, were more than sympathizers; they were secret believers. Therefore, it was not hard for the Rosenbergs to start their activities among the motherless and fatherless children of Hebrew Christians and fill the need which was unique under the prevailing circumstances. Thus it came about that a very extensive child evangelism effort began to parallel the evangelism of adults. The work of the Mission among children was placed under the supervision of the Rosenberg's daughter, Helen, who headed up the summer colony.

In the beginning of its ministry in Lodz, Poland, the Beth-El Mission served as a refuge for destitute, half-orphaned and otherwise very needy children. These children lived either with one of their parents or other relatives and attended public schools. After school they would come to Beth-El for a snack, rest and assistance with their home-work. On Sundays they all attended Sunday School and services at the Mission, and in summers moved to the country to live at the children's colony. Struggling mothers were grateful for the full care their little ones received from the staff at Helenoweck.

Many boys and girls from poor families were not used to having their very own soup bowls and flatware. At home they often had to share their dishes with other family members and took turns eating their meager meals. One little girl would not touch her bowl and sat quietly waiting for directions from those who were serving at the table. She was not sure if the bowl of soup was indeed hers or it was someone else's turn to eat first. When she was told that the soup was hers to enjoy, she smiled shyly in disbelief and then slowly began to eat. This home away from home was indeed very dear to many poor Jewish children who loved not only the warm meals but also the main emphasis which was made on the teaching of the Bible. Children learned God's principles from the Word of God and from its practical implementation by the deeply believing staff of this unique summer colony.

The older children soon gave their hearts to the Lord Jesus and took part in the worship services by reciting memory verses and singing.

To the Jewish children not only the New Testament but also the Old Testament seemed new. They took in the new teaching as parched earth takes in refreshing rain after a long drought. In the Jewish tradition, daughters were especially neglected as far as Bible teaching was concerned, therefore God's promises to *ALL* deeply touched their hearts.

Though newspapers wrote many articles against the missionary work of the Rosenbergs in Lodz and warned Jews against contacts with the missionaries, the fellowship of Jewish believers grew and more and more children were added to the original number. Touching conversions repeatedly took place and baptisms were frequently conducted by Pastor Rosenberg and his co-workers.

♈

Brother Hendel Reports

♈

Brother Hendel ministered to children at Beth-El in Lodz. In one of his reports in 1939 he writes the following:

"It is my chief task to distribute the printed Word of God, to deal with individuals, and to visit Jewish families. This gives me great joy and I thank God for the privilege and for His blessings.

"When children fail to come to our Sunday School once or twice, such absence always indicates that something is wrong with the poor children. Once I had to call on a good mother of two poor children, deserted by their father from whom they have not heard for some time. The mother has a hard struggle. Being left without livelihood and having no profession, she is forced to take any work there is to be found and at best she earns $1.25 per week. With this income she has to provide food and shelter for her children. The place they rent could hardly be called a home.

"The children were glad to see me and promised to come to Sunday School next Sunday.

"From this woman's house I went to two of her neighbors, also mothers with small children, and invited them to come to our women's meetings which Mrs. Rosenberg conducts, and let the children attend our Sunday School. Both agreed to do so. Now I pray that they will follow through. Every place I go, I leave a tract or a New Testament and Jewish families I visit never turn me down. This is indeed a blessed time of grace in our land and I praise God for it."

Such reports were many. This was a calm before the storm. Soon things began to change. 1939 was the year of the Nazi invasion of Poland. However, until the invasion there were several years in which the Mission in Lodz experienced many rich blessings.

ψ

Chapter 26

HARVEST OF SOULS

*I*n the early nineteen-thirties the work of the Mission experienced many marvelous life-changing new births among the attendees of the meetings. One such birth from above came to one secret believer in the Lord Jesus. It took him a very long time to gather enough courage to speak up about his faith in a public meeting and to concede to a baptism together with several others. He needed assistance on the path of righteousness and Beth-El was the proper place for him.

Another man, a tailor by trade, denied the very existence of God for a long time, but his inner dissatisfaction led him to the Beth-El Mission. After a relatively short period of time his heart melted from the living message of Pastor Rosenberg and others, and he asked to be baptized with two other new converts.

A third man was a rabbinical student who lived in the general area of the Mission. After a long struggle with the faith of his childhood, he accepted the Lord Jesus as his personal Savior. He testified to the power of the Gospel against the superstitions of the rabbis, and added that the light of the Cross alone could dispel this mortifying darkness.

One can hardly imagine how difficult it is for such Jewish "Bible scholars," who live in the bondage of the Talmud, to break through the labyrinth of rabbinical scholastics, full of hair-splitting assumptions, to the light of the Gospel and the saving grace of the living and loving God. Many hours of honest discussion between Pastor Rosenberg and this man, whose name was *"Gottlieb"* (God's-love), took place before he finally gave in and surrendered to Christ. The two-edged sword of the Word of God and the working of the Holy Spirit led him to acceptance of the Truth which alone makes one free. One day he came late and said: "Tonight I am here not to argue but to listen and learn from my Messiah." Convinced that Jesus, the crucified and risen from the dead, was indeed his Savior, he decided to venture "outside the camp" and to take upon himself the disgrace of the Cross of Christ.

This venture "outside the camp" was a costly one. The ceremony of "banishment" from the Jewish society and the Synagogue was degrading, to say the least. The chief rabbi would cover the door to the ark, in which the Holy Scroll of the Law was kept, with a black curtain. On the *"Omed,"* or the table, he would place lights draped in black shades. He himself would put on white robes as a sign of purity (or rather his rabbinical self-righteousness) and would blow sounds from the *"Shofar,"* or the ram's horn, which was normally used only on New Yearns Day and the Day of Atonement ceremonies.

Oddly enough, the cutting off *(niddui)* of the "unfaithful" was considered as solemn an occasion as these high holy days. The head of the subjects of banishment would be covered with *"Cherem"* — a sign of cursing and excommunication. (If the guilty one was not present, the ceremony was still conducted in his or her absence. (This ceremony is still conducted today just as it was then.) The "infidel" would be declared "unclean," worse than a leper, because he or she was believed to be cursed by God. The threat of this "casting out" hung over the heads of all of the new Jewish believers, yet the stronger ones could cite the words of the Apostle Paul, himself a Hebrew-Christian: "Who is he that condemneth? It is Christ that died, yea rather, that is risen again, Who is even at the right hand of God, Who also maketh intercession for us. Who shall separate us from the love of Christ? Shall tribulation, or distress, or persecution, or famine, or nakedness or peril, or sword? Nay, in all these things we are more than conquerors through Him that loved us." (Romans 8:34-37)

Where should such as these turn when love is not found even in the so-called "godly" circles? What should become of their children? That is where the Beth-El Mission came in and filled the gap and the need, being headed up by people of like mind and the same kind of experience.

℗

Reconciliation

℗

All of the new believers in Christ had to pay a high price for their faith, but no one knew this better than Pastor Rosenberg and his wife, who also paid a very high price for choosing to follow Jesus.

For nearly forty years Fanny Rosenberg was considered as dead to her parents because of her belief in Christ the Savior. Yet, in all that time, she did not give up praying for them. One day she received a happy note from her brother Harry in England, who was more than tolerant of his sister's new faith. In his note he suggested for her to go and see her parents in their advancing years before they passed away. He promised to go, too, and a visit was arranged.

To Fanny's regret, she could see only her mother. The father had by then passed away. And although the reunion with the mother was overshadowed by the death of her father, it was a great joy to be once again in her mother's arms and to know that her mother's heart rejoiced to see her beloved "Frymet" again. Fanny was told that her father also had spoken favorably of his long-lost daughter. Whether or not he trusted in the Messiah before he died, only eternity will tell.

☰

Chapter 27

PLANS FOR EXPANSION

Not knowing what the future would bring, the Rosenbergs made plans for further expansion of the work into areas where the Jewish population was large, such as the cities of Pinsk in Belarus, and Lutsk in the Volyn region. Two missionaries were sent there and made considerable progress in finding and organizing groups of Jewish believers. They came in contact with local churches and conducted meetings, facing once again opposition from the rabbis and persecution of those who made confessions of faith in Christ. However, this work was not destined to last very long. The dark clouds of yet another terrible war were looming on the horizon.

Meanwhile, the Beth-El Mission became well known not only in Poland but all over Europe, as well as in the United States of America. Traveling missionaries came to visit Poland, and to see this unique ministry in action. One of the more prominent visitors, after witnessing what God was doing among the Jewish people at the Beth-El Mission, told his friends in America of these great things, especially how the Lord had blessed every branch of the work.

The fame of the orphanage (which was a unique feature of the Beth-El Mission, being the only one on the Jewish mission field at large) was widely spread and aroused a sympathetic interest of Christian friends in many lands. To relate all the blessings among Jewish boys and girls would fill a large volume and should be a separate story from this one which is, more or less, a strictly biographical sketch of Pastor Leon Rosenberg. But this fame paved the way for a journey across the ocean and a visit to America in the late Fall of 1938 with a return to Poland in August 1939. But let us not run ahead, as all of this will be related to our readers in later chapters of this remarkable story.

Chapter 28

EYEWITNESS ACCOUNTS

*P*astor Frank came from Frankfurt, Germany, by invitation to visit the Beth-El Mission in Poland and the beloved Rosenbergs, whom he personally baptized. It was in Pastor Frank's church that Pastor Rosenberg was ordained after completing his seminary studies in Hamburg, Germany, and passing all the necessary exams.

Here are "word for word" impressions of Pastor Frank:

"Pastor Leon Rosenberg is the director of this important ministry, but at his side are three brothers who assist him in every way and replace him when he travels. Since my acquaintance with the Rosenbergs goes a way back, I was glad to respond to their invitation to see firsthand their work in Poland.

"I arrived in Lodz on a Saturday and was met by Mission workers who took me to the beautiful building of the Beth-El Mission on Navrot Street. Services were held on the Sabbath for the sake of the Jews who were free to attend them if they wished to do so. In a large meeting hall there were about 130 Jewish listeners. Being raised in synagogues, they were not used to peace and quiet, but here they were very quiet and attentive. I was the first to speak and then Pastor Rosenberg came to the podium and gave an inspired message. He was able to deliver the Gospel message in Yiddish, mother tongue or the jargon of the Eastern European Jews, and that was part of the reason why his meetings were so well attended, usually from 130 to 150 Jewish men and women. Personally Pastor Rosenberg preferred Hebrew, and in his family German was the commonly spoken language, but if Yiddish was the language of the local Jews, so be it, and he delivered his messages in the tongue of his audience, which was quite large, considering that the work here began only a few months before I arrived.

"After the meetings many guests visited the adjacent reading room where the missionaries were given an opportunity to speak to them personally and answer possible questions. Many already had committed their lives to Jesus Christ, but there were always some who didn't, or were confronted with the Gospel for the first time.

"Adjoining the reading room was a large hall where about 20 young girls and women flocked around Mrs. Rosenberg who was in charge of women's work: visitations of the sick and lonely and care for them as well as Bible studies at the Beth-El Mission. Jewish women had many religious questions and Fanny Rosenberg was able (and capable) to respond to them. She would spend about an hour with the women every Saturday after the morning service. No one was in a hurry to go home and many stayed on until the evening common Bible study period.

"On Sunday, at 3:30 P.M. the very first Jewish Mission festival took place in the Hall of the German Gymnasium (Middle School). The hall was overflowing with visitors and participants. After the choir sang a hymn and Miss Rosenberg read a fitting poem, Pastor Rosenberg came to the podium and greeted the guests. There were many Lutherans from their local church and also many other congregations were represented in the audience. This festive gathering gave great joy and encouragement to Pastor Rosenberg and his co-workers. The obvious blessing experienced in that meeting and later at 8:00 clock in the evening was further proof that the Jewish Mission in Lodz was pleasing to the Lord and was legitimized and crowned with His blessing.

"In the evening I was the second speaker not only on that day but also on Monday and Tuesday evenings, as the conference continued for three days. Every day the hall was filled with people.

"On the following days, after the conference was over, I was able to visit a private synagogue of the so called, *"Darshanim Chasidim."*

Many years ago they lost, through death, their chief rabbi, but continued to mourn for him by crying loudly, wringing their hands and dancing.

"We visited also a Reformed Temple, a rather impressive building with only a few men in it. Later we visited a large Jewish cemetery where, for a price, Jewish men were willing to "mourn" at the grave site of the famous "Wonder Rabbi," whose "sorrowing" followers preferred to do this in the comfort of their synagogue. We refused to take advantage of the services of these paid mourners and asked to be lead to the graves of the most honored rabbis. These graves were covered with notes and letters of requests for intercession before Almighty God. It was indeed a sad sight to behold.

"From time to time Jewish men and women came to weep and pray at these graves. They poured out their hearts before the dead in hope that they would lighten their burdens through intercession to God. Before the great Jewish holidays many thousands of Jews visited the graves of their loved ones seeking help and comfort.

"On all the streets of this large city one sees many Jews. In the Jewish quarters one hardly meets any

Christians at all, but mostly poor Jews and men in old-fashioned garb, reminiscent of the times of the patriarchs. In my ears rang the words of the Gospel, 'As sheep having no Shepherd.' (Matthew 9:36)

"Though the Jews have many rabbis, in reality they have no one to lead them out of the darkness of superstition and error into God's light and life. They live as their ancestors of old lived in Poland hundreds of years ago. It is heart-breaking to see so many intelligent men in whom many precious gifts slumber unused, when, if awakened, they could be applied for the good of the nation Israel and of the whole world. It is a deep mystery that the Spirit of God does not illumine the minds and hearts of these many people to lead them into full salvation through the Gospel of Christ.

"But it is in God's wisdom and will that those who received the healing touch of redemption in Christ should assist in the building of His Kingdom here on Earth, and this fact must encourage us even more to pray and work for Israel's salvation. Many did come to living faith during Rosenberg's ministry in Poland, as earlier in Russia, because they were given the opportunity to hear a clear and complete Gospel message, and especially have a chance to get to know better some real Christians, godly men and women who presented the best and living message, confirmed by the following illustration:

"The lady head physician of the Christian Evangelical hospital in Lodz, which I visited after seeing other important sights, introduced me to several Jewish patients and shared this story:

"A Jewish patient asked one of our nurses after a few days in the hospital: 'What kind of people are you? I have never in my life seen people like this. The nurse asked:

'What is it that drew your attention?'

'You care so much for our well-being, always ready to answer a call when we ring; you are never impatient with us, always nice even to the Jews.'

'We are not doing anything extraordinary, we are just returning a little from that which we have received from our Heavenly Father.' 'Is the God of Heaven your Father?' — asked the Jew whose name was Abraham.

'Of course!' — said the nurse.

'If God is your Father, then you must be children of God. Is that so?'

'Yes, we are.

'Am I also a child of God?'

'This I do not know.'

'But why? '

'Because I do not know if you believe in the Messiah Whom we call Jesus.'

'How can I believe in Him when I cannot see Him?'

'The Messiah has come and told us that God becomes our Father when we are born of Him by the power of the Holy Spirit on receiving forgiveness of sins by faith in His Son Jesus. We were not born God's children, but became His children through faith in Jesus. '

"One day the nurse was giving out Gospel tracts and Abraham asked her: 'Do you also have the good Book for me?' She gave him the book of the Gospel according to Matthew. He read it. Everything was new to him and very interesting, even wonderful, and the more he read, the more beautiful the story seemed to him, as if he had peeked into a new and strange world. When the nurse came to care for him, Abraham told her:

'He was a remarkable rabbi, this Jesus, wasn't He?' And she said: 'He was much more than that' 'Who was He then?' 'Continue to read and pray that God will open your eyes so you may see the Messiah.'

"At the time of his release from the hospital. Abraham said to the nurse: 'You must live, you must live a long life, sister.' 'What for must I live a long life' — she asked. He responded: 'You gave the good Book and it did my heart good.'

"Two weeks later Abraham returned to the hospital. The nurse asked him:

'Well, Abraham, are you sick again?'

'No, I am well, but I came to thank you for the kind treatment I received from you. But most of all for the good Book which is now my most precious treasure which I carry always close to my heart. It showed me that Jesus is indeed the Messiah. Now I am a happy man, and now I know why you were so good to me. You have learned it from your Jesus. May God bless you all.'"

Pastor Frank went on with the description of the facilities of the Beth-El Mission and could not say enough good things about the many ministries among Jewish adults, youth, women and children. He visited the Summer Colony and attended Sunday School classes where he was given an opportunity to speak to young and old alike. Very satisfied with his visit, he returned to Germany and for many years remained in close touch with the Rosenbergs until his death in the mid-nineteen-sixties at the age of 104. Both Fanny and Leon Rosenberg considered him their spiritual father, pastor and confidant, friend and advisor.

ψ

Sieuwert Slort

ψ

Another important guest, and later a co-worker, came from Holland in 1933, shortly before Christmas. His name was Sieuwert Slort. His brother Dauwe, while in Rotterdam, met Philip Trostianetzky, whom Pastor Rosenberg led to Christ some years earlier in Odessa and who assisted him in the ministry there. Both Dauwe and Sieuwert were taught by their father to love and respect the Jewish people and they had always been interested in the missions to the Jews. Pastor Rosenberg, after establishing his work in Poland, came to Rotterdam and Mr. Trostianetzky introduced him to the two young men. After Pastor Rosenberg heard Sieuwert preach and discovered that he was not attached to any organization, he invited him to come to Poland and help with the work there. German and Yiddish (similar to German) were spoken widely in Poland and Sieuwert spoke German. Pastor Rosenberg still suggested that Sieuwert attend a Bible school in Germany, but the red tape was so great that he went straight to Lodz instead.

The Beth-El Mission was a faith Mission and Pastor Rosenberg could not assure a regular salary to the young Dutch preacher with a heart for the Jews. He told him that as long as he himself had something to eat and a roof over the head, Sieuwert would be assured of the same. Mrs. Rosenberg received him like a son and took care of him lovingly and generously.

Sieuwert Slort's impressions of the Beth-El Mission in Poland are reported as follows:

"When I saw the Hall filled with so many Jewish men and women, I was quite impressed, but then the children filed in. There were dozens of them, big dark eyes shining with anticipation, faces radiant with joy. They sang familiar Christmas songs and recited poems and Scripture verses. When the treats were handed out, they received everything joyfully yet calmly. My heart almost burst with love for these little ones and

I could hear the Savior's voice saying, 'Let the little children come unto Me... as well as the command given by Jesus to Peter, 'Feed my sheep.'

"I became very active in the work. I visited poor families with the Rosenberg's daughter Helen, delivering material and spiritual help. In the beginning this was quite difficult, not because of physical weariness, but because I was seeing so much need, such as I had never witnessed before. It was very depressing for me, for often one was just helpless in the face of such misery. And yet, even there we found much faith which amazed and humbled us both.

"I was teaching a class to the older children and one of them, a lovely teenager named Niuta, used to translate my lessons into Polish, as the older children apparently preferred that language. In summer the Mission had a camp for these poorest of the poor and I frequently visited that facility. I loved those children very much.

"Ministry to the children and preaching in some local Protestant churches occupied my time, but being yet a very young man, I managed to fall in love with a photograph of the youngest Rosenberg daughter, Maria, who was in Switzerland at the time. I went even so far as to proclaim: 'When Maria comes home, we will have a wedding!' Somehow I had a feeling. Finally, in May 1934, Maria did come home and I fell in love not only with a picture but the person herself. Boy, was I in love! We were married in January 1935 and Pastor Rosenberg, Maria's father, performed the ceremony.

"After the marriage I went on a couple of missionary trips with Maria's uncle, Alfred Malcman. We preached the Gospel to Jews and Gentiles in many places, but predominantly in German and Czech villages where some years before many Dutch families had settled.

"Later I took a journey with my father-in-law and we visited two places, Lutsk and Pinsk, where he wanted to start new work among the local Jews. (By the way, Pinsk was the birth place of Golda Meir, future lady prime minister of Israel.) Standing there and gazing across the border, I was thinking of Maria's sister, Eugenia (Jenny), who did not leave Russia with the Rosenbergs in 1922, and lived with her family in the Ukraine. I thought I would probably never see them, but God's possibilities are limitless.

"After the birth of our daughter I became seriously ill and needed an operation. My thoughts went homeward to Holland. Rumors of war were already in the air and I had only a visitor's visa to Poland. Poles became increasingly suspicious of foreigners and I was denied an extension. Exactly at that time I received an invitation from Holland to take over a church in Friesland. In 1937 I left Poland with the warmest memories of a wonderful ministry and a wife who was the daughter of one of the greatest missionaries to the Jews."

Chapter 29

A MISSIONARY JOURNEY
TO AMERICA

As it has been mentioned before, the fame of a Hebrew-Christian Mission and Orphanage in Poland moved many prominent Gospel ministers to come and visit the place to see for themselves if the good reports about the work there were indeed true. Rev. Joseph Flacks, an American Hebrew Christian and Bible teacher, was among many who visited Beth-El in those days. It was he and several others who suggested that Rev. Rosenberg should travel to America and present his work there to churches and influential individuals who then, in turn, would perhaps be able to support this unique work.

By then Pastor Rosenberg had made many important contacts in Europe and established representative "stations" of his ministry in most European countries. Leaving the Beth-El of Poland in the capable hands of his wife and daughter, as well as two trusted brothers who assisted him on a daily basis, he was now ready to embark on a journey to America. Back in Lodz there was also a Board of Trustees, consisting of seven men called, "Friends of Israel in Lodz," who in 1926 initially formed a group of Christian brothers who agreed to help Pastor Rosenberg raise funds for the Mission, and to whom he would be ultimately accountable. (The name

"Friends of Israel," which was given to the Mission in Germany, was soon changed to Beth-El.)

An itinerary was prepared for Pastor Rosenberg by his friends in America and he began to follow it as soon as he arrived in New York in the Fall of 1938.

In addition to those whom he already knew, Rev. Rosenberg made many new friends among famous names in the Evangelical circles of North America. He met and was befriended by the then pastor of the large Moody Memorial Church in Chicago, Dr. Harry Ironside, Rev. MacIntosh of the First Baptist Church of Spokane, Washington; Mr. Robert Holt of Spokane, Washington, Charles Shoop, professor at the University of Minneapolis, Hal Williams, a mill owner in California; Lewis E. Derbee, director of the North-West Mission in Minneapolis; Mrs. D.C. Croker of California; Reamer Roy Mylan of California; Rev. Joseph Flacks, a well-known evangelist and Bible teacher as well as a highly esteemed Hebrew Christian; Rev. Russel Paynter, pastor of Bethany Temple in Philadelphia; and many others, who then formed an Advisory Council for the Beth-El outside of Poland. This Council was formed through God's providence and stood by the ministry of Leon Rosenberg in times of trouble and need, which were just about ready to begin.

On this missionary trip Pastor Rosenberg visited hundreds of cities and towns, numerous evangelical churches, congregations and fellowships, where he was allowed to speak in the morning services and present his work in great detail. He crisscrossed the USA and ventured into all provinces of Canada, covering more than 70,000 miles by boat, railroad, car and airplane. In the eleven months spent mostly in the USA, he learned much about the people and culture of this great and generous land, and laid a solid foundation for future support which was destined to sustain the Mission for many years to come. Even today in the early nineties, as we write this biography, the American European Beth-El Mission still draws some support from this old source.

☖

Chapter 30

GOD'S UNMISTAKABLE LEADING

*R*eaching yet another milestone in his life and ministry, Pastor Rosenberg wrote the following summary:

"As the dark clouds of a looming World War were ominously gathering on the world's horizon, I was still in America, but the circumstances made it absolutely necessary for me to return to Poland. With a short stopover in Holland to visit my youngest daughter, Maria, who was ill with tuberculosis and placed in a sanatorium, I reached Poland in August of 1939. An inner urging moved me not to delay my return. I had to oversee the work in Poland, and sensing the thunder clouds overhead, rushed home to my co-workers and of course my wife and daughter, as well as other relatives who assisted me in the ministry.

"As I came home, they could not comprehend how I dared travel in such a time, and I in turn could not give them any other answer, but that the Lord had urged me to return without delay. He had His way with me and my presence at home was in many ways very necessary.

"The Second World War, which began in September of 1939, was only one of seven major calamities in my life during the last 35 years. It was one of seven calamities in which I was directly or indirectly involved since the beginning of my ministry. Some of these have hit me and my work and family rather hard.

"It began with the war between Russia and Japan soon after my arrival in Odessa at the turn of the century, followed by Jewish pogroms and the Bolshevik Revolution with all of its consequences, arrests, persecutions and finally exile. All the dreadful and complete losses on personal and ministry levels could have thrown anyone into a deep depression or even denial of faith, as was often the case with many. But I was able, by the grace of God, to look back and in assessing the past, say with all sincerity of heart and mind: "and we know that *ALL* things work together for good to them that love God, to them who are the called according to His purpose." (Romans 8:28)

"As stated before, my return to Poland was the obvious leading of the Lord. There were many things to be arranged and earnestly considered which involved the whole Mission. The many tribulations in my past proved of great value at this time.

"We began to prepare bomb shelters, but soon realized that in our case, with so many workers and children, it would be wiser to claim the 91st Psalm and rest in the shadow of the Almighty. Though death and destruction reigned in many places, we were spared for the time-being, and God in His infinite mercy concealed from us the not so distant future.

"The fact that we were led by a Board and were an Evangelical Mission to the Jews as an "in-land Mission," served as a guard from the hatred of Nazi invaders, but only for a short while. Our orphanage in the country, ten miles away from the city of Lodz, drew the attention of bombers because of the close proximity of a railroad and woods. Our buildings quaked from the air pressure of the frequent explosions. We were all, young and old, in constant prayer, which the Lord graciously honored. Help kept coming to us from the most unexpected quarters and we held on as long as we could.

"For the Jews in Poland life was becoming increasingly dangerous and my co-workers began to suggest that something needed to be done to alleviate the distress. As the founder of the Beth-El Mission, I felt the burden of the work more than at any previous time. It became evident that HE would have me leave the war-torn Poland for the purpose of contacting our friends from whom we were entirely cut off.

I hesitated for a while because of the danger such a step would entail, having to go through the belligerent country as a marked and outlawed Jew.

"The way was utterly dark and fiercely dangerous. On the 8th of November we had a special gathering with the co-workers and Hebrew-Christians. After a season of prayer it was unanimously decided, for the benefit of the work, that I should undertake the perilous journey. I shall never forget this farewell meeting, which was, in many respects, similar to the one described in the Book of Acts, chapter 20. I was greatly encouraged by the bravery of my own family, especially of Mrs. Rosenberg, who again said: 'You belong to me, but first of all, to the Lord, Whose we are and Whom we serve.

"And so I leaped into the 'jaws of the lion' to experience once more that the God of Daniel was the same today as in his day. While detained along the way, I was greatly encouraged by the unique promise in Job 5:19: 'He shall deliver thee in six troubles, yea in seven there shall no evil touch thee. This was literally fulfilled on my behalf, as I found when recounting previous outstanding trials. The Lord truly saved me this time in the seventh tribulation.

"After three weeks I was freed and allowed to cross into Berlin. I could fill volumes with my experiences, but as I said, it was necessary to take steps toward going once again to America.

"But this plan seemed hopeless of fulfillment because of the prevailing conditions. The way was apparently blocked on every side. I was earnestly advised not to attempt to enter the USA without securing a non-quota visa. I claimed my favored promise 'All things work together for good to them that love God,' and things began to look up. My credentials as an ordained minister of the Gospel, proofs of my many years of service exclusively as such, and certificates issued by the police, as the, so-called, *'dossiers,'* showing my integrity, entitled me, according to the current immigration laws of the United States, to a permanent visa!

"So the Lord overruled all difficulties and paved my way to the United States. This too was God's manifest guidance for the sake of our afflicted ones back home in Poland.

"As for Mrs. Rosenberg, I thank God that before leaving Holland I was enabled to secure all necessary papers, including a permit to enter Holland and a non-quota visa for the United States. As soon as she is permitted to leave Lodz, God-willing, she will join me..."

Here the personal written account of Pastor Rosenberg stops, but from recorded history featured in the older copies of the "Bethel Witness" and from the verbal accounts of the Rosenbergs in the USA, we know that Mrs. Rosenberg was unable to join her husband in America for the next *SEVEN* years! They were reunited only in 1947 after the terrible war was over and after many tragic losses suffered once again by this remarkable family and this unique Mission.

ψ

PART
VII

A SEVEN-YEAR SEPARATION

Chapter 31

FORCED INGENUITY

All efforts to get Mrs. Rosenberg out of Poland were to no avail. She was kept under the Nazis until the end of World War II, but not without the Lord's greater purpose. The orphans needed their "mother." The missionaries, who were left behind to "hold the fort," and the large number of believers, belonging to the "Beth-El" family, needed her experience and support.

In the Orphanage she was assisted by her daughter Helen and several other workers. No one expected that the savagery of the Nazis would be so far-reaching and cruel as it turned out to be. Six of the "Beth-El" missionaries, most of the workers at the Orphanage and a great number of Hebrew Christian believers shared fully in the "bitter cup" of affliction with their Jewish brothers in the death camps, meeting violent deaths in the gas chambers, after which crematoriums became their final resting place without the common dignity of a burial or a funeral. To those who believed in the Lord Jesus Christ as their Messiah, death in Him meant life eternal and therefore a great gain. They went to be with the Lord!

Mrs. Rosenberg, though her life was spared, went through terrible agony, day and night witnessing and experiencing all the horrors, including news of the murder of her own daughter, Helen, and her husband Samuel Ostrer; sister-in-law, Theophelia, with her missionary husband, Alfred Malcman, and their three young children; Mrs. Rosenberg's brother-in-law, Herman Rosenberg with his wife Esther, (all of these relatives were led to Christ by Fanny and Leon Rosenberg) and many, many others.

But the most tragic and cruel was the death of over two hundred children whom Mrs. Rosenberg, together with her daughter Helen, nurtured both physically and in the Christian faith. Only eternity will reveal the reasons for the seemingly senseless slaughter of these innocent ones, and we shall receive the answers to all of our many "Why's."

As days passed and the suffering increased, the burden became heavier and heavier for Mrs. Rosenberg to bear without her husband. The vigilance of the Gestapo with its censorship made it almost impossible to communicate normally and regularly. Letters reaching her husband during those days were censored and mutilated, so she resorted to Bible names and episodes which would convey her messages to him. To do this, special wisdom from above was required, and it was given her in an amazing way and abundant measure.

The first "coded" message of this kind came through, and though sounding quite sad, was encouraging. Not being able to refer openly to Scripture, Mrs. Rosenberg was telling her husband that she "received a message from her uncle, the converted rabbi. His letter was forwarded at the close of the 8th month through Benito's friends and was greatly appreciated. This same message, she said, he also sent to you." No one else would know what she meant. She certainly had no uncle who was a converted rabbi, but she referred to the Apostle Paul, once a rabbi of Tarsus, and Benito's friends, the Romans, were the kin of Benito Mussolini. The date pointed to the chapter and closing verses. Yes, it was a message from Romans 8, and what a message it was!

This brought her husband to his knees in supplication and thanksgiving. In supplication, because the great trials expressed in this passage of Scripture, were "tribulation, distress, famine, nakedness, peril and death." These were the actual conditions which his wife and those with her were facing. But on the other hand, there was cause for thanksgiving for the triumph of her faith and the spiritual victory and fruitfulness, in spite of all these afflictions.

Other similar messages followed, referring to uncle David, the Singer, or to uncle Jeremiah, where dates and house numbers indicated chapters and verses in Psalms and the Prophets. A deeply painful message came after their daughter's husband, Samuel, died in a concentration camp and some time later Helen herself. Uncle David of this message, lived on Singer Street 55, apartment 4 or 8 (she couldn't quite remember which!), so Leon knew he had to look up Psalm 55:4-8 which read as follows:

"My heart is sore pained within me; and the terrors of death are fallen upon me. Fearfulness and trembling are come upon me, and horror hath overwhelmed me. And I said, Oh, that I had wings like a dove! for then I would fly away and be at rest. Lo, then would I wander far off, and remain in the wilderness. I would hasten my escape from the windy storm and tempest."

ψ

Chapter 32

THE GRIM CHRONOLOGY
OF TRAGIC EVENTS

*T*he years following the *"Blitzkrieg"* and Hitler's invasion of Poland, were a literal "walking in the valley of the shadow of death." Mrs. Rosenberg, together with her co-workers at the "Beth-El Mission" of Poland, endured unspeakable hardship and affliction. Their sowing of the "good seed" was sowing "with tears," however, the Lord granted them "a reaping with joy" — a great harvest of souls among the Jews, suffering under the Nazi occupation, and among hundreds of poor and orphaned children entrusted to the care of the Mission. These were indeed "sheaves of joyous harvest" to the glory of the Lord Jesus. Eternity will reveal the importance of this work, and even the seemingly odd timing. God *NEVER* makes mistakes!

Pastor Rosenberg went on to the USA and his friends there. The "Beth-El Mission of Poland" and later of Eastern Europe, was once again renamed in America and became the "American-European Bethel Mission" as it is known today. God had many wonderful surprises in store for the long-suffering Rosenbergs, but in 1939 things could not have looked bleaker, and had it not been for their deep faith and complete trust in the Lord, perhaps, they might not have been able to go on and start all over again with yet another ministry in still another part of the world. But these were not ordinary people or ordinary Christians; these were giants of faith and prayer, of unbendable and unbreakable spirit, and so the last years of their lives were a tribute to their Savior and a triumph of faith and glory over the direst of circumstances.

The first mission station for the new work in America was in Minneapolis, Minnesota. Congress ordered all organizations, which were receiving donated funds for people in hostile countries, to submit monthly reports to the Secretary of State. "Bethel Mission" immediately complied with this order and began to issue monthly financial reports to the State Department, showing amounts received and to whom they were sent abroad. As long as America stayed out of the war in Europe, it was possible to forward funds through international neutral channels and fill the needs of the Mission in Poland. But as time went on, news from abroad grew more and more grim because the needs were not only material, but also spiritual. Soon the country home of the poor orphans was requisitioned by the new authorities and the children were compelled to leave during the severely cold winter and move to the city in great haste. At the same time, in God's unfathomable foreknowledge, the number of suffering children had increased through the addition of those not of the Orphanage. These were being cared for by means of a soup kitchen.

In spite of these circumstances, there was still much reason for thanksgiving. The Lord had placed before the "Bethel Mission" a great task. It was the only official Mission in the land permitted to maintain its ministry well into 1944. In those dark times the Mission had a duty to perform: to allow the light of the Gospel to shine in this utter darkness, to alleviate in some measure the need which was crying out to heaven.

It is amazing that letters of praise and thanksgiving to God continued to reach Pastor Rosenberg in America practically until the end of the war, when most of what used to be a fruitful mission had perished in the flames and fury of hatred and war. Here is but one example:

"Dear friends, I know you will want to praise the Lord with us as well as keep in mind the need of praying for our poor orphans who are enduring great hardships and privation at this time.

"Give thanks to God with us for the protecting grace granted to our entire Mission family during the war in Poland.

"Praise God for His loving care in supplying our needs so miraculously through our friends.

"Kindly join us in praising the Lord for permitting our Mission to operate with a good testimony in these evil days which have befallen our people in Eastern and Central Europe. Pray that the good Lord may protect our workers here and supply their needs.

"Give praise to God for the Hebrew Christians of war-torn Poland who have not grown faint in their faith and trust in the Lord, but are yielding to Him more and more, regardless of the unbearable afflictions.

"Thanks to God for the Hebrew Christian youth who, because of these horrible events are learning to appreciate more and more their spiritual blessings in the heavenlies."

Such were the praises during the hardest times of suffering and loss. In her memoirs Fanny Rosenberg describes in detail all of the events during the seven-year separation from her husband. We could fill another book with stories out of that time, but choose to concentrate on the main events pertaining to the life and ministry of Rev. and Mrs. Rosenberg. Our focus is on the hand of

God in all these events, in order to give encouragement to the current and future generations of missionaries in this free land of ours, as well as all over the world.

Only God knows why the "Beth-El Mission" was allowed to conduct its ministry long after many other missions closed their doors. In times when food was becoming alarmingly scarce, more orphans kept coming to the Orphanage, adding to the original number, and many homes could have been filled with these poor Jewish children, were it not for the prevailing conditions in the land, which were becoming increasingly deplorable. The workers at "Beth-El" often asked "Why, Lord? We can barely handle the number You gave us before. Why more? What should we feed them?" But He kept adding and providing for the needs of more and more children.

All manner of restrictions were issued for the Jewish population and the Hebrew Christians were not excluded. Bread and other food stuffs became an ever growing scarcity. Lines in front of the stores and bakeries grew longer and longer, but there was no room in them for the despised Jew. At such times the sustaining power of the Heavenly Father was keenly felt. The God of Elias (Elijah) used *POOR* people to help the hungry orphans. One day a widow came from a distance on foot with some food products she had saved. It meant a real sacrifice for her and therefore was well-pleasing to the Lord. It also strengthened the faith of the children and adults at the Orphanage.

A Protestant pastor, a German, came like Nicodemus by night, though fearing not the Jews, but his own people. He brought some honey and other much-needed scarcities.

A German baker, who was closely watched by military guards while he was baking bread for the soldiers, managed somehow, for some time, to secretly add a little flour of his own to make a few extra loaves, as he put it, "for the poor Jewish children." He was very sorry when, because of new restrictions, he could no longer continue to practice his deed of mercy. Wave after wave of suffering came with increasing fury with no end in sight.

When the Orphanage, which the children called a "Paradise," was forcibly taken away by the invaders on a severely cold winter day, the order to vacate had to be carried out immediately. The children were taken to the Mission building in the city, a facility lacking all the comforts the children needed.

It was amazing that the little ones, who learned to love and trust the Lord Jesus in the Christian Orphanage, learned also more than some adults, to love their enemies. No bitter feelings apparently entered their young hearts over the loss of their "Paradise." One little girl said: "It is a pity that we no longer have our Orphanage, but I am glad the Lord protected it during the war time. It is now serving another good purpose." (During the enemy occupation, the Orphanage was converted into a hospital for non-Jews who were compelled to return to the Reich). One of the boys said: "if it is used for sick people, we can hope that sooner or later, when the sick recover, our Home will be returned to us." It was never returned to them but the faith of the children was something to behold and emulate.

Through valleys and shadows and severe testing in the fiery furnace of affliction, the Hebrew Christians of Lodz were led into deep spiritual blessings in a most tangible way. They enjoyed the spiritual fellowship with one another more than ever before, being drawn closer to one another by a common pain. As long as "Bethel" was still tolerated, it remained a beacon of the Gospel Light in the midnight darkness of suffering around it.

Jews were not permitted to leave their homes after five p.m., so the Gospel gatherings were conducted as much as possible during the day hours. On the Lord's day there were three meetings in succession — for believers, for evangelization and for young people. There was a Sunday School for all ages before each meeting.

Soon arrests and displacements of Jewish masses began and many workers were forced to move to Warsaw, Lublin and elsewhere, some even managed to escape to other countries, such as Britain and Palestine. This produced more stations of the "Bethel Mission" and a much broader outreach. God, Who knew the future, was spreading His Word abroad to as many Jews as possible prior to their destruction when many were quite receptive to the Gospel.

After a while, seeing that a reunion with her husband became more and more an impossibility, Mrs. Rosenberg moved temporarily to Warsaw, while daughter Helen, together with her husband, remained with the children at the Orphanage, until it was taken away and Helen was forced to return to the city which also proved not to be the final place for them. This constant instability due to frequent changes of the overall situation made Pastor Rosenberg very concerned for the fate of the Lord's work in Poland. Each new letter from his wife or daughter brought more and more terrible news. Help was still getting through via American Express in New York, Sweden and Switzerland, but not for very long. America was preparing to enter the war in Europe.

During the entire period of separation, Pastor Rosenberg neither sat on his hands, nor was he wringing them in desperation. He traveled extensively, visiting hundreds of American churches, arousing interest and raising funds for the faltering, suffering "Beth-El" in Poland. He was a dynamic and inspiring speaker, who appealed to the conscience of Christians in the free world, calling for prayer on behalf of the suffering Jews. The response was overwhelming with distant echoes reaching well beyond the immediate time of the current dire need.

Pastor Rosenberg's efforts to rebuild his ministry among Jews at any cost after each calamity which almost completely destroyed it, can be described with just two words: missionary resilience.

♆

Chapter 33

EXCERPTS FROM MRS. ROSENBERG'S LETTERS

*T*wo years into the war, in 1941, Mrs. Rosenberg wrote to her husband, though her letters were censored or confiscated:

"I am trying to write to you often to keep you informed about our situation. It greatly pains me to tell you that my beloved mother, nearly one hundred years of age, passed away recently. She deeply longed to see me, but I could not secure a permit to visit her. To think that my poor mother, in her advanced age, was exposed to so much hardship! Her home was destroyed by bombs and she ended up without a proper place to live, not to speak of the essentials which an aged person requires. (Later Mrs. Rosenberg was thankful to God for taking her mother home when He did, before all Jews were taken into the concentration camps and gas chambers. At least, her mother was given a dignified conventional burial at a local Jewish cemetery).

"We will be happy when this terrible war will end. Humanly speaking, there is not much prospect of surviving if conditions remain as they are now.

"Do you remember how our daughter Elizabeth (later a medical missionary in India), when she was a child during the famine in Russia, cried when we invited one of our brothers to share a meal of potato peelings with us? How she was comforted when I told her that the Lord would provide another meal for her. She stopped crying and said: 'Pray to the Lord that He really will.' Praised be His Name, He has never failed us, and so we will trust Him even under the present prevailing conditions.

"Our children do not look the same anymore. I doubt that you would recognize them now. Their lovely faces are pale and look very different. But they are still rejoicing in the Lord, cherishing spiritual blessings.

"I am certain you will be glad to know that we still enjoy our gatherings. Again, last Sunday was an oasis. Our brothers and sisters, together with the new converts, shared the Bread and the Wine, remembering our Lord Who so loved us, that He gave Himself for us. The Evangelistic meetings of last week were splendid. We really thank the Lord for the marvelous opportunities. I, personally, can truly say: 'The Lord is my portion. The lines are fallen unto me in pleasant places!' (Ps. 16:5,6)

"I wonder, what you would say of our singing? It is not as vigorous and powerful as it once was — but it is sweet singing in the Spirit. We miss you, yet we are thankful to the Lord that you are where you are. We remember you in our prayers, that the Lord will strengthen you, protect you and bless you together with all the friends and co-workers there."

From another letter:

"I am sorry to tell you, that due to circumstances, we were obliged to give up two places where we had soup kitchens. It breaks my heart to think of all those who needed this assistance so badly. However, it is really a miracle that we still do what we do. Praised be His Name!

"We have plenty to keep us busy here. Our time is well filled. I should say 'my time' — there is practically no limit to my time. After my long day's work is done, I am busy writing. Each letter must have a different message. Oh, there are so many who want a word from 'aunt Fanny.' Last month I wrote more than 140 letters, besides postcards and yet, I did not write to all!

"You will be glad to hear that the American Consul contacted me and gave me his advice regarding my emigration, but nothing can be done at the present time. As you know, the conditions have changed here again. The world is topsy-turvy. It looks serious but we claim the comfort of uncle Job in house number 5, #18, whose words have a calming effect on all of us here and may have the same effect on your heart. Job 5:18-21 was meant, and Pastor Rosenberg read the good counsel of Job's friend Eliphaz:

"For He maketh sore, and bindeth up: He woundeth, and His hands make whole. He shall deliver thee in six troubles; yea, in seven there shall no evil touch thee. In famine He shall redeem thee from death: and in war from the power of the sword. Thou shalt be hid from the scourge of the tongue; neither shalt thou be afraid of destruction when it cometh."

Towards the end of 1942 the letters began to sound more urgent and desperate. The Orphanage was still operating and Mrs. Rosenberg began to realize why she was left behind and unable to emigrate:

"A thousand thanks for your transfer of funds, which reached us promptly, and again let me tell you, it came at the time of utter distress and great need. But praise the Lord, when the need was at its peak, the help of the Lord was 'at the door.' We were waiting for another letter from you, dear Leon, but we can understand that under the prevailing conditions, even mail becomes scarce. It is not easy to live under such circumstances, especially when one has to take care of such a large family. Although our dear children (the orphans) are a source of great joy, I am often overwhelmed when I see my flock around me. To the sweet little lambs, who have no one else in the world, I am privileged in some measure to be their "mother." It is indeed a joy to have their esteem, love and trust, but these many children have also many problems, some typically boys' problems, others typically girls' problems, but nevertheless real problems, and worst of all is their physical condition: all are pale, undernourished, thin and unsmiling. This makes one forget all personal troubles and losses, and my daily prayer to the Lord is for patience and wisdom.

"We have again enlarged the number of children by taking in some of the utterly destitute boys and girls, as our dear children agreed to share their meager meals with others. This caring attitude is the fruit of their upbringing in our Orphanage. However, this also makes the soup thinner and leaner, but we still continue to dish out a considerable number of bowls and plan to do so as long as some help will continue to come our way. We are looking to the Lord for the provision of His daily 'manna...'" (A poem below was attached).

HIS CHOSEN PATH FOR THEE

He chose this path for thee:
No feeble chance, nor hard, relentless fate,
But love, His love, hath placed thy footsteps here.
He knew the way was rough and desolate.
He knew, the heart would often sink with fear,
Yet tenderly He whispered: "Child, I see,
This path is best for thee."

He chose this path for thee:
Though well He knew sharp thorns would
                              tear thy feet,
Knew how the troubles would obstruct the way,
Knew all the hidden dangers thou wouldst meet,
Knew how thy faith would falter day by day,
And still the whisper echoed: "Yes, I see,
This path is best for thee."

He chose this path for thee:
Ev'n while He knew the fearful midnight gloom
The timid shrinking soul must travel through;
How tow'ring rocks would oft before thee loom,
And phantoms grim would meet thy
                              frightened view;
Still comes the whisper: "My beloved, I see,
This path is best for thee."

♆

Chapter 34

GRIMMER NEWS
AND DEEPER CONCERNS

*F*or a while letters continued to come to the USA via Sweden and Switzerland. These were touching, heart-breaking accounts of the heading downward, deteriorating conditions, which eventually led to total destruction of facilities, staff and children. News from other areas, such as Holland and India, where two of the Rosenberg daughters lived during World War II, reached Pastor Rosenberg in the USA and he shared it with readers of the "Bethel Witness" throughout the seven-year period of separation. However, one area, namely Russia, kept silent, and the Rosenbergs knew nothing about the fate of Eugenia and Sergei with their girls, and this was an added source of pain for them. Would they ever know what happened to their eldest daughter?

The first death report arrived at the US Headquarters of the American European Bethel Mission in 1943. The first victim of Nazism was Samuel Ostrer, Helen's husband and right hand in the work at the Orphanage in Helenovek. His death was a great loss not only for his young widow but for the entire operation, and all the individuals involved in it. As a faithful soldier he fell on the "battlefield" of Christ against the prince of darkness, and regarding him, one can truthfully say of him that he that came out of the great tribulation, and washed his robes, and made them white in the blood of the Lamb (Rev. 7:14).

The saddest aspect of Samuel's passing was the loss of a father by the little Michael-Moses, an orphaned baby whom the Ostrers had adopted as their own. The baby was found in the gutter outside the Orphanage, exposed to the elements. The little boy had no tag or letter of identification attached to him, but he was circumcised and presumably a Jewish lad, abandoned by his mother (or parents). Samuel and Helen took him in as their own but, alas, not for long. Michael-Moses was destined to become an orphan once again.

Four years into the war, at the close of 1943, Pastor Rosenberg wrote in the "Bethel Witness":

"Since the *'blitzkrieg'* in Poland, this is a grateful and solemn anniversary for Beth-El. Solemn because of the unspeakable affliction and the appalling ordeals suffered by the Jews in Nazi dominated lands, a tragedy that brought anguish to men and women all over the world. The four years were in many ways the years of severe testings and trials for Beth-El. Forcible sifting, confiscation of property, evacuation of the Orphanage, loss of all belongings and separation from the director were indeed heavy blows. However, we are thankful because we know that the Lord had His purpose with Beth-El Mission in this particular area of His Vineyard. These were years of rich experiences for Mrs. Rosenberg and the faithful staff and workers to whom the words from the book of Job 5:10-21, quoted earlier, were quite fittingly applicable.

"It is indeed a miracle that Beth-El was left there as a Gospel Witness to the gravely-afflicted Jewish men and women. The Mission was enabled to rescue the perishing souls and to relieve starving orphans and other destitute children. We can truly say: The Lord hath done great things for us: He has bestowed upon us, day by day, His benefits and loving kindness. Though the burden of responsibility has been heavy, yet the Lord has helped us to carry it and He has sweetened our '*Marah*' (bitterness) and provided the daily '*Manna.*'"

ψ

More Trials And Tribulations

ψ

After a period of eerie silence, though help continued to be channeled through two neutral countries, Pastor Rosenberg began to feel real concern for his wife and the Beth-El Mission in Poland. Some coded alarming messages did finally arrive. One example was from the book of Psalms: "Serve the Lord with *FEAR* and rejoice with *TREMBLING*" (Ps. 2:11). This is usually understood as a warning to rebellious nations, but the reference made by a gravely afflicted loved one, was revealing, that although trembling in fear of the atrocious enemy, they were, nevertheless, rejoicing in serving the Lord.

From another cautious reference to Psalm 3:3, it was obvious that they truly learned the secret of "rejoicing in tribulation." But especially touching was the quotation from Acts 14:22 which reads as follows: "We *MUST* through much tribulation enter into the Kingdom of God." The brave sufferers had really learned to appreciate Hebrews 12:11, that grievous, painful tribulation "yields the peaceable fruit of righteousness unto those who are exercised thereby."

Soon another message came through: "A group of our orphans, aged 15, was taken today by the enemy to a camp for slave labor. These boys and girls were taken in addition to those taken previously, and whose destiny is unknown to us."

Mrs. Rosenberg considered this trial worse than the death of her own two children in childhood. She believed that the Scripture says we are not to weep for those who die in the Lord, who come out of great tribulation being faithful until death, and cautiously cited a passage from Jeremiah 22:10: "Weep ye not for the dead, neither bemoan them, but weep sore for him (them) that goeth away to return no more."

In closing she added a word of comfort: "What a comfort it is to know that the Lord blessed our efforts in bringing them up in the nurture and admonition of Him, Whom they learned to love and trust; they know that living or dying they are the Lord's and are prepared to meet Him. We can truly thank God for our Bethel Orphanage which is a 'nursery' for Heaven."

It was in 1944 that a new Mission station of the Bethel Mission was opened in New York. The missionary there was Pastor Rosenberg's youngest sister, Frieda, who several years before, in Los Angeles, experienced a spiritual rebirth. When her brother came into the area to speak in local churches, Frieda attended many of his appearances.

During one such guest-appearance, news came of the tragic death of his daughter Helen in a Nazi concentration camp in Poland. Pastor Rosenberg was awaiting his turn at the pulpit when a note about Helen's death was slipped into his hand. Hearing this latest piece of painful news, he gave out a deep sigh and yet proceeded with his message. Witnessing this reaction to the most painful news, Frieda was greatly impressed with her brother's spiritual strength. For the rest of her life she remembered this episode and often shared it with others.

It is quite possible, that in his quiet time, alone with God, Leon Rosenberg broke down and even cried, but in the pulpit, in front of a large congregation, he managed to conceal his feelings and give preference to the Gospel message which, coming from him, always glorified God and expressed thanks and praise to Him.

ॐ

PART

VIII

Chapter 35

END OF THE
HORRIBLE WAR

*I*n the Fall of 1945, the Editorial by Pastor Rosenberg in the "Bethel Witness" began with these wonderful words:

"Now the war is over! The day which we so eagerly anticipated, and for which we so fervently prayed, *IS HERE!* The announcement to this effect by our President, was accepted by Christians of our country with humble thanksgiving and prayer.

"The world was shocked when it learned what the Nazis did to the multitudes of innocent Jewish people in the gas chambers and crematoria, erected in Poland and elsewhere.

"While we cannot understand God's dealings with His chosen people, whom He called 'the apple of His eye, one thing is certain: His thoughts concerning Israel 'are thoughts of peace and not of sorrow' (Jer. 29:11). 'The Lord has His ways in the storms and the whirlwinds' (Nah. 1:3). He has His purpose with Israel whom He has destined for His glory and "to show forth My praise." (Isa. 43:21)

"God has made the horrible wrath of the wicked to praise Him. Eternity will reveal that the Nazi furnaces served, in many ways, as refineries for many precious Jewish souls. Through His prophet the Lord said: 'I will refine them as silver is refined; I will test them, as gold is tried: they will call on My Name and I will hear them;

He will say 'they are My people': and they shall say: 'the Lord is my Lord.'" (Zech. 13:9)

"Among the innocent victims were many who heard the Gospel message from our missionaries, who knew that the Lord Jesus can save to the uttermost, and that whosoever calls upon His Name, shall be saved. (Acts 2:21) We have heard that many Jewish people, miraculously escaping the places of cremation, turned to God."

Though the war was over, there was still no contact between Pastor and Mrs. Rosenberg, because of the precautions of the military authorities, who ordered a thorough black-out of communications. But when the black-out was lifted, a cable came telling of the miraculous liberation of Mrs. Rosenberg and those who survived with her. This joy, however, was dimmed, because of the loss of many precious lives in the ranks of missionaries, workers and orphans.

♥

First Letters From Mrs. Rosenberg After The War

♥

Poland, August 1945

"I have already written several letters, but realizing that mail delivery is not yet regular, I will try again, until one or the other letter will reach you. Not being certain of your address, I am sending my letters to my sister in England. She will get them to you.

"Now, beloved, I wish I could tell you something pleasant about myself, but I must tell you that the "black-coated beasts," the Gestapo, inflicted many deep wounds on my heart.

"The tragedy which has befallen our Bethel family, cannot be described. Most of our missionaries in Lodz, as well as most of those who belonged to the Beth-El family, together with most of our children, were brutally murdered by the Nazis. Of our workers, only Brother Choinatcsky, Brother and Sister Bakalarz and Esther Narve are alive.

"An eyewitness, one of the brethren who miraculously escaped, brought me the sad message, using the words 'I alone have escaped' from Job 1:19. He said, about three hundred lost their lives. Yet, it was comforting to hear him speaking so highly of Herman and Ester Rosenberg (Leon's brother and sister-in-law) and the Hendels who were, he said, 'as shining lights' in the Nazi darkness, among the tens of thousands of our people, whose suffering and death they shared.

"I wish I did not have to tell what happened to us here in Starochovice. You already know that our dear Helen and her husband were victims of the Nazis. Dear Samuel was murdered first, then Helen was arrested on her birthday. This happened when one of our boys, little Dave, who escaped the horror chambers of the Nazis, sought refuge in her apartment. The Gestapo "hunters" searched for the little victim and found his trail leading to Helen. There, before her very eyes, they shot him to death and took her away. She died as a soldier at his post, faithful unto death. Thank God that little Dave too was prepared to go "home" to be with the Lord Whom he, as well as all the other children of Beth-El, learned to love and trust.

"The terror of the Nazis increased in December of 1942 due to their setback on the Russian front. The blame for the defeat was laid on the "damned Jews." Those belonging to the Jewish race were hunted like wild beasts. They were taken to gas chambers or put in places where they could be cremated alive. I was made responsible for all the children in our Orphanage — that none should escape.

"Most of the children in our Home, from babies of two years and up to boys and girls, age fourteen and fifteen, were dragged away and never returned. They were taken away group after group. The last group was placed about twenty miles from us. A warm-hearted Polish peasant, who told us where they were, wept when he described the plight of these dear children, who were exposed to frost and snow. This kind man undertook to supply them with what help we could send, until they too disappeared.

"Though my deep consolation was in the Lord, the Good Shepherd of those dear little lambs, whom we were privileged to nurse for Him, preparing them for life and death — for time and eternity — yet, I suffered unprecedented agony for their sake. I then understood the cry of Naomi — I rather say 'Thy will be done.'

"On the 17th day of January of this year, the enemy planned to destroy all Jewish men, women and children in our community who were still alive, but early in the morning of the same date, the Russians came and the enemy fled. This was a miracle. If they had come but two hours later, none of us would have survived.

"I cannot describe how great our joy was and how our rescuers were greeted with warm handshakes, hugs, tears and kisses. So the 17th day of January, 1945, was the great day of liberation for us. What a wonderful feeling it was to be free from the 'Damocle's sword' which constantly had swayed over our heads!

"As long as we saw the 'black coats' with the emblems of the skull and bones and swastika, no one was certain from one moment to the next how much longer one would live. The Gestapo was certainly the agent of hell. Who can describe the inhuman fury?

"We experienced many miracles indeed. Besides those I have told you before, I think one is outstanding. During the last months of occupation our Orphanage was under constant surveillance of Hitler's henchmen. Again and again they searched for Jews and every search endangered our lives because there were always Jews with us.

"Once, on a Saturday afternoon, our brother Levin, the teacher, was in the back room giving lessons to some of our children. (We were teaching until we no longer could.) Suddenly a Gestapo man came in and determinedly said: 'There are Jews in your home now! I have been watching this house and know what I am talking about. I also know a Jew, a seamstress, came to your house today and she is still here.' "I did not say a word. He looked into nearly all the rooms, but not in those where some of our Jewish friends sought refuge. So they were able to escape. But the greatest miracle was that I myself was not taken away, though repeatedly beaten when trying to defend our little ones. I will never fully understand why I was spared.

"Until the middle of 1944 we were able to receive your assistance but nothing since then. Due to the havoc, robbery, plunder and pillage by the Hitlerites in our country, the prices are very high. A piece of black rye bread and a potato are considered a luxury if one can afford to buy them. The new friends who shared with us, trusting they soon would be reimbursed, are now in the like predicament. I hope you will not take this as a complaint. It is simply a matter of information and with whom else should I share my burdens? However, these conditions do not dim my gratitude to the Lord for the great things He has done for us in the past and what He is to us now.

"I found out recently that your sister Theophelia with her husband, Alfred Malcman, who served as our faithful missionaries, were killed by the Nazis along with three of their five children. The other two survived only due to the fact that they were not at home at the time of their parent's arrest.

"I had an unexpected visit from Philip, the eldest son of our dear Malcmans. He told me that he was rescued together with his brother Joseph. He urged me to move with our surviving orphans to his place which is not far from Danzig. I could plainly see the hand of the Lord in this and am now moving to Lamberg."

Additional information about the Malcmans came later from some eyewitnesses. Originally they lived in the city of Zdolbunov (Rovno region, Western Ukraine) but moved to Lodz to assist the Rosenbergs at the Mission.

Seeing that the Nazis were advancing, they went hack to Zdolbunov for a fact-finding "vacation." With the advance of the Nazi armies they did not return to Lodz but escaped in the dead of winter to Lithuania on foot through forests and fields.

By the time they made it there, Lithuania was in German hands. Their third son, Danny, was away from home at the time but missed his parents and joined them there. Just about then Nazis began to arrest Jews and separate them from other local population, placing them in one camp and Poles into another. Alfred Malcman served in the Polish army in his youth and actually was a ranking officer in it. He also took part in the Polish resistance. So, when the Polish refugees were herded together to be moved away and placed into a camp, Alfred joined that group with his family. Two older children were married by then and were not with the family.

In the commotion of moving to the Polish camp, Malcman's youngest son, Rudolf, quarreled with a Polish boy over something, as children often do. This enraged the father of the Polish boy and he began to shout: "These people are not Poles! They are Jews! Take them away!" The guards heard him well and immediately removed the Malcmans from the refugee crowd and killed them execution style.

Mrs. Rosenberg was not familiar with these details at the time of her writing in August 21, 1945:

"Indeed, I am spellbound! I do not know how to express my joy — yes, my exceeding joy — yesterday I received a notification from the Bank of Foreign Trade in Warsaw that money had come by cable directly from you. The joy was not because of money received, but because of the reestablished contact between us, which is indeed a great gift from the Lord! There were two checks for the Bethel Orphanage. Now I am looking forward with eager anticipation to a letter from you. Because the money was sent to my new address, I know that you must have received at least one of my letters.

"I wonder if I told you in one of my letters that among the surviving children, is little Michael-Moses, the adopted child of our dear Helen and Samuel. Lilian, the niece of our Herman, is also safe and both of these children are here with us. I am so happy for these and several others whom, by the grace of God, I was able to protect under our roof. Three more girls were rescued by others and came to me. Now we must start with renewed strength to rebuild our work. I plan to return to Lodz to reestablish our Children's Home and gather the destitute. There are many who need our care.

"How wonderful it would be if the Lord would again restore our Bethel and our Orphanage, where we could gather His 'little lambs,' His sheep, and lead them to His pastures — to the living waters of life! This would be the happiest experience in this, the final stage of my earthly pilgrimage!'"

Such were the lofty dreams of this ardent missionary woman, but the Lord had something else in mind for her. Her husband was finalizing her papers for emigration to America and re-unification with him there.

🕎

Chapter 36

GOD'S MARVELOUS WAYS

♆

"So the Lord blessed the latter end of Job more than his beginning..." (Job 42:12)

♆

Seven years were more than enough time for Pastor Rosenberg to establish new work in the United States and to obtain citizenship in that free and blessed land. For a while he too hoped that the work in Poland would somehow continue, but the new evil, which took hold of Eastern Europe, almost surpassed the previous one. Communism was an old familiar enemy which forced the Rosenbergs out of Russia, so hopes for the continuation of Beth-El's work in Poland eventually vanished.

Even Mrs. Rosenberg at one point realized that their ministry in Poland would soon become a closed chapter, just as their ministry in Russia had in the past. For someone with less faith this could prove emotionally and spiritually crushing, but the Rosenbergs were giants of faith and virtue, so they not only survived this new blow, but triumphed over it in the end.

During the first year after the war's end, Mrs. Rosenberg was able to travel through Poland in search of survivors of the Nazi Holocaust. She was able to locate quite a number of her Christian brothers and sisters in different parts of the country. They were all in bad shape materially, but at least alive after miraculously surviving the terrible catastrophe. Even some of the children surfaced, and she began to gather them around herself and some of the surviving workers, adding new orphans of whom there was no shortage.

Pastor Rosenberg traveled to Europe as soon as it was possible. In November of 1945 he visited many European countries, assessing the damage and looking for needs which the American European Bethel Mission could meet. He brought "first aid" to Europe soon after the war hostilities ceased, but his main concern was for his wife, who remained in Poland after the war, awaiting his coming for her liberation. His heart went out to her, because he knew how much she endured during the years of Nazi dominion. The sword of affliction pierced her mother's heart again and again. The Nazi murderers deprived her of nearly all of her relatives and killed many members of the Bethel family, including most of the darling little orphans. Those who survived, urged Pastor Rosenberg to come to their aid but, alas, an iron door was slammed in his face. The Soviet-controlled Polish government refused to issue the necessary passport, which would enable Pastor Rosenberg to join his wife. He spent four months in Europe and had to return to America without seeing her.

☙

God Answers In Due Time

☙

Back in the United States it became evident that it was God's leading that Pastor Rosenberg was unable to enter Poland during that first postwar visit to the European continent. It would have been dangerous to him personally, and he would not have been able to bring help to Mrs. Rosenberg, nor to the other survivors. His personal intervention before the government authorities on behalf of his wife, a Polish citizen, and himself only recently having obtained US citizenship, could have drawn him, and even more so Mrs. Rosenberg, into a maze of unpleasant complications.

For the liberation of Mrs. Rosenberg the Lord used as His instrument a friendly neutral government, which took her under its official protection, making it possible for her to leave Poland with two rescued orphans: Mike, the adopted son of Helen and Samuel Ostrer (both killed in Nazi concentration camps), and Lilian, the orphaned daughter of Leon's half-brother, David, who was killed by the Nazis, and whose wife committed suicide shortly before an order came to take her away to be killed. With these two surviving children Mrs. Rosenberg was brought to Sweden, from where it was easy for her, as the wife of an American citizen, to proceed to the USA. The children, however, due to some immigration restrictions for Polish citizens, were not permitted to travel there with her. They were ordered to wait for their own quota. Soon they were admitted to England and enrolled there in a private Christian school, courtesy of the friendly British government. Later Mike came to the USA and, as of today (early 1994), lives near Los Angeles, alone, after losing his wife to heart disease. Lilian remained in England and lives there now.

After a four-month badly-needed rest in Sweden, Mrs. Rosenberg boarded a Swedish ocean liner, the "Gripsholm," and in August of 1946 landed in New York. The port was a beehive of great commotion. Hundreds of friends and relatives came to meet their kin. They were on one side of the fence and the "free, liberated" arrivals — on the other. Only after hours of painful waiting, Mrs. Rosenberg was finally in the arms of her husband, who did not give her much time even for a "good cry." "This," he said, "you will do later if you will still need it, but now let us try to get out of here as quickly as possible and proceed to 'our home' in California."

And what a nice home it turned out to be! Through God's marvelous leading, an "estate without an heir" was offered by the city court to the highest bidder. Pastor Rosenberg made a down payment offer towards a total price of $4,000.00 and the three-bedroom house with everything in it became a home and the new headquarters of the Mission in the USA. Later, three more rooms were added: a large office, a study for Pastor Rosenberg and a guest bedroom for the constant flow of guests. The house came with fine furniture, rugs, quality china and silverware. It was conveniently located on a street corner with a bus stop, not far from the centers of both Los Angeles and Hollywood. The address, *252 N. Dillon Street,* somehow reached Eugenia and Sergei in the Ukraine where they lived with their four girls until the Fall of 1943. It was etched in the mind of Eugenia and came in handy at the right moment in God's perfect plan.

After five days the Rosenbergs reached their destination. At long last Mrs. Rosenberg was once again in her own home and with her husband! One could hardly ask for more. One by one friends and prayer partners were introduced to her, and she was able to thank them personally for the years of diligent prayer. She was still concerned for the work in Poland where Paul and Waly Bakelatz were left in charge of Bethel and a new group of orphaned children. So, while thanking them for past prayers, Mrs. Rosenberg requested continuing prayer, until things would be resolved one way or another under a new regime in Poland.

Through extensive correspondence, Mrs. Rosenberg maintained a close contact with many Jewish people in

Europe: Hebrew Christians, as well as with some of the boys and girls from the Orphanage who went through the same trouble and miraculously survived the Nazi ordeals. This "ministry" was a blessed one for "mother Rosenberg." She received letters in Yiddish, Russian, Polish and German, and was able to answer each in the same language. In addition, she mailed many parcels of food and clothing to the suffering displaced people in many European countries, and in the US she often spoke in churches about her war experiences in Poland. In the evenings she attended English language classes at a local night school, where again she was able to make many contacts with Jewish refugees, who later gladly came to her home and invited her to theirs. Many came to know the Lord personally through these casual contacts with this remarkable missionary woman.

Summarizing her first year in America, Mrs. Rosenberg wrote in the "Bethel Witness" in 1947:

"It is but one year, yet, while comparing this one year with the seven previous years under the Nazis, so full of painful and bitter experiences, severe testings and trials, I see God's marvelous protection all the way until He safely brought me to these shores, and I am at a loss for the right words to express my gratitude to Him. I just keep repeating the words of the Psalmist: 'Bless the Lord, O my soul, and forget not all His benefits' in Ps. 103:2, and my favorite Psalm 124.

"After all the tragic and irreplaceable losses, what a blessing and joy it was to be reunited not only with my husband, but also with two of my still living three daughters and their families, for whom the Lord also opened the doors into this country and our open arms. I had not seen Jenny and Sergei for over twenty-two years during which time we barely had any contact, because they lived in the faraway Soviet Union, and we had no hope of ever seeing each other again. Now they are here with us, together with some of their children. And Maria, from Holland, whom I did not expect to see among the living, came with her family to join us here. Others are soon to arrive, and I can hardly wait for the day when all of our family who survived the war will be around Leon and me here in this free and blessed land. My God, how good You are!

"After my arrival, I thought it would be difficult for me to communicate with my American friends without the knowledge of their language. It seemed impossible that one of my age (she was 73!) could learn another language, when my brain is already invaded by several other languages. But with prayer and diligence, after attending a night school for several months and studying at home, I was enabled by my Lord not only to keep up a simple conversation, but to teach and preach the Word of God to groups of Jewish women. I discovered that English is a beautiful language — befitting such a beautiful country as the USA.

"Of course, in the international environment of our family, where many languages are spoken on a regular basis, I am somewhat hindered in my learning progress. But by-and-by, my children and grandchildren too will adjust to the new conditions, and soon we will have our own little American colony."

Writing all this in the nineties, we cannot but marvel at the appropriate attitude of this unique immigrant woman, who did not demand that the American School System should adjust to her, the newcomer, and cater to her ignorance of the English language. Rather, she rushed (at 73!) to adjust herself and her family to the new and beautiful country, hurrying to learn its language and way of life.

While Mrs. Rosenberg basked in the warmth of her new-found home, her family and the ever growing circle of friends, Pastor Rosenberg continued to travel in the USA and abroad, not imagining in his wildest dreams *WHAT* was lying ahead for him and his Mission in the not too distant future.

The Mission still had representatives in many European countries and even in the Middle East: in Palestine, in a suburb of Haifa, called *Kiriat-Chaim*. So, regular reports were reaching Los Angelès from many directions. The Mission station in New York, the so-called "Bethel Center," was manned by professor Solomon Birnbaum who, prior to this ministry, for fifteen years taught Hebrew Missions and Bible at Moody Bible Institute in Chicago, Illinois.

Here we should mention that on one of Pastor Rosenberg's missionary journeys to Europe, in September 1947, on board the Swedish ocean liner "Drottingholm," he met Rev. Peter Deyneka Sr., the director of a Russian missionary society (Later the well-known Slavic Gospel Association), who was also traveling to Europe. The two Christian brothers, both ardent missionaries, enjoyed precious fellowship, sharing in the study of the Word of God and prayer. They parted in Sweden, but later both attended the same conference in Warsaw, Poland, where delegates from 64 Evangelical churches from all over the country gathered for postwar fellowship and planning. Through the years Pastor Rosenberg and mission director Peter Deyneka continued to stay in touch with each other.

☰

Chapter 37

A MIRACULOUS ESCAPE

When in the year of 1947, Eugenia and Sergei arrived in America with two of their daughters, Lydia and Katie, it was finally possible for the Rosenbergs to find out how they managed to survive as Christians under the Soviets and escape to the West in the middle of the war. After having lived for two-and-a-half years under Nazi occupation in the Ukraine, they then lived for almost two years under the Nazis in Sudetenland.

Eugenia's survival was no less miraculous than that of her mother in Poland. Both ladies were Jewish, albeit believers in Christ, which meant nothing to the Nazi butchers. As it turned out, not long before the Nazis marched into the town where Eugenia and Sergei lived, towards the end of 1941, Eugenia gave birth to her fourth daughter, Katie, fourteen years after the birth of her third child, Vera. Moving inland, away from the front, in the dead of winter, as was suggested by the communist authorities, was out of the question because of a small baby in the family, especially since the means of transportation were open unheated coal cars and the train was heading for Siberia!

It was decided then and there that Eugenia and Sergei would stay put, awaiting what might come. And many things did come! We wish only to tell at this point, that when the German armies began to retreat out of the Ukraine in September 1943, among hundreds of thousands of refugees who were moving west was the eldest daughter of Fanny and Leon Rosenberg with her four children.

Sergei was not with them. But on their way out of the country, far from their hometown, without any prior consultation or agreement due to the war-time circumstances, the family "ran into" him by God's providence, and together they continued their journey westward — from the clutches of Stalin into the clutches of Hitler!

The end of the war for them came none too soon in August 1945. Events in between would fill another book, but this is not their story or our purpose. To demonstrate how God performs His miracles on behalf of His children, we have decided to share one more important episode, which eventually led to Eugenia's reunion with her parents in America.

The town in which Eugenia and Sergei lived with their children at the end of the horrible war, was liberated by the American army. After shelling the town all night, Americans marched in victoriously under the cover of tank artillery. The soldiers mowed down with their tank the fence in front of the house where the family rented a flat, knocked out the door with the butts of their rifles, demanded to use the flat for themselves until morning, took all the food out of the cupboards and ordered the family out.

The top sergeant in German flyer's boots (war trophy), put his feet on the table in front of Eugenia, who using her rusty English, tried to convince him, that he was "God-sent to her," and therefore must immediately notify her father in America that her family survived the war and was alive and well in Sudetenland (later turned over to the Red Army and returned to Czechoslovakia). She told the sergeant, that she had not seen her parents for over twenty years and had not heard from them in over five years, that she remembered her father's address in America, and would he "please send him a message."

The sergeant was adamant in his refusal, called Eugenia "crazy" in a loud voice and ordered her out, insisting that "the war is not over yet," that "this is the front and all mail is censored..." But all to no avail; this time he had met his match. Finally, while reluctantly giving in, he told Eugenia to write the note to her father herself (hoping she wouldn't be able to do it), and he would see "what can be done about the censor." She wrote the note, he added one for the censor, gave his field number as return address, and a month or so later an affidavit arrived from America with a letter from *"Father."* The rest is, as they say, history.

One more escape and two years later Eugenia and Sergei came finally to America with their eldest and youngest daughters, Lydia and Katie. Two other daughters, Irene and Vera, got married in Germany during the two years of waiting to emigrate, and followed three years later with their husbands.

Several years later, on one of her missionary journeys on behalf of the AEBM, Eugenia looked up this American sergeant somewhere in Washington, where she located him through military records by the number he left on the envelope. A snapshot of him, her note and the famous envelope with his scribbling on it for the censor, became "historic treasures" of the family and will be passed on to future generations as proof of God's overruling and intervening on behalf of His children.

ψ

Chapter 38

OTHER ARRIVALS

*T*he next family to arrive in America, were the Slorts, Sieuwert and Maria, with their two children, Anita and Jan, who since 1937, during and beyond the time of war, lived in Holland.

Shortly after the birth of their second child, Jan, Maria was diagnosed with tuberculosis and placed in a sanatorium. When in 1940 Holland was invaded by the Nazis, Maria wanted to return home because she was getting better and was no longer contagious. But her doctor advised her to stay, thinking she would be safer there. Her ID bore the revealing letter *"J,"* indicating her Jewishness, and the authorities issued her a yellow star with the word *"Jood"* (Jew) on it.

Remaining at the sanatorium indeed proved life-saving for her, and when the war was over, the Slort family began inquiries about the possibilities of emigration to a country with a warmer climate than Holland. Attempts to enter Switzerland proved unsuccessful, so they went to California to the utter joy of the Rosenbergs. From the onset, Sieuwert became active in his beloved Mission and Maria continued her recovery, gaining strength month by month until she too was able to participate in the ministry of the Mission well beyond the life span of her parents, who never thought she would outlive them. Again God's ways proved higher than man's.

One more living daughter of the Rosenbergs at the end of the war, was Elizabeth Vick, who was a missionary doctor in India. After receiving excellent medical training in Germany before the war, she applied for service with a British mission and was commissioned to go to India where she trained nurses and was a head physician in a large hospital in New Delhi. When Nazis came to power, she was unable to marry her German fiance and remained unmarried until age forty when she met and married a British gentleman who held a high position in New Delhi until India regained its independence from Great Britain.

Serving in India saved Elizabeth's life. Keeping her there was God's timely protection. It will forever remain a mystery why some Jews perished and some were miraculously protected and survived the most dangerous situations virtually untouched. God is indeed sovereign!

During the war, the contact between Elizabeth and her parents was minimal, but as soon as it became possible, she came to America to meet with them and her two sisters from whom she had been separated for many years. She came in 1948 for a short visit and then once again in 1950 to stay for several years, during which time she was active in the Bethel Mission. But after a while, she returned to the mission field in Pakistan for another three-year term of medical service and returned to the USA only after being stricken with cancer which eventually took her life. Elizabeth, or 'Vicky,' as her friends called her, was a typical Rosenberg woman, possessing unbridled missionary zeal coupled with a strong character and an extraordinary capacity for serving God. Like the rest of them, she spoke several languages and in addition, loved sports, books, piano playing and above all — people!

The next visitor to the Bethel Mission in Los Angeles was Helen Weinman, Mrs. Rosenberg's sister, whom she and Leon led to Christ at the very beginning of their Christian ministry. She actually was their "first fruit." During the war Helen lived in Britain and therefore was not in any danger. She was a missionary in her own right, an ordained deaconess, who led many Jews and Gentiles to Christ.

Helen did not stay long in the USA, but was a joy to meet and to get to know by the relatives from distant countries, who knew her only from pictures and accounts given by her sister Fanny and her nieces, Jenny, Maria and Elizabeth. Soon after the State of Israel was established, Helen moved to Jerusalem and ministered there for many years until her death in the mid-sixties.

Many more distant relatives and friends assembled in Los Angeles during the fifties and early sixties, and Leon and Fanny felt like the Job of old, that their latter years were more blessed than the earlier ones, for many wonderful things happened to them during the last twenty years of their lives, not the least of which was the birth of a Jewish State in the land of Palestine.

ॱ

PART
IX

Chapter 39

THE ULTIMATE
BLESSING
AND JOY

At this point we wish to interject a little bit of history, not necessarily known to most readers of current events.

It would be worthwhile to note, that some Jews never left their' "Promised land." Small Jewish communities always remained in that land during several captivities of the distant past, as well as during the last two thousand years after the destruction of the Temple in Jerusalem. A slow but steady trickle of immigrants into the land continued throughout the centuries. Due to severe persecution in many Arab lands, thousands of Jews emigrated to Palestine. The newcomers joined the existing communities in all parts of the land and together they waited and prayed for the restoration of their nation. This ancient longing, called 'Zionism,' was not the modern kind, practiced by Herzl or the European Jews millennia later, but rather a 'spiritual Zionism,' which lived in the hearts of Jews everywhere, especially in the hearts of the Sephardim, who always spoke Hebrew and whose prayers always included a plea:

"...Sound the great Shofar for our freedom... bring our exiles together and assemble us from the four corners of the earth. Blessed art thou, O Lord, Who gathered the dispersed of the people Israel to return in mercy to the city of Jerusalem...; rebuild it soon in our days... Blessed art thou, O Lord, the builder of Jerusalem."

Another popular misconception concerns the term "*Palestinian.*" For centuries it described the Jews, and history forcefully repudiates the present common usage of "*Palestinian,*" denoting exclusively the Arab refugees. The fact that the most of Palestine is today's Jordan, is largely obscured by popular propaganda, and Jews are almost never considered as "*Palestinian.*"

This is yet another fact about Jews deliberately underreported by those, who try to discredit their prior claim to the land. But the Bible is clear on this subject, and only those in whose interest it is to disregard biblical truths, will insist that the land was never Jewish. (Useful reading on this subject: "From Time Immemorial," the origins of the Arab-Jewish conflict, by Joan Peters.)

ψ

Birth Of The Israeli State
And New Vision For The AEBM

ψ

As we mentioned before, one missionary was placed by the AEBM in Palestine since 1947. This man, brother Weber, who was of rabbinical background and a survivor of the Polish Holocaust, had to overcome many almost insurmountable obstacles while living in Palestine. His early letters from the field in Haifa were usually quite negative and sad, though he managed to lead some Jews to Christ. In August of 1948, after the birth of the State of Israel, when a wave of new immigrants from Europe began to flood the land, a new kind of letter from brother Weber reached the AEBM in Los Angeles. It read in part as follows:

"When I meet newcomers from Europe, it awakens in me the old sorrow which I experienced while in Poland. It reminds me of the inhuman cruelties in the places of torture, the forced labor camps, ghettos, gas chambers and furnaces. When I see little children arriving, I am reminded of those places where the Nazis with their diabolically methodical exactness ordered Jewish mothers and fathers to sort huge piles of children's clothing, shoes, etc., of those little ones who passed before them to be gassed and cremated.

"It was only by a miracle that we came through and survived these ordeals. None of us can explain how it was possible to go through such torment, moral torture and humiliation. This miracle we will never be able to fathom.

"I do rejoice to have these fellow-sufferers with me here, SHARING WITH ME THE MIRACLE OF THE ESTABLISHMENT OF THE ISRAELI STATE. No one, including the 'old-timers,' can explain or understand by human reasoning, how this could come to pass. NOW IT IS AN OVERWHELMING JOY TO BE WITNESSES FROM THE VERY BEGINNING, IN SPITE OF THE HARD STRUGGLES, OF THE REAL PROGRESS WHICH THE NEW STATE IS STEADILY MAKING IN ALL THE PHASES PERTAINING TO A WELL-ESTABLISHED GOVERNMENT.

"It is my earnest prayer, that soon the greatest miracle might come to pass — the miracle predicted in the Holy Scriptures regarding our nation — namely, the miracle of the new birth, the returning to the Lord with prayer and supplication, accepting Him as their Savior, the promised Redeemer, by our people."

Rejoicing With Trembling

Knowing the Holy Scriptures, Pastor Rosenberg put down his thoughts in the "Bethel Witness," issued shortly after the establishment of the Jewish State:

"It is very significant that in the Jewish struggle for Palestine the United Nations found no better solution to this problem than the partitioning of the Holy Land. This decision is absolutely contrary to the will of God (Joel 3:2).

"Still more significant is the fact that Jerusalem was not included in the section allotted to the Jews. Without Jerusalem, modern Israel was deprived of the very heart of the nation, the core of God's revelation.

"God said: "I have chosen Jerusalem that My Name might be THERE" (II Chron. 6:6-8). "I will dwell in the midst of Jerusalem" (Zech. 8:3). Jerusalem is the "key-note" of Israel's worship. During the centuries they chanted the solemn pledge, "If I forget thee, O Jerusalem, may my right hand forget her cunning." (Psalm 137:5)

"How sad that Jews have to fight even for the little corner allotted to them.

"While there was rejoicing in the Jewish Quarter when the Jewish State was proclaimed by the Israeli Government, yet many earnest Jews stood aghast — realizing the seriousness of the situation, knowing in their hearts that partitioning was not the solution of the nation's problem. They feared the complications which would arise for those Jews in the various lands of which they were citizens.

"Jews who believe in God's promises, know that this is not a fulfillment of the predictions made by the prophets, but only the beginning of things to come.

Deep in the heart of the very earnest, religious Jews, the Messianic hope is rooted. Their expectation is directed to the "King Messiah" and they await a solution that will include the entire nation and the entire Promised Land.

"The earnest Jew knows also that the greatness of a nation is vested in the greatest of books, his Bible, given by God through the great prophet Moses and the other great Jewish prophets. Concerning this, he confesses daily: 'I believe that all the words of the prophets are true.' In the same creed he confesses that he awaits the coming of the Messiah. The Jews know that annulment of this by them will make them the greatest question mark to the nations.

"The cause of Israel's troubles and the remedy for it are recorded most graphically by the prophet Hosea. In this, which might be called "the most romantic" book of the Bible, as to the affectionate love of God for Israel, the nation is compared to a disloyal wife, who deserted her loving husband. By doing so, she brought upon herself sorrow and affliction. Israel, because of her disobedience is dispersed, and the prophet says that the nation shall be without a king, without a ruler and without her sanctuary (Hosea 3:4). This condition, the prophet predicts, will continue UNTIL the nation WILL TURN BACK TO GOD. The Hebrew word "teshubah" used here by the prophet, literally means "repentance." "They will seek their God" (indicating the desertion, their turning away from Him). It is also very significant that the same prophet says, "THEY WILL ALSO SEEK... THEIR KING DAVID." (HOSEA 3:5)

"It is also noteworthy what the prophet says concerning the King.

The very term "return and seek," which is applied to the King, as to God Himself, suggests that he speaks of the MESSIAH, King of the House of David, and that He too was rejected. The nation will have to SEEK Him and to RETURN to HIM. It is the rejected King Messiah Who returned to His place whence He first came: "I will go and return to My place till they acknowledge their guilt and seek Me." This national return to the rejected King Messiah will take place in time of great trouble. 'IN THEIR AFFLICTION THEY WILL SEEK ME.' (Hosea 5:15)"

Such were the thoughts of Leon Rosenberg, as he contemplated the current events in 1948. Needless to say, declaration of the establishment of a Jewish State was the greatest news the Rosenbergs had ever heard. News of great numbers of destitute and orphaned children touched the familiar sensitive cord in the hearts of Leon and Fanny Rosenberg, who always felt called to this particular field of ministry. They did not know that the work in Poland was in the last stages of its existence. Though encouraging letters continued to come from all who still labored there, the noose of Communism was steadily tightening around Poland's neck, and soon the buildings would be confiscated and missionary activities ordered to cease.

♆

Chapter 40

THE FIRST JOURNEY
TO ISRAEL

After visiting all the Mission stations in Europe, including one in Greece, Pastor Rosenberg discovered that the "Iron Curtain" was about to fall between the East and the West. In the Spring of 1949 he was still able to visit the restored Orphanage in Lodz, Poland, which the Bethel Mission faithfully maintained as long as it was possible.

Then he moved on to Israel to see brother Weber and his wife in Haifa. Reporting to home and family, Pastor Rosenberg wrote:

"Approaching the Holy Land, viewing the historic mountains of which Mount Carmel was the nearest, the people on board began to jump and shout, some with tears in their eyes: "Look! Look! We are arriving in OUR Israel!" Some started to sing the national anthem, *"Hatikva,"* which means 'hope' and the first line of which says, "We do not give up our hope." This national hymn is a contrast to what the Jews in the Babylonian captivity cried in their despair, "Our bones are dried up, our HOPE is vanished." (Ezekiel 37:11) Now hope seemed again revived.

And although *"Hatikva"* is sung in melancholy minor key, to the weary Hebrew exiles returning home from the Diaspora, it sounded electrifying, filling them with hope and enthusiasm. Alas, it was not the real living hope, which fills the heart of a believer in the Lord Jesus Christ. Ignorance, spiritual blindness and misinterpretation of the Scriptures by rabbis was the cause of their drifting from the Messianic promises and rejecting Him Who is the "Hope of Israel."

"However, one cannot help sympathizing with their enthusiasm. What the word 'home' means to a Jew is very difficult for others to understand. It is more than just a 'home' for the 'homeless.' Approaching the land for me, a Hebrew-Christian, was awesome, for I realized that this is the *LAND* promised to my ancestors, Abraham, Isaac and Jacob. Sacred history passed before me. Heroes of the Bible, Moses and the prophets, and all the historic places in this land, reaching back as far as 4,000 years, kaleidoscoped before my very eyes. Looking at the old Mount Carmel brought me at once into association with the prophet Elijah, the man who more than all the other prophets lived in the minds of the nation, in hymns and synagogue liturgy.

"Furthermore, as a Hebrew Christian, I vividly realized that I was approaching not only the land of my ancestors, but the land of *EMMANUEL,* the land where Jesus, my Savior, moved with compassion for the lost sheep of the House of Israel, went about doing good and preaching the Gospel; the land where He gave his life a ransom, died as the Lamb of God to take away the sin of the world, and rose again from the dead.

"It also made a great impression upon me that the land to which I came was no longer Palestine, but *ISRAEL!* What a change had taken place there! At this point in my thinking tears began to flow freely and I began to pray to my God for new doors for a ministry to my people."

There were many "firsts" for the Jewish people: the very first Jewish government, a first sovereign parliament and a new national emblem with a *menorah* (lamp stand) framed by olive branches — the biblical symbol of peace — and the word "Israel" in the center. This was indeed a dramatic achievement, and the feelings of pride and confidence of Jews everywhere were immeasurably lifted. The world was impressed with the way in which the people of Israel organized their government and established a firm system of administration and lawmaking under the most difficult conditions.

But, alas, there were also many problems. Not the least of these was the confusion in ideas concerning the future structure of the State of Israel. The religious segment insisted on a strictly religious structure, a type of theocracy, void of secularism. The secular segment insisted on the creation of a democracy. The newcomers were from all possible backgrounds and cultures, and spoke many languages. The question arose almost immediately what language should become the national tongue of the new State. It was decided that Hebrew should become the national language to the chagrin of the religious sector who believed that the language of the Bible should never become the language of the street.

The strictly Orthodox Jews in Jerusalem started a new movement under the leadership of a rabbi. The group called itself *"Neturim Kartah,"* or "the guardians of the Holy City." They were not impressed with the founding of a secular state, and to this day, as of this writing in the early nineties (1994), stand in opposition to it, refusing to serve in the army and restricting their habitation to separate quarters. They actually wait for the Messiah's coming and the fulfillment of His promise regarding the rehabilitation and restoration of the Israelites in the Holy Land. Their leader said then, and it is reiterated today: "We cannot take part in the Government of the newly established State because we would have to do the same things which the others do — things which are not in compliance with our Torah, namely with the Law of Moses. Jews are only then Jews, when they are 'Bnai Torah' (meaning: children of the Torah, or Law). We cannot compromise, and therefore must be separated. We must 'draw the line' — otherwise it will jeopardize the very existence of our nation more than at any earlier time."

♆

The Problem Of Hebrew Christians

♆

The least welcome were, of course, the Hebrew Christians. The hardships and trials regarding their conditions, economically and spiritually, became a matter of very earnest concern to Pastor Rosenberg. Confessing Christianity in a totally Jewish environment, they faced social, spiritual and economic hardships. There were Jews of influence, not the least of whom David Ben Gurion, the first president of Israel, who said: "The Hebrew Christians belong to the Christians more than they belong to us. To us they belong only racially, but religiously and ideologically they belong to Christians. Therefore, it is Christians who should care for them."

After seeing the country and making the necessary observations, Pastor Rosenberg returned home with mixed feelings of joy and "heaviness of heart" for those multitudes who returned to their homeland after such severe testings and trials, and have not yet found their way to the Lord, their Messiah and Savior.

While in Israel, Pastor Rosenberg felt the significance of the word in Isaiah 22, where the prophet speaks of "the burden of the valley of vision." The prophet had many glorious visions but was heavily burdened when he was given the vision of the valley. His heart was heavy seeing the spiritual need among the people of Israel in his time. Still greater was their need now, at the onset of life in their newly-found homeland. The entire setup there seemed very serious to Pastor Rosenberg, for the nation looked like a "valley of disbelief in the Messiah" There was much unbelief in general, but mostly unbelief in God. The leaders did not recognize the danger signal which God gave to His people at the time of the first entry into the Promised Land — namely, not to say "I have achieved this with my own strength," but always to remember that these accomplishments were made by God's hand, and only because of the Covenant which He made with their Fathers. (Deut. 8:17,18)

Also, while in Jerusalem, Pastor Rosenberg came upon a wonderfully dedicated, Hebrew-Christian couple. He felt in his heart that this couple must join the AEBM, but he could not make such a decision alone without the consent of the Home Board and the people themselves. In his report to the Board he suggested that the couple be approached, and the Board agreed. And so, the Kofsman family was approached by the Board of the AEBM and asked to join the Mission's ranks in the effort to win more lost sheep of Israel to Christ, their Messiah and Savior. The Kofsmans agreed but remained in Jerusalem, while brother Weber conducted his ministry in Haifa.

Another concern was gnawing at the heart of Pastor Rosenberg: concern for many children of Hebrew Christians in Israel and for those of them who were orphaned by the war and the Holocaust. A plan began to form in his mind and heart — a plan to open an orphanage in Israel. He shared it with his wife and then with the Board of the Mission, and a fund was opened for purchasing an appropriate facility, perhaps in Haifa. Pastor Rosenberg felt the need to go to Israel again.

♉

Chapter 41

SECOND MISSION TO ISRAEL

*T*he vision for new work in Israel became clearer and clearer to Pastor Rosenberg. The Board of the AEBM shared it fully and agreed to send the Mission's director once again to Israel to make this vision a reality. Fervent prayer for the Lord's guidance and wisdom followed and sustained Pastor Rosenberg on this his second journey abroad.

While in New York he visited his beloved missionaries there, Solomon and Rosalie Birnbaum. Professor Birnbaum was recovering from serious surgery, but was feeling much better. Pastor Rosenberg's visit with them and a group of friends in their home was a real treat. Supported by their prayers, excited by the prospects of a new outreach in the Holy Land, Pastor Rosenberg shared his dream with his trusted friends and co-workers and arranged his sea journey from New York to Europe with renewed confidence and faith.

The "SS Queen Elizabeth" offered excellent accommodations in a second class cabin. The giant ocean liner made its way steadily through a storm which it encountered on the high seas. There were many opportunities for Gospel sharing en route. People who fear the elements are usually more receptive to Christ's message of hope.

The journey from Cherbourg to Paris was continued by train, which was filled to overflowing with passengers, most of whom smoked pipes, cigarettes and cigars. This was extremely disagreeable to Leon Rosenberg, who only smoked once, when he tried it as a boy of twelve years, having been enticed to do so by a schoolmate who convinced him that "this was the way to become a real man!" On tasting the stuff, Leon threw it away once and forever.

In Paris Pastor Rosenberg was met by a few friends who kindly took care of him for the duration of his stay there. Through them he had precious opportunities to serve the Lord by contacting some Jewish friends and testifying to them about the saving grace of the Messiah. They were attentive listeners and invited Leon to have further meetings with them.

From France he chose the way to Israel through Italy. This for a two-fold reason: traveling by boat was less expensive than by air, and going by boat offered more opportunities for ministry, as most of the passengers to Israel would be Jews from various countries, needing a word of encouragement and the message of salvation.

From Italy he embarked on a boat to Genoa. There he had ample time to make all the necessary arrangements for the further shipment of the trunks and boxes of clothing etc., in order to have them on his arrival in Israel. Lacking the technical facilities commonly available in the USA, Italian workers were slow in moving things, but eventually everything was loaded and our weary traveler was once again on his way to his final destination — Israel!

As was anticipated, nearly all passengers on the ship were Jews bound for their ancient homeland. But what a variety! From many countries and diverse walks of life they were bound for their long lost ancestral patrimony.

Truly, it was the Lord's way to place Leon Rosenberg, a Hebrew Christian missionary, "into the belly of a boat" with so many unsaved souls, so that he could spread the light of the Gospel among them.

The various languages Pastor Rosenberg spoke came in very handy. Jews love to talk, and a missionary must talk as a witness and messenger of the Lord. He must at all times be ready to tell the story of the Messiah and His love.

The news that there was a missionary on board soon spread around. This was done by the cabin mates. Earnest, as well as simply curious persons, religious and infidels, "rightists" and "leftists," became very interested in a Jew who spoke favorably of Christ.

The journey lasted seven days and Pastor Rosenberg heard many stories of suffering and woe. What a depth of sorrow came to light from those burdened Jewish hearts! — woe which can only be expressed in the words of Lamentations 2:13: "Thy breach is great like the sea; who can heal thee?" Little wonder that many were numbed and hardened by all they had endured at the hands of the, so-called, "Christians." What a stigma on nominal Christianity!

There was plenty of opportunity to "weep with those who weep" and to share the warmth of the Messiah which melts the icy crust like the rays of sun in the Spring. To see a tear in the eye of a Jewish listener or to feel the warm grip of a hand expressing gratitude, gives the heart of a missionary great encouragement. The "key" to the heart of an anguished soul is knowledge of the *SAVIOR ALONE!*

After stopping briefly in Naples and Pompeii, the ship moved on to Greece with a stop in Athens, giving the passengers an opportunity to visit the historic city including the Acropolis. Athens, the famous city, seat of philosophers, writers and artists of ancient Greece, had been destroyed many times but again and again survived to be rebuilt.

The antiquities of Rome may be more ornate, those of Babylon more mysterious, those of Persepolis more romantic, but the ruins of classic Athens remain unrivaled for the highest beauty of conception and perfection of execution, enhanced by the loveliness of the surrounding scenery, which Pastor Rosenberg filmed with his movie camera to share later with his family and friends back home.

The ship had entered the Aegean Sea through the modern Corinthian Canal which shortened the journey to Israel. How different is traveling in modern times from what it was in the time of the Apostle Paul!

From Athens the ship passed the Isle of Rhodes. On the way from Rhodes to Cyprus Pastor Rosenberg, for a change, had a great time with some little Jewish boys — telling them interesting Bible stories, which they liked very much.

Three evil names are indelibly written in the heart and mind of every Jew — Pharaoh, Haman and Hitler. The freedom from the bondage of the Egyptian Pharaoh is commemorated by the Passover feast, the *"Haggadah,"* the victory over Haman by the festivities of *"Purim"* (meaning: casting lots), recorded in Esther 9:24,25, but the defeat under Hitler and then victory over him were events tinctured with painful resignation and contempt, because of the tragedy which befell the nation at his hands, having no precedent and exceeding all the centuries of suffering.

The feast of Purim fell at the time of this second journey to Israel by Pastor Rosenberg. A program was arranged on board ship and every talented musician took part in it. But the program did not satisfy all, because the main thing was omitted which would signify the meaning of the feast. It was suggested that the Megilath, the Book of Esther, be read and a lecture given on the historic event. The Book of Esther was read by a rabbi, but the lecture was assigned to Pastor Rosenberg. This gave him a wonderful opportunity to magnify and exalt the Lord Who provided redemption for everyone.

♆

A Happy Arrival

♆

Many spent a sleepless night from sheer excitement as the boat approached the Port of Haifa. Pastor Rosenberg later wrote that he would not miss this sight for anything in the world. It was indeed exciting to see hundreds of hands lifted and waving in greeting to the newcomers, and then the embracing of friends and relatives at the debarkation. This thrilling sight also was captured on film.

Some time was spent on shore before friends could take Pastor Rosenberg to their home. The usual inspection by the immigration and customs officials took some time. People always try to smuggle something illegal and it takes forever to examine everyone's baggage.

Finally the port was left behind and Pastor Rosenberg could attend to his main business which was the reason for his coming to Israel again. The main purpose in the director's going to Haifa this time was the establishment of an Orphanage in memorial to the many slain orphans who had fallen victim at the Orphanage in Poland at the hands of the Hitlerites. For those surviving the great calamity, wherein millions of Jewish men and women lost their lives, and hundreds of thousands of innocent children were killed, the newly-established State of Israel became the *ONLY* haven of refuge.

Among those miraculously-surviving boys and girls lamenting the loss of their fathers and mothers were children of Jewish parents who were Christians and yet drank of "the bitter cup" at the hands of the same cruel enemy. To undertake something for those children by means of a Home wherein they could be reared in the "nurture and admonition of the Lord," became a real spiritual concern of the AEBM in the early fifties. It became more and more evident that it was a vision from the Lord, and that it was His will that this matter should be presented to the praying constituency through which God would supply the necessary means for the carrying out of this project.

This idea was not new to the Rosenbergs who for years had the privilege of caring for orphans and destitute children. However, as in the past, the enemy, who always hinders God's work, tried to stop it here before it began. Even some nearsighted missionaries believed that such work in Israel would not be necessary, "because the Israeli Government takes care of all Jewish children." These well-meaning friends had overlooked an important factor, namely, that no matter how much the Government or Jewish Benevolent Societies may care for destitute Jewish children, they would never provide the one thing most needed for Hebrew Christian children — rearing them in the spirit and truth of the Gospel, stressing the need of salvation in Christ Jesus.

This was Pastor Rosenberg's main task, and towards this goal he was pressing step by step, following the Lord's leading. Remembering the words of David Ben-Gurion about the Hebrew Christians being the concern for those of the same faith and not of the Jewish Government, Pastor Rosenberg stressed this point before the Government authorities, going all the way to the top and obtaining an audience with Ben-Gurion himself. Permission was obtained and a search for a suitable property was begun.

By that time the Lord had something very special in store — a beautiful, comfortable two- story house with large rooms, high ceilings and a view of the port of Haifa on the Mediterranean Sea. The property was fenced in as a separate private estate and had a nice garden with a concrete play-ground on a lower level, giving ample space for outdoor recreation and, if necessary, for extension.

Underneath the house were two large cisterns hewn out of the rock so the property had its own artesian well with fine water, which was important in that country.

The location of this property was also ideal. It was nestled at the foot of Mount Carmel, the mountain where the prophet Elijah in the zeal of the Lord achieved great things among the people of Israel in that Land.

The price was only 8,500 English pounds. And though this was more than the Mission had available, its leadership felt keenly that they should trust the Lord and not let this excellent offer go unaccepted. Much prayer was needed and Pastor Rosenberg urged his friends at the United Missionary Worker's Meeting to bring this matter before the Lord. A few days later, a missionary told about the property under consideration that it belonged to a Britisher, a Christian man who wanted to leave the country, and was looking for a reliable purchaser, who could meet his requirements. After a thorough inspection by experts, the price was agreed upon, a contract was signed and a down payment given. The rest of the money would be transferred behind the scenes by banks in Great Britain and California. Since the former owner's lawyer demanded that no mortgage be left on the property, because his client was leaving the country, all funds had to be in by midsummer. (Proceedings began in the Spring.)

To comply fully with the laws of the young land, Pastor Rosenberg had to obtain a special permit from the Minister of Finance and the General Controller of Foreign Exchange. One verse from the Book of Proverbs came to Pastor Rosenberg's mind: "The king's heart is in the hand of the Lord, as the rivers of water: He turneth it whithersoever He will." (Pr. 21:1) Believing that the Lord could do "abundantly above all that we ask or think" and that He alone gives us the "spirit of discernment," he appealed to the constituency of the AEBM. Several concerned souls responded with generous gifts and the purchase of "Bethel" in Haifa, Israel, became a reality!

In those days the Mission was highly recommended by all missionaries in Israel. They were happy and grateful to know that this facility, a strictly evangelical interdenominational institution, would serve any destitute child brought in or recommended by them, as well as by others who complied with the spiritual character of the orphanage.

The Kofsmans rejoiced over the "House of God" on Hagefen Street and wished it to be a "place of security, peace and love for many years to come!" They were also happy to have a garage (no car yet), and a meeting hall for proclaiming the Good News of salvation in Christ Jesus to men, women and children.

After the visit by Pastor Rosenberg, they wrote in the "Bethel Witness":

"We have been greatly benefited by the presence of our Director in our meetings, and so were others in all the places where he ministered the Word. His messages brought us good and wholesome nourishment. All of us needed them and they were appreciated by all."

Pastor Rosenberg returned home enriched by his new experience in the newborn land of Israel. His heart was deeply satisfied and grateful to God for all He did so soon and so fast on behalf of "Bethel" and for the benefit of many orphaned and destitute children.

Reassured by the Jewish Government, particularly by the Prime Minister, David Ben-Gurion, who issued a statement in favor of full freedom of religion in Israel, Christian missionaries in that land did not foresee any problems. However, there was one segment of the Jewish society, which disagreed with the Prime Minister and conspired to issue its own statement forbidding ALL Christian missionary activities.

℣

A Manifesto Of The Chief Rabbis Concerning Christian Missions In Israel

℣

One newspaper wrote:

"The highest Rabbinical Court in Jerusalem issued on the 20th day of December 1952 a manifesto concerning the activities of Christian Missions in Israel. It was signed by Chief Rabbis Herzog and Uziel and the General Secretary of the Rabbinical Court, Rabbi Schesuri. This was addressed to all the Rabbis and religious functionaries. It is a war cry against all the missionaries."

The Manifesto read in part as follows:

"More than 400 messengers of Satan *("Schlitchej ha Satan"),* missionaries... among whom there are baptized Jews, traitors of the nation... came to this land like locusts and are now here..."

The following was a comment of a newspaper in Tel-Aviv:

"Upon seeing this manifesto, the thoughtful Jewish reader will with dismay and astonishment learn of this insulting cannonade — which is not really becoming such an institution as the Upper Rabbinical Court in their religious struggle. Such an insult against the Christian Missions is truly shameful and ill-considered. Imagine if the Pope of Rome were to call the High Rabbi and his colleagues "messengers of Satan," or if ministers of Protestant Churches were to speak in such a way of the Zionists and their propaganda in the USA! Surely we would lift up our voices to protest against such violent insult. We can only say with Voltaire: 'I do not agree with your convictions, but I will say with my last breath that you are entitled to have your convictions.' The methods which the Rabbis adopted are against all the principles of democracy."

The same paper continues:

"Two days after the manifesto was issued, the Prime Minister, David Ben-Gurion, declared solemnly in the *Knesseth* (Parliament) that the new Government IS IN FAVOR OF ABSOLUTE RELIGIOUS FREEDOM AND THE RIGHT OF THE INDIVIDUAL TO HAVE HIS OR HER OWN OPINION; BUT BY NO MEANS WILL IT BE TOLERATED TO USE ANY PRESSURE

OF A RELIGIOUS NATURE UPON ANY ONE. WE WILL NOT ALLOW SUCH MEASURES TO BE USED. AS TO DIFFERENCES OF OPINION IN MATTERS PERTAINING TO THE SAFETY OF THE STATE OR THE DIGNITY OF AN INDIVIDUAL, THE GOVERNMENT WILL DECIDE. THE UPPER RABBINATE HAS THE RIGHT AND DUTY TO PROTEST AGAINST MISSIONARIES AND TO MEET THE ISSUE WITH ALL EARNESTNESS AND RELIGIOUS WARFARE DECISIVENESS, BUT NOT BY INSULTING THE MISSIONARIES. MUST BE SPIRITUAL, BUT NOT IN HOT PURSUIT AND INSTIGATING ACTS OF VIOLENCE."

This last statement left a tiny loophole for action on the part of the Rabbinate and all religious zealots. Though it was in no way a "green light" for abusive action, they managed to bypass its intent and in the course of future years conducted many vicious attacks against missionaries and their activities in the new democratic State of Israel.

More debates followed and missionaries, in turn, responded to the hateful manifesto with an appeal for mutual understanding, stressing their loyalty to the Jewish State and a genuine desire to serve the Hebrew Christians and their children whose needs otherwise would be neglected. They also expressed their desire to assist in distribution of material relief in an honest and fair manner, but in the eyes of the Rabbinate active Christians remained forever under suspicion.

ψ

Chapter 42

REPEATED JOURNEYS ABROAD AIMED AT SUPPORT AND EXPANSION

*F*ollowing 1952, many more trips to Israel were under-taken by Pastor Rosenberg with the sole purpose of giving material, moral and spiritual support to the estab-lished work and the missionaries involved in it. At the same time the director tried to find the kind of staff that would correspond with the high standard of the AEBM at home, being able to run the facility in Israel smoothly and aboveboard.

In 1953 Pastor Rosenberg took with him to Israel his wife, Fanny, and his secretary, Miss Laurine Volker. It was an urgent necessity for both, especially for Mrs. Rosenberg who was an experienced foster mother of many orphans, having supervised a Mission Orphanage in Po-land for many years. She had to go to Israel to strengthen the hands of foster-mothers in Haifa, while Miss Volker had to take care of important business with the Israeli Government in connection with the Mission property and the Orphanage there.

ψ

Something Different

ψ

Upon their return Miss Volker wrote in the Bethel Wit-ness:

"The caption for this narrative should be 'Something different,' because this phrase is peculiarly applicable to our Orphanage.

"This children's home came into being in an unusual and even miraculous way. It is in the fullest sense 'A Christian Home' for needy boys and girls with a background entirely different from that of other children. These have been snatched from the scorching fire and the gas-chambers — from the hands of the enemy who desired their extermination.

"It is a Home where children are reared 'in the nurture and admonition of the Lord,' and cared for morally, physically and spiritually. In this Home we endeavor to fulfill this three-fold task in the best manner possible.'"

Mrs. Rosenberg, on the others hand, felt that the Lord had blessed her life beyond all her expectations by allowing her, in her advanced age, to visit the land of her forefathers, the land of the Patriarchs and of Jesus Christ, her personal Savior and Lord. She was able to travel through the land and see the most important sites, such as the Tomb of the Patriarchs, the empty Garden Tomb of Jesus, and Gethsemane.

The next couple of years were difficult ones for the Rosenbergs and the Mission. The ever so energetic and dynamic Director fell ill and had to be hospitalized to undergo a serious operation. Though he recovered in time, less than two years later he had a severe heart attack and was again laid on his back and unable to travel. He was a little over eighty years old and many of his co-workers were very concerned for him and the future of the work in Israel and at home.

Towards the end of the nineteen fifties Pastor Rosenberg was again "shipshape," considering his age, and ready to travel again. It was in 1958 that he stayed in Israel for almost nine months, during which time his dream of expansion was finally fulfilled. A Christian lady who lived across the street and helped at the Children's Home, dropped a hint that the building next door to "Bethel" might be for sale. Pastor Rosenberg took the hint and asked the owners, who were from Switzerland and were planning to move to Europe, if a purchase would indeed be possible. The price for the property was more than the Mission could afford at the time, so, our wary Director began to pray. He felt after the prayer that the Lord wanted him to do "what he was able to do himself!"

He remembered that back in the United States he owned a house and could take out a mortgage on it. The house was paid for by then, but the bank was not loaning the full amount that was needed. He took what he could, happy that he had a personal part in the purchase, and the rest was swiftly raised through faithful friends. Soon a roomy and beautiful property, adjacent to "Bethel," was artfully connected to it with stairs and concrete platforms, forming one complex on Hagefen Street in Haifa. The two-story house with a beautiful view of the Haifa harbor was fulfilling the need for expansion and Rosenberg's gratitude to God knew no bounds.

Overjoyed, deeply grateful to his friends and to God, Pastor Rosenberg returned home to rest and prepare for a missionary itinerary in the American Midwest. He was able to fulfill the task quite successfully, but bad news from Israel grieved him deeply and he shared this burden with his trusted friend and Assistant Director of the Mission, Professor Solomon Birnbaum, whose work at the New York mission station was coming to a close due to a change in circumstances. The bad news from

Israel came expressed in a brief note: "Kofsmans are leaving the work in Haifa and are moving back to Jerusalem." No further explanations were given. Ties with the Mission were severed and the search for a replacement began in earnest.

The following year Professor Birnbaum traveled to Israel with his wife, Rosalie, and both of them so fell in love with "Bethel" in Haifa and the children, that soon they were more than willing to commit themselves to a ministry there. They spent the next ten years at "Bethel," working with the children and conducting meetings and Bible classes for adults. They returned to the United States only after being forced to do so by drastic changes in the treatment of "Bethel" by the Israeli authorities.

☱

Other Faithful Servants

☱

God had provided many faithful servants for "Bethel" in Israel in the course of time, filling the recurring needs. When prayer rose to Heaven for helpers and teachers, an answer came almost miraculously.

A seasoned missionary, who also "happened to be" a trained teacher from America, had lived in Palestine since 1946. Her name was Olga Barnett. Through the "coincidence" of many circumstances she was eventually led to "Bethel" with a newly-opened Grade School for orphaned and destitute children. Here she found her place for the next decade or more, and her contribution to the AEBM in Israel defies any human evaluation.

The year the Birnbaums arrived in Israel, she was finally able to leave on a furlough and get some rest, but returned to "Bethel" and served for several more years.

Many others came to serve and try their missionary "wings" at "Bethel." Not all worked out, but quite a few stayed for long periods of time and made significant contributions. Some were local women who came daily to cook meals and clean the facility. Others came from abroad, from America and Europe, and the Lord preserved the new work among children for almost 20 years before changes had to be made.

Having the Assistant Director himself at "Bethel" gave the Rosenbergs a tremendous sense of confidence and peace of mind. Both of them were getting older. Christmas of 1958 was a triple celebration which brought their children and grandchildren together. First of all, of course, it was a joyous celebration of the miraculous incarnation of their Redeemer and Lord, Jesus Christ. Secondly, it was the 86th birthday of Mrs. Rosenberg and thirdly, it was the 60th wedding anniversary of Fanny and Leon. Unfortunately, during this celebration Pastor Rosenberg was in Israel bringing to completion some important matters in the Lord's work there. However, when he returned, he was compensated in a very joyous way on his own 84th birthday in February of the following year. Once again the whole family gathered around its senior head. All were used to his frequent absences, and no one more so than his wife, but they always remembered that their lives belonged to the LORD, and that He Who blessed them with added years had His purpose therein:

"Those that He planted in the House of the Lord shall flourish in the courts of our God. They shall still bring forth fruit in old age; they shall be fat and flourishing; to show that the Lord is upright: He is my Rock and there is no unrighteousness in Him." (Ps. 92:13-15 KJV)

The early sixties brought more illness to the aging Director of the AEBM. He recovered enough to continue his work on the book "The Various Manifestations of the Deity," dictating final portions of it to his secretary. One more attempt to travel abroad was made but a heart attack forced Pastor Rosenberg to remain at home.

Until 1967 he struggled to stay relatively healthy, but eventually became bedridden and unable to continue to lead the work. His eldest daughter, Eugenia, who had already worked in the office of the Mission full-time since her arrival from Europe in 1947, and who was the voice of the AEBM on the radio, was appointed Acting Director by the Board of the Mission. In May of 1967 Pastor Rosenberg quietly died in his sleep and went to be with the One Whom he served most of his life so diligently and faithfully. His wife, Fanny, cared for him at home with the help of an able live-in servant of God. Mrs. Rosenberg followed her husband one year later.

This dedication to God's service and the persistent pursuit of His glory through it speaks of a deep faith in the God Who said to Abraham: "Fear not, I am thy shield, and thy exceeding great reward."

ψ

EPILOGUE

*I*t is appropriate now to reveal the identity of the one who compiled these lines for you, dear readers. It was I, Vera Kuschnir, one of the five granddaughters of Leon and Fanny Rosenberg, the third daughter of Sergei and Eugenia Abramow who one day, after the going to Glory of my mother, found in the old safe of the AEBM a stack of loose pages yellowed by time, in the English and German languages and I began to read them.

Mother, together with an able and active Board of Directors, led the AEBM from the death of her parents until she herself retired at the age of 80. About that time she invited me to serve on the Board of the Mission to represent the family of the founders.

I was very busy, being involved in radio ministry to the former Soviet Union and translation into Russian of Christian books for the benefit of believers there. But Mother was persistent, and really needed help, so I agreed to assist her in grandfather's Mission. After she moved the Mission's headquarters to Santa Barbara, I did help her at the office part-time, and even in the past, back in Los Angeles, I often went to the Mission to help with mailing of the then bimonthly magazine "The Bethel Witness," and with other odds and ends. Seeing the hand of God in this new "call," I agreed to join the Board and assist at the office, and as of today, while I am writing this book in 1994, I am still quite active in the work of our Mission.

Soon after involving me in the work of the Mission here in the States, Mother and the Board decided to send me to Israel to see the work there and with God's help correct some problems that needed to be resolved. When I arrived in Haifa, "Bethel" was no longer a Children's Home or an Orphanage, but a Youth Hostel for local and international young travelers. You will probably want to know what happened to the work that Pastor Rosenberg established with such love soon after the birth of the State of Israel.

The benevolent attitude towards Christian Missions changed when David Ben-Gurion was no longer the Prime Minister of Israel. Those who followed him were much less interested in protecting Christian missionary activities. So, one day in 1967, a large group of religious Jewish zealots stormed our buildings in Haifa, assaulted Mrs. Birnbaum and other workers, and demanded that the facility be closed, or that it would at least stop educating Jewish children in the Christian faith. Police were summoned and the offenders were arrested, but when the case went to court, "Bethel" lost out against the onslaught of hostile zealots — even in the halls of justice.

However, all was not lost. The final judgment contained a permission to operate a Christian facility for youth over 14 years of age, and that is when the Board began to consider a change from children's work to youth work. One Board member was sent to Israel to help make the transition. "Bethel" became a Youth Center and later, even to this day, AEBM operates a Youth Hostel on Hagefen Street in Haifa and another one in Eilat, called "The Shelter," which was added several years later. As answer to prayer, both places have wonderfully reliable staffs of dedicated souls.

When this transition took place in 1967, Pastor Rosenberg was on his deathbed and fortunately knew nothing about the change. Grandma Fanny, as we all called her, was upset at the time but still confident that the Lord was in charge and a blessing would come out of this new situation as many times before in the history of the Mission. She was right! The Mission is still very much alive today and just as fruitful, and we pray that it will endure until the second coming of the Lord. What would doubtless make the Rosenbergs especially happy, is the fact that once again their Mission is ministering to Russian Jews who come to Israel from all over Russia and the Ukraine, and that this story will go in book form, in the Russian language, to Odessa (Ukraine) where the work began at the turn of this century!

The attack on "Bethel" in 1967 was not the first one, nor was it the last, but previous ones were easily repelled as long as David Ben-Gurion was in charge. Some attempts by the enemy to close the work in later years also failed, but periodic attacks continue to this day.

The Birnbaums returned to the States in 1969 and Professor Birnbaum went to be with the Lord three years later. Rosalie, as of this writing, is 90 years old and lives in Washington DC.

So far I have visited Israel five times and seen the land and its people close-up. My involvement with the Bethel Mission produced in me a deep concern for the salvation of Jews everywhere. I became the voice on the AEBM's radio broadcast here in the States, replacing my mother after her death in 1985. Father died in 1974. I feel I must carry on the good work until I am no longer able to do so. My prayer is that the work of the Mission may continue for many years to come, and I feel sure that the Lord will continue to provide workers here and abroad because it is *HIS* work which He has protected and preserved for over 90 years!

When I found the old manuscripts which were intended by their writer to become a book, I was deeply moved and determined to finish this task, unfinished by my grandfather and not tackled by those who followed due to extreme busyness with many other tasks at hand.

I organized the pages into a chronological sequence, translated many German ones into English, edited out nonessentials, and added information from many old issues of the "Bethel Witness" and from my own and Aunt Maria Slort's memories. The result is this biographical sketch which could be much more appropriately called: "A Story of Missionary Resilience," the name we chose as its subtitle.

And yet, the story would not be complete without my personal observations of the Rosenbergs as family people, as those whom we knew as our grand and great-grandparents. The reason I mention this is that many wonderful servants of God are often negligent parents or spouses. In the case of the Rosenbergs it wasn't so. On the contrary, they were loving and attentive parents and grandparents, devoted to detail and keenly interested in all family members no matter how remote the relationship might have been.

I met my grandparents for the first time in April of 1949, when my husband and I arrived in Los Angeles from Germany. Grandfather was our sponsor and he arranged for us the best accommodations possible on our train journey from New Orleans to Los Angeles. We were the only ones from a huge number of *DP's* (displaced persons) who had tickets with sleeping accommodations, and the only ones who were actually met by someone, when our ship (a Navy troop Transport) docked in New Orleans. A retired missionary couple waited for us there and took care of us all day until we boarded our train at 11 PM. It may be a small detail for some, but for us, who were coming out of six years of war, from bug-infested barracks and DP camps, straight from the open grave of burying a second child in two years, this "detail," of being met by someone in a strange country (the language of which we did not speak), and then being allowed to sleep comfortably for two nights on a train, was no small matter, but a never-forgotten act of kindness and great sensitivity.

My husband was not yet a born-again believer in Christ. He was not an atheist, being brought up a Greek Catholic, but he did not believe in Christ in a personal way. Nevertheless, he was received as one body with me and part of our family on an equal basis. (I received Christ as my personal Savior three years prior to our arrival in America.) Grandma showered him with love and kindness and grandfather answered all of his questions until ten years later the miracle of his spiritual birth took place. Both grandparents exercised extreme patience mixed with much love, and not only with Stan, but also with all our unbelieving friends. "Your friends are our friends" was their usual reply after an introduction to someone new.

Another lasting impression was left by my Grandmother's way of pronouncing the name of Jesus. She put so much tenderness and sweetness into the name, that it always sounded like a name of someone she really loved. She never used her Savior's name glibly or lightly, and we all eventually learned to do the same.

Neither grandparent ever missed an opportunity to share his or her belief in Christ with others. As if afraid that an opportunity might be forever missed, they spoke of Him almost right off-the-bat. This was another useful example for all of us to follow.

Since Grandfather traveled often and was gone for long periods of time, Grandmother learned through the years to support him and their Mission in prayer. In his absence she held morning devotions with the staff at the office, read her Bible during the day and prayed on her knees before bedtime even in her old age, though kneeling was not an easy exercise for her due to a bad hip she had ever since the breech-birth of my Aunt Maria, her last child.

Most touching were our family gatherings on special holidays, birthdays and baby dedications. On Christmas Grandma filled little bags with goodies for all the little ones and personally distributed them from a stool under the Christmas tree. We sang Christmas carols, listened to the Bible story about the birth of Christ from one of the Gospels read by Grandfather, if he was at home, and by others if he was away, and then we sat down around a huge oval oak table in the dining room for a festive meal with the grandparents at the head of the table. Grandfather prayed loudly with much feeling and emphasis on the occasion, giving all glory to God for His bountiful blessing showered on our family.

Each newborn child was dedicated to God by grandfather himself. If he was gone at the time of the birth, we all waited for his return. Again we would all assemble at the grandparent's house on N. Dillon Street in Los Angeles, and grandfather Leon, as the patriarch of his large immediate and extended family, would take the newborn into his arms, holding the little head (size of an orange) in the hollow of his right hand, and pronounce one of the most moving benedictions I have ever heard. All of our children were dedicated to God in this unforgettable way.

Grandfather Leon was a devoted patriarch in the old Jewish tradition. From time immemorial, he owned a photo camera and later bought a movie camera. He produced hundreds of pictures of his family, ministry and travels and many reels of 16*mm* movie film. In Los Angeles, we were often "herded" together in front of the house on the front lawn (or inside the house) and were ordered to "move" (these were *MOVING* pictures!), while grandfather directed the production of yet another family "documentary." Hundreds of feet of this kind of home movies are kept as "reliquiae" to be shown only on special occasions to the now adult and even old grandchildren and great-grandchildren. They see themselves learning to walk on wobbly baby legs, or riding a rocking horse in the back yard, or pushing a rattling toy "lawn mower" down a sloping front lawn.

In America, the Lord granted my grandparents 20 years of blissful life and fruitful ministry to which all of us are witnesses. When we first arrived, the Mission was busy with the loading of huge containers with relief supplies for many impoverished war survivors in Europe and Israel. We all helped. The garage was packed with donated clothing and shoes, blankets and toiletries. We called it *"Maison de Garage"* in the old tradition of fashion houses in Paris! Being war refugees ourselves, we were allowed to dress from this "fashion house" until we were financially on our feet. There was no welfare system as we know it today, and our men worked from day one in any place they would be hired.

In God's ultimate mercy and love He provided a tender caretaker for the Rosenbergs in the person of a fine Christian lady, Elizabeth Waltner, a German Mennonite. She lived with them the entire time they were in the Mission house in Los Angeles, and took care of them when they were ill and dying. Elizabeth's lone figure in a dark suit at Fanny Rosenberg's grave site will be forever etched in my mind. She stood there when everyone else was leaving. Her job was done. Through tears she said to me: "Now I will rest some place and let the loving Lord take me." But this would not be in her nature. Before she finally rested in the arms of her Lord, she took care of her blind brother until he died, and also cared for two other needy relatives. What a beautiful servant of God!

Finding the torn, yellowed pages of my grandfather's biographical notes was like finding a gold mine on the Klondike, during the gold rush. I firmly believe that his remarkable story will touch many hearts and will point them in the right direction: towards the foot of the Cross of our Redeemer, Savior and Lord, Jesus Christ.

Though I shared some of my personal glimpses into the lives of these two seasoned, tried and proven missionaries, my desire was not to glorify them, but the One Who called them unto Himself to do His work of leading sinners to Christ here on earth. May He alone be glorified!

I wish to close this story with my grandfather's motto, adapted from the First Epistle of the Apostle Paul to the Corinthians, and with the blessing he pronounced over his and Fanny's posterity at the time of his first serious illness when he thought that he was going to die. First, here is his motto:

"For though I preach the Gospel, I have nothing to glory of: for necessity is laid upon me; yea, woe unto me, if I preach not the Gospel." (1 Cor. 9:16)

And now, the blessing which each descendant of the Rosenbergs can rightfully apply to him or herself:

"The Lord bless thee, and keep thee:
The Lord make His face shine upon thee, and be gracious unto thee:
The Lord lift up his countenance upon thee, and give thee peace." Numbers 6:24-26 (KJV)

"These are the blessings which the High Priest Aaron and his sons were commanded by God to pronounce over the children of Israel while serving in the Holy of Holies. These are the blessings which I, your father and grandfather, pronounce over you in the hope that the Lord will allow them to come over you.

I would love to see you all once again but I let the Lord decide whether this should ever be made possible. I commit all of you into His keeping. I have much reason to be thankful to Him: for all my years, all my days, which He graciously granted to me. May His name be praised in all eternity, for His goodness endureth forever. Amen."

(These words father Rosenberg dictated on Sunday, January 8th, 1962, from a hospital bed. But the Lord granted him five more quiet years, calling him home in May of 1967).

ψ

A young Jewish man with phylacteries

Studying the *Torah* (the five books of Moses).

The *Torah* is always hand written on a large scroll.

The Passover table (*Seder*).

Leon's father,
Eleazar Rosenberg

Fanny's parents,
Moses and Lea Weiman.

Pastor Frank,
who baptized
Leon and Fanny
Rosenberg.

Helen Weiman,
Fanny's sister,
the "first fruit"
of Leon and Fanny's
missionary activities.

The Rosenberg family in Russia.

Young Leon on the left in front of his Christian Bookstore; his daughter
Elizabeth is seen in the doorway.

Association Mildmay's free cafeteria and clothes-making factory for Jewish refugees and war victims. *Odessa, 1906.*

Inside the Odessa prayer house.

A document issued by Russian authorities giving permission for the Hebrew-Christian church to hold their services. A correction from *'Christian'* to *'Evangelical'* can be seen.

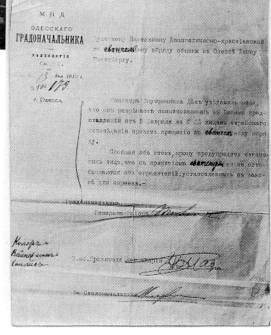

The Jewish Congregation:
Mr. Rosenberg and Mr. Kudaschewitz in the front.

THE MILDMAY MISSION TO THE JEWS.

CENTRAL HALL, PHILPOT STREET, LONDON, E.1.

Hon. Director and Treasurer—Rev. SAMUEL HINDS WILKINSON.

À tous ceux qui s'en intarressent.

Le porteur de cette note M. Leon Rosenberg est un
missionaire fort bien accrédité de la Mission ci-dessus,
qui dans une liaison de longues années est devenu un des
representants de la Mission les plus eprouvés. J'ai l'honneur
de le recommander au tous ceux qui sont en état de l'aider
de quelque façon quoi qu'il en soit.

Signé

Directeur.

Various documents
dealing with
Pastor Rosenberg's
missionary activities.

Pastor
Rosenberg
performs
baptism.

Mission School
in Odessa, Russia
(starting point,
left, and how it
has grown,
below).

Fanny Rosenberg leads
the Women's Bible
Study group.
Fanny and her sister,
Helen, are seen
in the front, left
and right, respectively.

Christian youth
group founded
by W.F.
Marcinkowski
(center);
Rosenberg's
daughter
Eugenia is seen
in the top left.

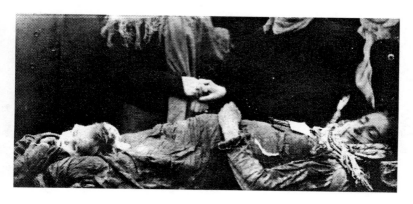

Victims of the *pogroms* in Odessa, 1905.

Germany. Rosenbergs' house in Blankenburg, Harz. *1922-1929*.

(From upper far left) Maria (Slort), Sergei and Eugenia Abramow with
daughter, Lydia, during the Abramow's visit to Germany.
Fanny *(front left)* is holding their daughter, Irene.

Left: Leon in Germany.

Below: Missionary group in Frankfurt.

Below: First meeting of Hebrew-Christians in Germany. Among others, there were Leon Rosenberg *(center right)* and Fanny *(behind him, left)* with their daughters *(sitting at both sides of Leon, first row)*; also, Mr. Gitlin *(upper right)*.

Orphans
in Poland.

Right: Burned down factory
that became "Beth-El."

Below: Beth-El in Lodz, Poland.

Right:
Helen Rosenberg gives bath
to orphan children in Helenovic, Poland
(see below).

"Beth-El" at Lodz,
Poland.

During a meal.
Lodz, Poland.

"Beth-El" Orphanage
Lodz, Poland.

Victims of Nazi terror.

Mission workers in Lodz. Top, second from right, third row — Sieuwert Slort.

Congregation in
Lodz, Poland.

Children participate
in the church service
during a holiday.

First conference
of Hebrew-Christians
was in London,
England.

Hebrew-Christian
conference
in Warsaw, Poland.
1926

Helen and Samuel
Ostrer
(*both fell victims
to Nazi terror*).

Below:
The Malcman family.
Five members were
killed by Nazis.

The Birnbaum
family,
New York.

Dr. Solomon Birnbaum *(right)*
preaching in the Bethel Center
in New York *(below)*.

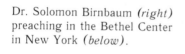

The extended family of Rosenbergs in front of the Mission building on North Dillon Street, Los Angeles, California.

Leon Rosenberg liked photography. The family still has his cameras.

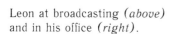

Leon at broadcasting *(above)* and in his office *(right)*.

Prayer house in Los Angeles,
California *(left)*.

Right:
Shipping of containers with aid.

Below:
Leon Rosenberg represents
"Beth-El" Mission
at a conference.

Right:
Birnbaums in Haifa, Israel.

Center:
The children of the "Beth-El"
children's home in Haifa, Israel.

Bottom:
Children gathered in the new
"Beth-El" dining room;
Dr. Birnbaum and Dr. Rosenberg
are in the background.

"Beth-El" children
sing together with
Mrs. Rosenberg
and Mrs. Volker
(Leon's Secretary)
during their visit
to Israel.

The "father" of orphans, Dr. Leon Rosenberg.

Right:
Leon Rosenberg after
a heart attack, together with
his wife and daughters. *1962*

Below:
The last illness.

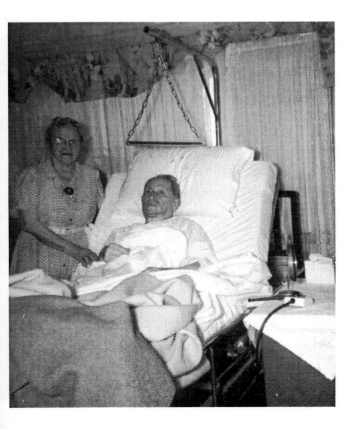

"Beth-El" youth in Haifa today.

Inside the "Beth-El" cafeteria.

"Shelter" in Eilat, Israel.
Below: Church services in Eilat.

AEBM Board today. The author is third from the right.